A HISTORY OF IDEAS
IN AMERICAN PSYCHOLOGY

A HISTORY OF IDEAS
IN AMERICAN PSYCHOLOGY

Ernest Keen

Westport, Connecticut
London

Library of Congress Cataloging-in-Publication Data

Keen, Ernest, 1937–
    A history of ideas in American psychology / Ernest Keen.
      p. cm.
    Includes bibliographical references and index.
    ISBN 0–275–97205–4 (alk. paper)
    1. Psychology—United States—History—20th century. I. Title.
BF105.K45   2001
150′973—dc21   2001021160

British Library Cataloguing in Publication Data is available.

Library of Congress Catalog Card Number: 2001021160
ISBN: 0–275–97205–4

First published in 2001

Praeger Publishers, 88 Post Road West, Westport, CT 06881
An imprint of Greenwood Publishing Group, Inc.
www.praeger.com

Printed in the United States of America

The paper used in this book complies with the
Permanent Paper Standard issued by the National
Information Standards Organization (Z39.48–1984).

10 9 8 7 6 5 4 3 2 1

The author and publisher gratefully acknowledge permission for use of the following
material:

Excerpts from *Psychology in America* by Ernest Hilgard, copyright © 1987 by Harcourt, Inc.,
reproduced by permission of the publisher.

Excerpts from *The Psychology of the Child* by Jean Piaget. English language copyright © 1969
by Basic Books, Inc.

Every reasonable effort has been made to trace the owners of copyright materials in this
book, but in some instances this has proven impossible. The author and publisher will be
glad to receive information leading to more complete acknowledgments in subsequent
printings of the book and in the meantime extend their apologies for any omissions.

To my colleagues whose friendship
has nurtured my intellectual life
Douglas K. Candland
Joseph P. Fell
John Kirkland
and
Douglas Sturm

Contents

Preface   ix

Introduction   xi

Part I   The Mind and the Body: From Wundt to Gestalt

1   What Is the History of Psychology?   3

2   Late Nineteenth-Century Psychological Theory   17

3   The Psychology of William James   31

4   The Psychology of E. B. Titchener   49

5   American Psychology in 1910   63

6   The Psychology of John Watson   75

7   Koehler's Gestalt Psychology   89

Part II   Clinic and Laboratory: From Freud to Skinner

8   Completing the First Century   101

9   Sigmund Freud's Psychoanalysis   111

10   The Psychology of Edward Tolman   123

11   Clark Hull, Carl Rogers, and the 1960s   135

12   The Psychology of Donald O. Hebb   147

13   The Cognitive Developmentalism of Jean Piaget   161

14   The Psychology of B. F. Skinner   175

Part III Specialization and Fragmentation

    15 Ideas and Identities in Psychology   189

    16 Phenomenological Psychology   201

    17 Feminist Psychology   215

    18 Postmodern Psychology   227

    19 Toward Some Conclusions   241

    References   249

    Name Index   261

    Subject Index   265

Preface

A narrative grasp of the history of psychology is important for students of psychology because this story contextualizes the questions they ask. All who wrote American psychology were themselves students, with questions as well. There have been many lines of questioning, and answering that ceased only because the immediate question was unanswerable or because the outcome seemed inconsequential. In light of later developments, of course, the unanswerable question may become answerable or already answered, but without knowing the history it too might seem inconsequential. Or the consequence of a neglected earlier finding may now seem obvious in light of later ideas. What seemed a dead end may become a vital connecting link in a new theory.

Since this account of the history of ideas in psychology is necessarily partial, only some of the benefits of knowing history can come from reading this book. But many important ideas are represented here, and knowing them makes other forrays into the dense thicket of this history less disorienting. In addition, this narrative is, like that of all sciences, a heroic one: psychologists overcoming great obstacles, stumbling on astonishing facts, persevering in the face of ambiguity until a new idea is born. We sometimes come to understand something about which we formerly did not even ask.

Ideas summarize findings. But ideas also lead to them. What follows is a summary of ideas that offer a general picture of American psychology since the late nineteenth century. It is clear that the accidents of publication—always a wild card in the progress of any science—have a magnified effect in the writing of histories. In fact, scientists studied here in detail are, for the most part, those whose books were available in paperback for a course in the history of psychology I taught at Bucknell University over several decades in the late twentieth century.

It is an exciting story—for those for whom ideas are exciting. Ideas are, of course, the stuff of our intellectual lives, but a history of ideas is but a small part of the larger history of a period. As human history goes, ideas track the threads of continuity and the radical breaks in continuity that come from abrupt dead ends and accidental or hard-fought new starts in our cultural life. As occupants of the planet, we are also occupants of this cultural history, a crucial part of which is the story of human scientific effort.

With science, of course, we are more than occupants; we are creators, hemmed in by the limits of the possible, driven on by the force of the necessary, and inspired by the narrative of which we reckon ourselves to be part. To know the history of ideas, in psychology or in general, is to know with some accuracy and crucial depth who we are, and what it means to be a psychologist, or even a participant, in the twenty-first century.

Introduction

There are many ways to write a history of psychology. Every attempt necessarily chooses what to include and why, thus enacting a certain concept of what psychology actually is. Since there is no fixed essence of psychology, each such vision requires assumptions about what really has happened, and it looks forward to what ought to happen in the future. These assumptions ought to be seen as arguments, aimed at criticism here, praise there, and whether the historian knows it or not, they argue for a certain kind of future.

In addition, historical work constructs narratives. The narrative constructed here has come late in my study of the history of psychology, as I realized that I care what has happened and what will happen. In describing the history of psychology, I focus mainly on the twentieth century, where the tentative beginnings of the late nineteenth century became expansive visions. Such narratives are of interest to psychologists of the present because we still care about what has happened and what is to come.

I wrote much of this book before I was aware of my own advocacy. My advocacy appears in my being a psychologist, however, and you are urged to recognize it and to recognize that it has shaped my account of what happened, thus making this historical record (like all historical records) a somewhat political document.

I divide the history of (primarily American) psychology into three periods. The first, from James to Gestalt, must struggle with the historical problem of dualism. In the late nineteenth century, science, invented for physical things, was applied to the mind, and that application was not without its agony. It was a time of struggle with a philosophical issue of long standing: the metaphysical character of the human mind (Chapters 2 and 3). Like many other thinkers since that historical origin, these psychologists (Chapters 4 and 5) often solved the philosophical problem by ignoring it, thus smuggling the metaphysical issue in surreptitiously. Wundt, who did not, was a dualist explicitly, and his work focused on the realm of consciousness.

On the other hand, Watson (Chapter 6) was clearly a materialist. But he more adamantly eschewed metaphysics altogether. This intentional neglect amounted to denying he had a metaphysical view. His lack of a philosophical sense of psychology was accompanied by a scientific view that science speaks for itself, that it need not account for its own existence. Refusing to deal with the consciousness within whose scope his own work occurred was, of course, a convenience. But it was also a decision to create a science that was entirely separate from philosophy. Much of American psychology has followed this path, and psychology has continued to flourish as a science like physics, which has no inherent obligation to explore itself. Gestalt psychology (Chapter 7) is an exception. But like most physicists simply take "the physicist" for granted, psychologists have tended to take "the psychologist" for granted.

Our way back to our beginnings will try to break through "Watson's convenience," a convenience that erects barriers against taking the psychologist into account. And we shall see that even though Watson's behaviorism inspired much of American psychology, we have also vastly outstripped the limits he saw.

The second period, from Freud to Skinner, less intentionally and yet more visibly escapes and ignores philosophical issues, and tries to actualize the vision of a science that does not make metaphysical commitments. Watson's convenience, so useful in the beginning, became more invisible as it became more assumed, and its rather ad hoc character was forgotten. This convenience has also become more problematic as psychology has developed.

In this second period, because of the increasing and simultaneous popularity of both Watson (Chapter 6) and Freud (Chapter 9), psychology polarized between two large paradigms of experimental scientists versus clinical therapists. No longer arguing about the status of the mind in a science invented for bodies, some sought to make the science into an accumulating body of verifiable knowledge, while others sought to make it into a way to help people. People, of course, are mental beings, again introducing consciousness. The ghost continued to haunt the machine.

The fact that the scientists imitated Watson and the therapists imitated Freud, however, shows a continuity as well as a change from the first to the second period. It is not a repetition but a modification of the beginnings, now confidently celebrating the new established science of psychology. Attention to the mentalistic–materialistic dichotomy waned in this context. Any struggle with metaphysical dualism seems to become irrelevant. In retrospect, however, it is hardly invisible in the new polarization, but further complications are deeply obscured.

Therapists tend to be mentalists, and experimentalists tend to be physicalists. Outcomes of therapy are mainly mental; outcomes of experiments are mainly physical. At the same time, behavior therapists are not mentalists, and cognitive scientists are not materialists. The big fact, however, is that we simply do not dwell on the historical or metaphysical roots of our internal quarrels. In fact, we ignore them—even as we sometimes enact them.

The immediate successor examined here to the behaviorist (that is, physicalist) legacy of experimental psychology was Clark Hull, whose work also led to the extension of learning theory beyond the laboratory in Dollard and Miller's work. Tolman (Chapter 10) makes important efforts toward an unformulated middle. And Rogers, clearly a mentalist, can usefully be contrasted with Hull (Chapter 11). All this is examined in Part II, which takes us from these idea systems through Hebb (Chapter 12), Piaget (Chapter 13), and finally Skinner (Chapter 14).

In the middle to later part of the century, an entirely new pattern may be discerned. An increasing number of diverse specialties engulf and eventually make obsolete the experimental–clinical polarity in the same way that that polarity made obsolete the mind–body polarity. Cognitive psychology, presumably mental, is no longer embarrassed about that fact, but cognitivie psychologists do care that they are experimental, even as the clinical application of cognitive psychology ("cognitive therapy") is accepted along with the computer and other mechanical analogs of cognitive processes.

On the therapy side of mid-century psychology has come and gone a stage of therapeutic psychology that sought to treat the family, even entire communities. Personality theory is, variously, mental, bodily, behavioral, experimental, and clinical. Mental life appears not only in cognition, but also in social perception and phenomenology. Behavioral measurements, however, remain the insignia of scientific objectivity. Clinical work is, variously, mental, social, existential, and, on the materialistic side, sometimes behavioral and increasingly psychopharmacological. Dualism has disappeared from the language of this conflict, but continues as an implicit metaphysical format that shapes and informs various conflicts itself.

Each of these is a perseveration from the past, but an extension into new territory. What began with competing ideas became at the end of the century a proliferation of careers. The theories have become practices, the professions have become APA divisions, curricular innovations have become subdepartments, all eventuating in a quite complex mosaic of a discipline that has established itself as not only viable, but as an integral part of American culture.

From competing theories about mind and body in 1900, to competing paradigms of experimentation versus helping people in 1950, to competing professions in 2000—this is a complex narrative that needs to be told to our students. Psychologists are often not very interested in the historical dynamics still operative in their discipline, and they certainly do not care to own the mind–body problem. In spite of all these developments, it is not clear, however, that they escape it. Nor are they interested in the fact that the history of psychology is a version of the history of American culture, largely through the twentieth century.

We shall see that the larger cultural context has profoundly shaped psychology. Psychology became what the culture allowed and encouraged. That culture, of course, contains other professions that have experienced shifts from academic to professional status, from theory to practice, and from ideas to incomes. It is a cultural history of secularization and specialization, increasingly capitalistic in character and dominated by corporations. It was a century in which we increasingly privatized the professions in an American economy oriented to profits, and as a culture we have also weakened our commitment to the notion that some things command an attitude of reverence. This is simply the story of American culture, if not all Western cultures. Psychology has been a part of the modern world in the West.

One cannot write a history without caring about the future, and caring enters into anticipating the future even more than describing the past. My account, therefore, of phenomenological psychology (Chapter 16) as an effort to deal finally and decisively with dualism expresses a hope more than it describes a reality of a visible center in the future of American psychology. Feminist psychology (Chapter 17) will never be a center of all psychology, but nearly all psychology has indelibly learned and been changed by feminism. Postmodern trends in psychology (Chapter 18) are even more open-ended.

I do not envision the future of psychology in this book. That future depends both on how accurate our sense of this history is and on any continuing relevance dualism is allowed to have. Should this unspoken, divisive issue matter to psychology? At the same time, we must appreciate that the future of American psychology also greatly depends on the future of American culture.

PART I

THE MIND AND THE BODY
From Wundt to Gestalt

1

What Is the History of Psychology?

IN SEARCH OF A CENTER

Psychology has no center. The study of the history of psychology is a study of psychologists trying to create one. Psychology was born of philosophy; the early psychologists were all acquainted with philosophy, and they all saw psychology as a specification of the philosophy of mind, with the addition of a scientific approach. William James (Chapter 3), in his *Principles of Psychology* (1890), is the prototype of such a pioneer, although the idea had already mobilized Wundt in Germany, and was elaborated further by others. In this book, we shall focus on the Americans.

In the second decade of the twentieth century, John Watson (Chapter 6) began to think of experimental science as the only method for psychology, and he further used that method to pronounce what could and could not be known scientifically. He sought to establish behaviorism, and thus psychology, as no less a science than biology or physics. In order to maintain this level of scientific rigor, Watson had to restrict psychology to the study of overt behavior, excluding particularly everything "mental," and including all overt behavior. This definition of the subject matter of psychology simply followed the limits of the methodology.

As a prohibition against studying things that Watson thought could not be studied scientifically, this definition provoked doubters. The controversy had an ideological tone, and by the time of the second edition of Watson's book, *Behaviorism* (1930), those American psychologists who desired to be "scientific" outnumbered those who were more philosophical. Even at the expense of not studying certain subject matter, such as human consciousness, those who favored rigorous method outnumbered those who wished to include such problematic subject matter at the expense of method.

Thus, American psychology became behavioristic, a move that grafted together two almost incompatible points of view: (1) an old idea that the "psyche" in "psychology" is the mind, which ought to have its own field of study, and (2) the new idea of "-ology," which is appended to the science of the earth (geology), of life (biology), and of society (sociology) as an indication that the discipline is a science. Therefore, Watson's behavioristic redefinition of psychology stated that science must study behavior, not the mind, because the latter is "subjective." In taking this behavioristic turn, it was hoped that psychology would be capable of attacking the perennially puzzling problems of human affairs scientifically—by making behavior its object of study.

Thus, psychologists had first put the mind, as subject matter, in the center (Chapters 2, 3, 4, and 5), and then in an effort to be a science, psychologists led by Watson (Chapter 6) put science, the method, in the center. Many psychologists (e.g., Gestalt, Chapter 7) maintained that to give up the mind is an error, while others saw that doing so was the only way for psychology to become a science. Two centers, such as subject matter and method, are possible in a field, even if they are incompatable. Such a situation may yield healthy competition, mutual contempt, or both.

There have been, in twentieth-century psychology, numerous examples in which scientific method and mental content are not incompatible. Psychologists therefore celebrate the "resolution" of the tension between subject matter and method. However, this tension between method and content has remained in other cases of mental life, now less obvious perhaps than in earlier times. The tension echoes on the fringes and is latent even in the centers of psychological subject matter.

The tension was of course made much worse by developments in positivist philosophy that defined scientific knowledge very rigorously, in fact, modeling all knowledge on physical sciences like physics and chemistry. As a philosophy, positivism has both flourished and floundered, but as a methodological definition of psychology it has definitely flourished. Nearly a century later, positivism still shapes the mainstream definition of "real knowledge" within the community of psychologists.

Decade after decade, departments of psychology kept getting enrollments for this new science, well before the misfit between positivist method and mental content was resolved. In many cases, of course, it remains unresolved. People were hired to teach the courses, textbooks were written, and the content of it all accumulated into a body of subject matter. Its outlines were never determined by a settled sense of positive science in light of mental subject matter, nor by a settled study of mental life in light of positivist methods.

For years the accumulating literature of psychology excluded the mind, in spite of the fact that the name of the discipline, the major, the profession—the title, "psychology"—names a science of the mind. This incoherence between a subject matter (psych-) and a method (-ology) was resolved only in spots, and yet literature accumulated. The field expanded vastly, but without an actual center. As psychologists, we fail to find a center because the two centers, mental lilfe and scientific methods, are separate compartments of modern intellectual discourse.[1]

Now, over a century later, let us look again. To return to historical roots enriches only those disciplines that have come to be embarrassed by them. Psychology has distanced itself from its roots so thoroughly that it is not embarrassed. That lack of embarrassment socializes most new recruits into a justifiable pride in their discipline, but it does not teach them about this history. Psychology is enormously popular because it is among those disciplines whose roots are more deeply seated in human curiosity than the field itself has come to explore.

Every theorist in this book has had to deal with this issue, and each pretends that there is coherence here, that psychology is a coherent science. In time there has in fact come to be a coherence, but it is a coherence among efforts to create coherence, not a coherence between subject matter and method, or between a language of subjective "mental" experience and a language of physical facts about which scientific methodology is so adroit. Therefore, psychology sometimes enacts a kind of pretense, and one that most flourishes when this history is ignored.

Philosophy, of course, is larger than science. Its questions go where science cannot go. But every psychologist trades on the prestige of science, as compared with philosophy, and thus the pretense becomes compounded with every generation of psychologists who prefer not to worry about this historical anomaly. Every important theorist must negotiate a peace between two incompatible demands, but most psychologists ignore the history of these demands. By the new millenium, we had forgotten most of this history, and the practice of "the science of psychology" in the twenty-first century has become so traditional, well established, and successful as a science that this historical amnesia is nearly total.

UNASKED QUESTIONS

Psychology may be the only science whose central issue that inspired the origin of the field is almost totally neglected. William James clearly struggled in the 1880s with the nature of the mind and its connection to the brain and to the world, as intelligently as anyone can imagine. The issue would be simpler if we could simply forget the mind, for the brain is a material object obeying laws we understand as scientific, in fact, as laws of physical reality in physical space and time.

If psychology and its theories of method and definition of knowledge had had a different model than the physical sciences, the methodological constraint on subject matter may not have been so severe.[2] But mental life simply is not a thing, and to apply thing-methods to its study is bound to cause trouble. James's intellectual struggle with the relations of the human mind to the brain, and to objects in the world, was not uncommon. Today it still often inspires many new recruits to join psychology and thus guarantee psychology's continuation. They come to psychology in the spirit of profound curiosity. What is human consciousness amidst a world of material things which it knows so well?

James's struggle with the nature of the human mind is not incidental; it takes on the always present but rarely acknowledged problem of metaphysical dualism. And yet, after James's psychology the mystery remains how the reality of consciousness (whatever the nature of that particular reality is) interacts with the reality of the material world—either the material brain or the material objects of perception. Dualism may be descriptive of the appearance that there are two realities: mind and material things. But such a dualist starting point leads to traditionally unanswerable questions.

It is as if psychologists a century ago read James and appreciated that he asked the questions they most wanted to ask about the mind. They also realized that he could not solve the problem of dualism, and therefore they found some other problem within psychology to occupy their time, leaving the mind–body problem—but not getting too far away. In that process, the accumulation of other problems came to define their field, and to substitute for what originally attracted them to the field. Many fields of psychology emerged from this sequence, and as these fields created career tracks in their own right, with their own central questions, psychology became a discipline with a common ground we have forgotten, and about which no one speaks.

It is as if we celebrate our commonalty as psychologists without there being much more in common than the name; as if the original impulse, which has been abandoned, is a dirty secret we all share and are ashamed to speak of. It is as if James, his question, his struggle, and his failure to resolve the tensions between mental and physical analysis is our original sin, harped on only by fundamentalists, whose commitment to personal and historical origins guides their thought.

Of course, psychology is not the only discipline to have wandered away from origins that became unworkable. Sociology was inspired by Marx, and/or by Spencer, and by the ideological split between the two of them. Sociology has also debauched into fragments as diverse and disconnected as those of psychology. The methods of science offer us little in resolving Marx's and Spencer's deep and enduring controversy: Should the basic unit of analysis be the individual or the social collectivity? However, there remains among sociologists, unlike psychologists, a consciousness of the continuing relevance, in the science of sociology, of this controversy and this origin.

In economics, the split between, say, followers of Adam Smith and of Robert Owen constitutes a similar polarity as that of Spencer and Marx in sociology, with the same results: This question of our moral commitment to ourselves as individuals or to the collectivity that nurtures us never really leaves the fringe of academic reflection on economics. To be sure, in these fields, as in psychology, there are specialties that seemingly erase such origins, in academic departments of economics and even in the economy itself. And yet the original issue is not an academic taboo, in economics or in sociology, as is the question of dualism in psychology.

Psychologists, in hastening to abandon a seemingly unanswerable question from our history, have become much less anchored in our own origins, and thus have found the interface with biology much more congenial than that with philosophy. Psychology is more comfortable as a "life science" than as a "mental science." Darwin is not an embarrassment to even the hardest of scientific exclusionists, the way that James appears to be to psychologists. James disappears from our modern intellectual map in psychology, and Darwin does not.

We reject James not because he soared off into wild speculations with mystical and theological overtones. His philosophy of pragmatism is as easy to live with as mainstream American culture. It is James's struggle with the mind–body problem that is hard for psychologists to live with, and Darwin, while leaving us with "Social Darwinism" as an embarrassing and renegade legacy, did not leave biologists with an unspeakable dilemma.

The affinity between biological and psychological sciences itself begs the mind–body problem, but biology does not have this sort of ancestor. Darwin easily objectified his subject matter, the world of organic life. That world, the animals themselves, suffered a loss of our reverence in such objectification. In psychology, the loss of focus on the subjectivity that intrigued James (and the rest of us) so intensely yields not just a loss of reverence. We have lost our minds. In biology, animals, not interested in science and careers or in what we think of them, do not protest. However, psychologists study people, who do protest if their consciousness is neglected. In short, James's work is neglected because the methodological innovations, inspired by positivism and behaviorism, are incompatible with the many questions of mind, issues that inspired James's original vision. We tend, therefore, to see him as a colorful but usually inconsequential founder.

Thus, we have abandoned, not solved, the mind–body problem. It has not, however, ceased being important, even though it leads to no political ideologies (like Social Darwinism) that are an embarrassment to science. It is rather the case that we psychologists have, as a discipline, a profession, and an intellectual pursuit, picked our way through the minefield of psychological issues, always careful to turn away from this central problem. We have done this for so long, with such energy and even creativity, that this buried beginning is simply no longer visible to us. This is true the longer psychology exists, and the longer one has been a psychologist. The invisibility of this origin, both collective and personal, becomes reduced to a certain pride in ignoring the mind–body problem, as if the progress in our field has made it irrelevant.

In a way it has done just that. The progress of psychology has made irrelevant our historical and, for many of us, our most intensely personal involvement with the field. To become a psychologist today is to take an oath that burns both historical and, for many (but not all) psychologists, personal bridges, bridges crossed before our reflections were "disciplined" by the discipline. After that discipline, we abandoned our personal struggles with the nature of the mind and became intrigued instead with the ability to predict and control behavior. For many of us in psychology this was reward enough for abandoning the mind. Others of us found our way back to studying the mind through one of our famous indirect, inferential routes. Still others of us stayed with the mind and only pretended to be scientists.

That earlier curiosity opened out into the mysteries of how I, here, at a distance, grasp visually, intellectually, and emotionally, a material object. And as if that were not enough, we have become convinced that the brain is involved in that grasping, but just how that physical organ creates my mental life is as obscure as ever. Such a question is now irrelevant to many psychologists. James's relevance is of no consequence to most psychologists, except as an old family problem that is quaint at best, naïve at least, and, in some contexts, James is the occasion of obligatory contempt. He is seen as part of our prescientific heritage, allied with theories of religious salvation and other superstitions. These views of James are certainly not universal, but most of us are capable of selling them to our students in the spirit of pride in how far we have come.

We have, indeed, come far since James. We have not, however, made him obsolete. His *Principles of Psychology* (1890), seen perhaps as too difficult for undergraduates, is most impenetrable to those who don't read it. By failing to assign it to our students, we are depriving them not only of a worthy intellectual task, but also of a sense of obligation to our history, and of our rootedness in the nineteenth century. Most of all, we are often depriving our students of the very issue in their own personal intellectual histories that led them to believe that psychology may address some questions everyone else in the scientific world neglects.

Although we rarely own up to it, psychology's dirty little secret is one of our most precious legacies for the future. In spite of our frantic production of more text and numbers, psychologists share a secret desire to understand the mind in its relation to the rest of nature. In spite of our official rejection of the question, it was that curiosity that drove most of us, years ago, to ask that first psychological question and to take that first psychology course.

THE HISTORY OF PSYCHOLOGY

The history of psychology has been written many times. Current texts deviate in tone and emphasis, but the actual narrative told in each case tends to praise our progressive sophistication, differentiation, and specialization. This narrative is not wrong, of course, as long as the positivist methods of psychology define the field. The narrative is correct from the point of view of psychology as a natural science. But psychology will never escape being a mental science and a cultural science, even though "real knowledge" in psychology remains limited to positivist imitations of physics. Thus, psychology distances itself from the "cultural sciences," like anthropology.

Furthermore, by omitting the cultural context, both of what we study and that we study, the conflict of ideas is portrayed in psychology as a free-standing phenomenon that occurred as it did according to scientific processes, omitting the historical origins of psychology in the dualistic dilemma and other factors in the culture that sometimes proved decisive. In fact, new directions, new theories, and new divisions of the American Psychological Association, as well as new areas of research and new professional elaborations increasingly throughout the history of psychology, became integrated with, and thus influenced by, if not selected by, the attutides and values of the larger culture.

If psychology is in some sense superficial because of its tendency to ignore its own history, the same is true of the American culture with which it has become allied. In both cases, the "progress" accomplished in the "new" preempts an appreciation not only of this history but also of the enduring intellectual problems posed, struggled with, and abandoned there. This book hopes to appreciate what was accomplished without forgetting the history that has been ignored.

The traditional perspective in previous histories of psychology implies that this science would have developed as it did in any modern nation from the late nineteenth century to the early twenty-first century. In fact, American culture and its peculiar American foibles can be seen in these histories. The cultural context shapes the questions asked and ways of asking them more than do the obvious scientific findings. Therefore, it is intellectual folly to pretend that the science evolved in a cultural vacuum.

The history of psychology is a version of the history of American culture, largely through the twentieth century. The shift from academic to professional status, from theory to practice, and from ideas to incomes mirrors the secularization, specialization, and capitalizaton of all of America in the twentieth century. We Americans have, in that century, weakened our sense that it is important to have reverence, at least about something: We weakened our historical perspective, which enables us to recognize old errors as they persevere into the present. And we have weakened our collective identities, which were embedded in whole disciplines (like psychology) in favor of increasing loyalty to subspecialties, and even private profit. Like the modern world in general, psychology is populated increasingly with human beings who have little remaining sense that we (psychologists, not to mention everyone else) are all in this together.

SCIENTIFIC PRIDE

The problem with scientific pride is that it leads scientists to see themselves as insulated from the pushes and pulls of the culture. In the second decade of the twentieth century, when Watson's work was becoming known, such an island of insulation seemed anything but frivolous. The political contentions in Europe had exploded into war in 1914, and most Americans were but a generation or two from European origins.

The conflicts in Germany, France, England, Italy, and Austria-Hungary unleashed centuries-old animosities that had festered into regional and national disputes about which populations were all too willing to fight, to reorganize their economies into the production of modern techniques of combat, and to die.

Armies, organized on a mass scale with lethal and eventually toxic enthusiasm, decimated each other. Governments that did not participate in the conflagration failed to protect their populations, and the absurd mass destruction of cities, death of entire families and communities, recruited able-bodied citizens in "glorious sacrifice" for their sacred ethnic heritage. In a word, World War I broke out, spreading over and consuming Europe.

In the face of such events, Americans felt insulated by the Atlantic Ocean. Having only recently forgotten its own birth at the genocidal cost of the Native American population, the United States appreciated its insulation from the European chaos. American involvement in the European war was hesitant and very late, although it consolidated the defeat of Germany. While we participated, our sense of both connection and detachment was complex.

The connection was familial and historical. Many Americans are of European descent and have personal acquaintances with immigrant family members from the old country. At the same time, an ocean crossing took weeks, and so the disaster filled the pages of newspapers and radio reports and American consciousness with violence and death, side by side with a feeling that it was all very far away. Our familial connections to Europe were close, but the war was half a globe away. Personal anxieties and personal safety, side by side, made American insulation enormously valuable and American avoidance of deathly conflict very special.

The irrationalities in Europe were grounded in ethnic, religious, and nationalistic loyalties. Science was used in the war, but equally by all sides. Science has no nationality nor religion. Its truth stands above such messy human foibles, and thus the prescientific, the emotionally explosive, the uncompromising obligations, and the ultimate sacrifices, family by family in Europe, made the detachment of science and the solidity of its truth, like the insularity of the nation, a place of safety.

In this climate, American behaviorism was not seen as a technological science; it was seen as an island of sanity and rational mastery over the explosive potential of human existence. Watson was, in addition, a salesman. Behaviorism was an expression of the detachment of science, the rational mastery of what in Europe had gone up in flames, and an avoidance of those depths that promise so much dangerous explosion. Behaviorism connected the purist of science with enterprises like medicine and manufacture, and this gave it enormous appeal for American culture in general, as well as for American psychologists in particular. Science was the key to a safe and sane future; it seemed impossible to have too much or too pure of a good thing. So Watson's behaviorism, like science everywhere, seemed a liberation from threats of human meddling in superstitious and unpredictable irrationality. It was safe, it was practical, it was detached—and it was American.

Philosophy, like religion, dealt with mysteries. Behaviorism dealt with practicalities. Life needn't get bogged down in ultimacies, or consumed by imponderables. Rational practicality is also a human possibility. In this way, science can be proud. If it is not exploited by agents of political ambition or ethnic glorification, science is the answer to human tragedy. Pride in science, as it developed in the American context of American psychology, also came to express a contempt for religion, philosophy, and other dangerous ultimacies. This pride was exploited by Watson, and by others in small but frequent contexts, across American psychology. This pride fed a ridicule of all psychology that was not scientific.

PSYCHOLOGY, CULTURE, AND SECULARIZATION

In taking psychology's cultural context seriously, we must also recognize a larger and slower central ideological change that accompanied the evolution of what we call "modernity": namely, secularization. The struggle with religion by intellectuals since the Renaissance has been a struggle for basic definitions of human life and all its accoutrements of knowledge and morality. Secularization was not merely a rejection of religion, nor another reaffirmation of Greek rationality. Most important, it was the elevation of humankind into competent and accomplished knowers whose knowing was of the world, was disciplined, was independent of religion, and came to be embodied in the social establishments of science.

I was most recently led to a new appreciation of secularization by Hilgard's (1987) account of the introduction into psychology of "personality" by Gordon Allport (1937), and the introduction into psychology of "cognition" only in the 1950s, provoked largely by the translation of Piaget's works. In both cases, a rebellion against an orthodoxy had to occur, an orthodoxy cast in the form of a very strict behavioristic science that was suspicious of psychological realities that did not yield to physical measurement. In both cases, a violation of the orthodoxy had to overcome a fear that old religious notions of the human soul would be revivied, or that it would be labeled "religious," even though neither "personality" nor "cognition" are religious concepts.

Of course, "mental tests," including IQ, were already established, but their legitimacy came from their educational usefulness, thus granting them legitimation not only among educators but also among engineers of mass education. The testing movement had to overcome fears of lost status to those born into advantages of wealth, but it also was fought in the name of human science and its role in replacing religion with rational mastery.

In this much larger historical arena of secularization, William James had already staked out a claim for psychology as a science, but Watson's retreat from the mind was a way to be less radical, not more radical, than James. Ironically, Watson's claim that the mind is merely an extension of the body left a place, beyond the reach of science, for those believers in the human soul. In contrast, Allport wanted a psychology of the entire single person: body, mind, and soul. He disliked Freud and sought language to describe his subject matter. Soul was an option "already under something of a taboo," in Hilgard's (1987, p. 493) terms. "Self" was an option taken up by Rogers and others later, but Allport chose "personality." In the 1930s the only use of the term "personality" was in the literature of "multiple personality" studies by James (1890) and Morton Prince (1906), and "psychic research" that claimed proof of survival of "personality" after death (Myers, 1903). The important point was to avoid what Hilgard called the "taboo" that surrounded "soul."

Like "personality," the cognitive processes so common in psychology since 1960 also suggested a religious tradition of the "human soul" in the 1930s and 1940s. Of course, perception and intelligence implied consciousness as well, and James (1890) and Dewey (1896) had already made a thinking mind important to psychology, but the return to the mind after behaviorism had to be strictly scientific to avoid suggesting the soul. Thus, the reappearance of cognition was tentative, appearing first in adjectival form. Lewin's (1935) "cognitive structure" was a reference easily forgiven by secular enthusiasts because Lewin was, after all, a German. American authors first used the word two decades later: "cognitive style" (Lewis, 1954) and "cognitive dissonance" (Festinger, 1957). Criteria of scientific legitimacy in American psychology banned the word "mind" for years. "Cognition" and "personality" came to be accepted in the face of a taboo against the unspoken sense of religion and the human soul. Culture plays a heavy hand in psychology.

This interaction between the larger cultural whole and its psychological part has been there from the beginning. The sciences all influence and are influenced by culture. Such interaction is so complex that we have not mapped out the terms of that complexity. In fact, no simple part–whole relationship can be seen here. Therefore, various parts (or fits and starts) at various levels—the culture as a whole, science in general, the social sciences, psychology, behavioristic psychology, Skinner's behaviorism (to suggest just one series of increasingly specific parts)—can be seen. Each of these parts has a history during which each interacted with others and with the culture at large.

The matrix of things to understand in order to understand contemporary psychology looks so rich, full, and complicated that it seems hopeless to get on top of it sufficiently to know what one is doing when one is doing psychology. Making sense of psychology is always partly historical. It involves the construction of a history and a future that gives one's current work its meanings.

Any psychologist's action—running an experiment, treating a patient, teaching a course—is performed within some sense of prior attempts upon which the present is an improvement and within some sense of subsequent ones that will improve on the present. This sense of psychological work is not always explicitly negotiated in the mind of the psychologist, but it is always there, because, if for no other reason, modern persons are like this; we construe our action as taking place in historical time, and we construe time as progressive.

All this was officially unspoken and rarely published in the first half of the twentieth century. Since psychologists generally do not dwell on their own history, in the twentieth century they did some strange and wonderous things. An explicit articulation of how we came historically to do what we did will surely help us to better understand our own science. But it is also important to see that such understanding does not automatically lead to an improved orientation, for what we find in taking these questions up are more and more questions. Finally, that ultimate ambiguity about the "meaning of life" or the "purpose of human existence" seems to shine through, of which we have heard much from Europeans, toward whom our ambivalence remains unchanged.

Every psychologist and psychology student today must make his or her private peace with the ultimate ambiguity; that is our modern condition. If some chose to do it by ignoring it, by refusing to ask certain kinds of questions, I am not confident to judge them badly, even if they appear to us to be dangerous, as indeed some of us appear. But whether we can judge others or not, we shall in this book take up the questions and try to deal in the currency of competing simplifications against the backdrop of an ultimate ambiguity. And we shall try to achieve some sense of doing psychology, some sense that is informed by a fairly rigorous attempt to understand what we can about all these questions.

The history of psychology is a version of the history of American culture, largely through the twentieth century. The shifts in psychology in the twentieth century from academic to professional status, from theory to practice, and from ideas to incomes all mirror the secularization, specialization, and capitalization of all of America in the twentieth century.

NOTES

1. Of course, psychologists have achieved a kind of "measurement" of "mental life" in such obvious examples as measuring IQ or measuring the accuracy of sensation and perception. And yet quantitative units of measurement have no more affinity to mental life than the fact that children learned them and science uses them. The quantification of mental life is possible, but

it is secondary to the mind's more native categories of meaning. Measuring aspects of mental life is successful in understanding the mind as metaphorically like phenomena of the physical sciences. Meanings in mental life, in contrast, are categorical, not linear; qualitative, not quantitative. Indeed, the distinction between meaning and quantity in psychology is a major one, as it is in human culture. The incommensurable character of these properties itself reflects an origin in mind–body dualism. Scientific psychology's use of body (quantitative) methods on mental life has become more developed every decade since the beginning of psychology, and the field has become so successful that we have lost touch with the metaphoric nature of scientific psychological knowledge, not to mention questions about what it all means.

2. Only in Part III are nonscientific (or postscientific, postmodern) psychologies explored.

2

Late Nineteenth-Century Psychological Theory

THE SCIENCE OF MENTAL LIFE

William James (1890) defines psychology as "the science of mental life," both of its phenomena and their conditions. James (1892) called it, "the description and explanation of states of consciousness as such" (p. 1). Both versions, about "science" (description and explanation of) and about "mental life" (states of consciousness as such), contain many of the questions and answers that characterize the birth of psychology in America.

If we were to ask the question why James and others wanted a science of mental life at all, we would no doubt respond that thoughtful persons have always been curious about themselves, and that science in the nineteenth century was the avant garde mode of expressing curiosity, as opposed to poetry, theology, and metaphysics. These answers say no more than one climbs a mountain "because it's there," but there is a good bit more to say. A science of mental life was a matter of more urgency and excitement than, say, a science of pine needles. Why this urgency and excitement about the necessity and possibility of a science of mental life?

Western secularism, as mentioned in Chapter 1, is a key context. Renaissance figures like Copernicus, Descartes, and Newton envisioned the world as an orderly place whose order could be discerned through the application of mathematical and geometric intelligence. Ever since, an entire worldview has rested on the integrity and success of science. A worldview is not, of course, merely an idea system, a series of articulated philosophical notions appropriate for academic debate. A worldview is the very basis of the intelligibility of life. It becomes a remarkably concrete and personal investment in which your and my very identities are at stake, our presupposed reasons for doing virtually everything we do.

The collective agreement about the scientific worldview has always been partial, peaking perhaps in the twentieth century, and always subject to attack from such groups as believers in God, or in poetry. The combination of certainty and dissent about the scientific worldview has characterized modern Western culture, and continues to this day. In the nineteenth century, there was an acceleration of science, an intensification of the resulting tension, and a new vision within science itself about how to win its battle against nonscience, including superstition. That new vision engaged a science of mental life.

Already in Descartes, but especially in the British empirical philosophers who followed him, the extension of scientific discernment of order to mental life itself, to discernment itself, was envisioned. But it was only in the nineteenth century that the concrete form of this science became visible. E. G. Boring (1950), in his exhaustive *A History of Experimental Psychology*, devotes an entire chapter to the "personal equation." He begins, "At Greenwich in 1796 Maskelyne, as every psychologist knows [*sic*], dismissed Kinnebrook, his assistant, because Kinnebrook observed the times of stellar transits almost a second later than he did" (p. 134). This event began a century's concern, in scientific circles, with the personal equation, a concern that culminated in the reaction-time experiments of Wundt, the whole field of psychophysics, and ultimately the establishment of psychology, the science of mental life.

The importance of the personal equation, however, is not only that it led to psychology, nor even that it played a part in the development of Einsteinian physics. The problem of the intervention of persons into the perfect sphere of scientific knowledge reminded scientists of the tentativity of the scientific worldview itself. But it also offered the opportunity to successfully meet this challenge and hence to complete the scientific victory once and for all. Granted, persons interfere with the perfection of scientific knowledge; the knower, the mind itself, has its limits. But to overcome these limits becomes possible by having a science of mental life according to which the necessary adjustments can be made, and the soundness of scientific knowledge can be more assured than ever. The science of mental life was not, therefore, just another science, but the "queen of sciences," the "propaedeutic science," the first, the basic, the prerequisite science. If all knowledge is somehow dependent upon a knower, it will not do to leave knowers, mind, and consciousness unexamined if that knowledge is to be certain.

The breakthrough in the nineteenth century, the emergence of a concrete form for this old idea of a science of mental life, came in the application of experimental methods to the body, the nervous system. When Helmholz, in 1850, demonstrated that the speed of nervous transmission was not only not instantaneous but measurable, and, to everyone's surprise, slower than the speed of sound, he not only demonstrated the success of experimental methods for investigating the nervous system and hence the material basis of knowing. He and his colleagues were also winning a long-standing battle with their respected scientific mentor, G. E. Mueller, who held the view that life cannot be reduced to matter and energy but remains a special, extraphysical phenomenon. Mueller's vitalism was not religion or theology, but it stood in the way of materialistic hegemony and, seemingly, in the way of scientific progress itself. Once the nervous system is brought under the control of scientific concepts, the knower, knowing itself, would presumably no longer remain a mystery.

This vision is reductionistic; mind is reduced to the nervous system, while a mental event, experiencing itself, is reduced to the activity of the brain. Nothing will remain unknown about knowing itself, and the language and worldview of Newtonian science will be that much more secure. Here, "reductionistic" is not merely a pejorative word. It is science's goal to "reduce" the amazing complexity of life to comprehensible and comprehensive principles. And yet not all nineteenth-century scientists of mental life believed that this reductionistic vision was the only one. Wundt himself resisted reductionism and was a dualist, if reluctantly, while Fechner, whose work in psychophysics makes him memorable to us, was a spiritualist who sought to persuade his materialistic century that the materialist worldview was a *Nachtansicht*, a vision of night and of sleep, in contrast to his *Tagesansicht*, which was seeing by the light of his spiritualistic day.

The increasing momentum of secularization was bound to win. We must, of course, dwell a bit on Wundt, that encyclopedia organizer and systematizer of nineteenth-century psychology, to see what was meant by the notion of *Erfahrungswissenschaft*, a science of mental life.

DUALISM AND METAPHYSICS

Boring (1950) offers us an intriguing view of Wundt's psychology and why Wundt called it "physiological psychology." Boring notes that there were really two roots of modern psychology, one in philosophy dating back to the Greeks but clearly accelerated in the concerns of Locke and the British empiricists—concerns known even then as "psychological"—and the other stemming from the scientific breakthroughs in physiology in the first half of the nineteenth century. According to Boring, it was only in the 1860s that it became clear that the "psychology" of the philosophers—primarily a set of questions, issues, and concerns—and the "physiology" of the early 1800s—primarily an approach, the experimental method—were deeply related, if not about identical things. The fusion of the traditional questions of psychology with the nineteenth-century methods of physiology yielded the hybrid "physiological psychology," as Wundt titled his voluminous work. The adjective "physiological" should therefore be read as "experimental," rather than denoting a particular hybrid of separate disciplines, physiology and psychology, such as "physiological psychology" is today.[1]

If you were a scientist in the nineteenth century, nothing would be more understandable to you than the impulse to extend the methods of natural science to the psyche. Some scientists then, as now, were thoroughgoing materialists, for whom the term "mind" was at best a convenient label for the functioning of the brain, or at worst, a superstitious holdover from prescientific times. Most scientists, however, understood the manner as Wundt (1904) did, namely, that the mind, the subject matter of psychology, is not identical to the brain and, therefore, that psychology is not physiology: "The fact that the naive consciousness always and everywhere points to internal experience as a special source of knowledge may, therefore, be accepted for the moment as sufficient testimony to the rights of psychology as science" (p. 17).

Many Americans, however, were quite unclear about Wundt's placement of psychology in the scheme of the sciences. This placement depended on the difference between the data of physics, which were mediated by theory, and psychology, which dealt with immediate (unmediated) experience. Laws of physical science, mediated by language, were clearly stated in deterministic formula. In contrast, laws of psychology, which undercut language, in Wundt's view, "express purposes, preferences, and values," as Hilgard (1987, p. 67) puts it. The science of mental life was therefore precisely the science of knowing, that special source, internal experience, which Kant (1724–1804), in the late eighteenth century, said could never be studied scientifically.[2]

Kant's view was that studying the mind actually changed it, and therefore it was unlike the natural objects to which science is applicable. Fichte, Schelling, and the nineteenth-century Romantics generally agreed with Kant that the mind is therefore "transcendental," a view that was understood by scientists, reductionistic materialists, and dualists alike to be antiscientific. Kant also argued that the mind must be understood in terms of qualities instead of quantities, to which Wundt replied that Fechner's psychophysics demonstrated the contrary.[3]

Fechner had appreciated and elaborated on Weber's law, which states that there is a precise and regular relationship between mental events and the physical properties of the stimulus of which they were conscious. Since such a "law" exists, Kant's vivid distinction between "qualities" (read "mental") and "quantities" (read "physical") seemed unnecessary, at least to some. They were not only related in an orderly way, they might somehow be two aspects of the same thing. The entire discipline of "psychophysics," which attempted to elaborate Fechner's findings, had an at least implicit agenda to overcome dualism, if not all metaphysics, with the light of science. Psychophysics has been largely abandoned in this country, partly because psychology no longer needed to establish its legitimacy by resolving dualism. The issue was simply relegated to philosophy, a nonscientific discipline in most academic circles.

Returning to Wundt's view, which clearly dominated the early decades of psychology in Europe, physiological psychology was a science that brought the methods of measurement and experimentation to mental events as these are experienced directly in consciousness, without reducing the mind to the material brain. This was the promise of the propaedeutic science that could secure, once and for all, the scientific worldview. The reservations of Kant and his successors in poetry, philosophy, and religion were hardly appreciated by the growing number of enthusiastic scientists of mental life. A notable exception was Fechner, who actively sustained both scientific and philosophical–spiritual interests.

One major theme that emerged as a corollary to the new science was that metaphysics is irrelevant.[4] This theme was given further impetus from the fact that serious study of the mind had heretofore been done by philosophers, and psychologists, as scientists, were not merely repeating their work. Scientific methods were vastly different from the philosophical methods of rational argument and speculation. And the kinds of questions asked by scientists, as well as the kinds of things that qualify as answers, were notably different from those questions and answers of philosophy. It therefore became important for the midwives of the new science to avoid falling into the traditional patterns of metaphysical thought.

THE HISTORICAL PROJECT

The difference between the late eighteenth century of Kant and the late nineteenth century of Wundt (and the late twentieth century of recent thinking) is instructive. Between Kant and Wundt stands the French Revolution, the great advances in physiological science, the appearance of Hegel and Hegelians and the Romantics, and Karl Marx and Charles Darwin, to name only a few important events. Between Wundt and our own time stand two world wars, the emergence of global interaction, and a technological remaking of much of the environment in advanced nations. Further, the twentieth century saw the emergence of technologically disadvantaged nations, Einsteinian physics, enormous advances in scientific medicine, and the development of modern psychology. Here we want only to think briefly about Kant, then Wundt, then ourselves; the remainder of our work will detail the history of ideas in psychology, one aspect of the twentieth century.

Kant's question was something like this: How can we know anything at all? By Wundt's time, the question had become, How does the mind work? By the end of the twentieth century, we asked, What causes behavior? What is the relation among these three questions? Are they really the same question in different forms? Is there some kind of progressive order to them? Are the questions based on different presuppositions? Is there an order to this series of presuppositions?

One might see a progressive sharpening of the question in such a way that we have increased the likelihood of arriving at a meaningful answer by ruling out the imponderables that only serve to retard our progress. That is, Kant's question engages our thinking about a kind of ultimate issue. It tries to ask everything at once, and it is clear from Kant's philosophy that in order to proceed with the work, Kant had to answer everything at once.

By Wundt's time, the whole area of metaphysics had been marginalized.[5] Specific Kantian formulations about the nature of the mind (transcendental, not a part of nature as nature is usually conceived) and the nature of the world (knowable only in its phenomenal appearance and inaccessible as it is in itself) had become less central to Wundt's science of mental life. Now, in retrospect, we see these as incidental or even irrelevant to Wundt's science. The mind was not the body or the brain, nor was it physiologically approachable. However, its metaphysical status, the philosophical view that the mind has a different nature from the material world, was irrelevant. The same scientific methods that led to the mastery of the world and the body, it was believed, would reveal the workings of the mind and yield up the envisioned propaedeutic science. Science thus abandonded, then replaced, but did not resolve, mind–body dualism.

Through much of the twentieth century, the mind was no longer the focus as it was in Wundt's time. Our assumption tends to be that insofar as we know about the mind at all, it is only through behavior, and insofar as we want to know about the mind at all, it is in terms of how it affects behavior. It has certainly been possible since early in the twentieth century to have a psychology without a mind at all.

Many see this as an elimination of irrelevancies, and therefore as progress. As our thinking has tried and failed and evolved, we have come to see more clearly what questions can be answered and what questions cannot. This discrimination has emerged through a progressive application of operational strategies, which asssume that questions can be answered only through the testing of hypotheses cast into the language of operational variables. By Wundt's time, the nature (metaphysically understood) of mind and world disappeared from the list of answerable questions, and by our own time, the mind itself as an object of science has disappeared, and we work only with its functions and externally visible manifestations—if we work with it at all.

This sequence of Kant's, then Wundt's, then late twentieth-century questions can, therefore, also be seen as a loss, perhaps a loss of radicality and a progressive narrowing of scope to less and less basic questions. The narrower one's focus, the more must be taken for granted. Wundt's science of mental life no longer asked whether the mind is of such a nature that it can be studied by scientific methods. It is simply assumed to be studiable in this way. The science of the causes of behavior, which populated so much of American psychology in the twentieth century, did not even ask how the mind works until after mid-century. The focus had become the causes of behavior. It was often assumed that the working of the mind is not really important apart from the real business of the science, overt behavior.

By the end of the twentieth century, the cognitive revolution had been firmly established, and questions of how the mind works have reappeared in psychology, although the methods of science still demanded a behavioral index for research variables. This return to important questions about the mind from earlier formulations about mere behavior suggests that the future of psychology may reverse the sequence of progress from the nineteenth to the twentieth centuries, revisiting with more sure-footed methodology an exploration of questions seemingly unanswerable in the twentieth century. We shall take this up at the end of this book.

Wundt's science of mental life may, in summary, be seen as part of a larger trend from Kant's time to our own. Did he purify the science by ignoring metaphysics, or did he contaminate it by presupposing a metaphysical postion which, in its inexplicitness, biased his science? Must one ask everything at once, or does this lead to the paralysis of mere speculation? Must one focus on some apparently answerable part, or does this lead to unexamined assumptions and, hence, bias? These two questions are also on the agenda for the end of the book.

Wundt himself can hardly be accused of naïveté. He taught and published philosophy for part of his career, and he never believed that the science of mental life that ran through the laboratory, parallel to the science of physiology, was the whole story. Indeed, the higher mental processes, where the propeadeutic promise of psychology would be fulfilled, would only be clarified in *Voelkerpsychologie*, the science of the natural and social history of man. Wundt was also quite conscious of taking a metaphysical position in saying that the mind, the subject of psychology, is exhausted by the predicates we can scientifically demonstrate to it. That is, if we strip away from the mind that which is demonstrable, there remains no entity or reality. Metaphysics, the attempt to discern the ultimate nature of reality, is reduced here to science.[6]

Wundt's science was, we can now see, transitional. It both was and was not metaphysics. It was metaphysics because the nature of reality is at stake; the mind is not the same thing as the brain. It was not metaphysics because that very hypothesis assumed that the nature of the mind is such that it can be revealed by science. Thus, the older metaphysics became superfluous, but the study of the brain became irrelevant. Eschewing Kant's metaphysics of a reality that transcends nature did not reduce the mind to the brain.

Is Wundt's position defensible? Can one ask how the mind works while assuming its nature is such that this question can be answered by scientific methods? While Wundt assumed that mind is not body but is studiable by science, by the mid-twentieth century we assumed further that mind is scientifically comprehensible only as it is related to behavior, and that behavior is comprehensible by studying its causes. Perhaps psychologists should more sharply distinguish Wundt's dualism from Kant's. The mind needn't be transcendent of nature (Kant) to be nevertheless different from the brain (Wundt), or from the objects it perceives.[7]

Wundt, in rejecting Kant's notion of the mind as transcendent, affirmed the proposition that the mind is a natural, and not a transcendent, object. Today, in making all psychology scientific, psychology appears to affirm the further proposition that this natural object, the mind, is essentially embedded in a network of causes and effects, as are physical realities. But here a resurgence of old doubts arises.[8]

Wundt's psychology–physiology (mind–brain) dualism was technically a parallelism, the notion that the two run through nature in a parallel fashion. Every event in one is accompanied by a congruent event in the other. This too is metaphysics—but not really. It presupposes a metaphysical doctrine for the purpose of making possible the progressive development of the science. Wundt simply couldn't ask all the questions at once, and the ones he chose to ask were those answerable, he thought, by science. But if science then flourishes independent of metaphysics as a discipline, can science do so without metaphysical suppositions? And can any such metaphysical presuppositions bias science? Even more to the point, has science itself really become independent of its philosophical underpinnings? Has today's psychology, in its successful establishment of itself as an independent science, compounded or resolved Wundt's problem?

Titchener (1929), in his *Systematic Psychology: A Prolegomena*, pits Wundt's psychology against that of Franz Brentano. Brentano was a Kantian if one looks behind him, and a precursor of Wuerzburg psychology, Gestalt psychology, and contemporary phenomenological psychology if one looks ahead of him. What was at stake between these two psychologists, Wundt and Brentano, was, Titchener notes, a method, but behind the methodological difference lies a disagreement about the nature of the mind, a difference we must call a metaphysical difference. If one assumes, with Wundt, that the mind is a part of nature, then it stands in nature, to be studied by experiment, guided by, say, mathematical conceptualizations.

The focus of Wundt's psychology is therefore immediate experience, most notably sensations, images, and simple feelings. These elements were not conceived by Wundt to be things, substantive bits which, like so many tiles, make up the mosaic of living experience. For Wundt emphasized again and again the movement and activity of the mind. However, as a part of nature (as we have conceived nature in natural science), the elements are subject to natural law, and, while not bodily, they are closely analogous to the mechanics of bodies.

Brentano (1874/1960), in vivid contrast to Wundt, distinguished all Wundt's phenomena (which he called "psychic content") from "psychic acts," which he conceived to be the more important part of psychology. Psychic acts are "intentional," or less ambiguously referential. They refer to content, such as sensations, images, and feelings. These latter, then, the content of experience and the focus of Wundt's psychology, are physical, not psychic, phenomena. The mind, the psyche, is intentional. It is that which refers to physical phenomena and, hence, also to the world. The psyche is not, therefore, in nature, a part of nature or the world at all, but rather is that by virtue of which nature and the world can be sensed, perceived, and known by us. This argues that rather than in nature, the mind is logically, strategically, and even metaphysically, prior to nature. Thus, perhaps as we see Kant's, we may see Brentano's mind as "transcendent."

As psychological theory, the Wundt–Brentano difference seems small, especially since Wundt spoke of elements as processes and activities. As metaphysics, on the other hand, the two positions were vastly different, for "intentionality" (Brentano's word for referentiality), as the nature of the mind, makes it different from any other object in nature. And from that difference follow very different notions of how to have a science of mental life. Brentano, while empirical and loyal to phenomena as they appear rather than, say, the truths of authority or tradition, was not experimental. Experiments depend on having control of the variables. Psychic acts are not experimentally controllable, although they are, Brentano would argue, both observable and capable of being understood.

If a metaphysical difference lies at the root of the Brentano–Wundt disagreement, and if one's methodology depends upon this prior metaphysical difference, then it follows that the difference itself cannot be settled by one method or the other. The method is as much in question as the theory it derives from. It therefore made no more sense then to insist on an experimental demonstration of Brentano's theory than it does today to insist on a scientific finding about God. But what are we to do with such differences as those between Brentano and Wundt? We shall watch the development of the history of psychology in this country to see that Wundt and Brentano were both rejected in the face of behaviorism.[9]

THE AMERICAN CLIMATE

A great deal of Kant, Wundt, Helmholz, and Fechner was known to physiologists and philosophers in this country during the nineteenth century. It was not, however, known outside academic circles, as were the medical–technical improvements that steadily refined American medicine. The birth of the new science of psychology, however, made a more general impression, and William James's (1890) *Principles of Psychology* was an event in American letters and American self-consciousness. Onto what sort of soil did that fertile seed fall?

Even more salient in American culture than the thinkers we have discussed, for scholars and laymen alike, was the Darwinian theory that extended to all spheres of life. The Civil War over, Reconstruction presumably accomplished, and American transcendentalism in its twilight, the resistance to Darwinian ideas faded in the face of the immense popularity of Herbert Spencer's Social Darwinism. Louis Agassiz, the renouned naturalist who held out against Darwin, died in 1873, to be replaced by religious objections such as C. Hodge's (1874) *What Is Darwinism?* which in turn gave way to Henry Ward Beecher's pulpit approval of Darwin and Spencer. By the turn of the century, every intellectual was a Darwinian, a Spencerian, or both, and William James was not the least of the enthusiasts.

Of course, Social Darwinism, as preached by Spencer and William Graham Sumner, the "William James of American Sociology," was not simply Darwin's theory of the origin of the species. According to Sumner, humanist impulses to reverse the exploitations of laissez faire capitalism could be immediately laid to rest by the view that some individuals are less fit than others. The argument went on to say that to artificially perpetuate the stock of the less fit would be to weaken the gene pool as a whole and to interfere with the natural processes of selection merely because of short-sighted sentimentalism. It is no wonder that John D. Rockefeller and Andrew Carnegie, the giants of American capitalist free enterprise, were both Spencerian Social Darwinists. In its worst form, Social Darwinism made it possible to feel self-righteously attuned to natural law, or even to God's law, by being insensitive to the suffering of the "less fit" in society's process of "evolution."

Even as Social Darwinism was "conservative" in the sense of justifying policies that did not interfere with the "natural selection" of the capitalist economy, it also contained an inherent optimism about the inevitability of progress. Thus, as an apparent scientific basis for a practical social policy, Darwinism struck two responsive chords in American popular thought: free enterprise and progress.

However, Darwinism had different ramifications elsewhere. As eventually written by James in 1890, American psychology "had inherited its physical body from German experimentalism, but it had got its mind from Darwin," in the words of Boring (1950, p. 506). American psychology was not about the mind as a theoretical problem whose workings could be discovered by Wundtian experimentalism. American psychology was about the mind in use, as a part of the adaptive equipment of the organism in the environment as it struggled within the great game plan of evolution. Although E. B. Titchener imported Wundt's less practical notion of the mind into psychology, which dominated for a decade or so at the beginning of the twentieth century, the more practical orientation, seen clearly in James and Spencer, was eventually to predominate.

James's psychology was clearly more American than Titchener's, and the temporary Titchenerian hegemony only gave more impetus to the Watsonian revolution when it was to come in the second decade of the twentieth century.

NOTES

1. This terminological matter is even more complex. Today's physiological psychology uses behavior as the dependent variable in research. Hence, much contemporary psychology is really a science, not of the psyche but of behavior, and should be called "behaviorology." Nevertheless, the old prebehaviorist term, "psychology" survived the behavioral revolution. Hence, both Wundt's physiological psychology and current physiological psychology are misnamed, the former because "physiology" was a metaphor for a method, and not a subject matter, and the latter because "psychology" is a metaphor for a subject matter which, for many psychologists in the twentieth century, was not the psyche at all.

2. Hilgard (1987), repeating Wundt, puts this hope this way: "Because natural science treats the objective data as derived from subjective experience, the data of science may be considered to represent mediated experience, that is, mediated by the observations of the scientist. In Psychology, however, experience is treated as immediate and underived, that is, based directly on the experience of the knower" (p. 41). Thus, Wundt's psychology, in studying consciouseness itself, was about the psyche. Wundt's psychology was believed to bridge the knower and the world that is known, and thus to ground the knowing of objective science in science itself. None of this is true today, nor does it seem to be understood today.

3. Hilgard (1987) cites Fries as the first step in graduating from Kant's doubts about a science of the mind, followed by Herbart, then Beneke, and finally Lotze, whom James (1890) quotes in several chapters of his *Principles of Psychology*. The point here, however, is that psychology, which was to secure *knowing* scientifically, was aimed at overcoming Kant's transcendentalism, which was of course a vivid metaphysical dualism. The early psychologists were ambitious indeed. By themselves they accomplished little of their ambitions, but the secularist wave they were riding did indeed succeed in the twentieth century.

4. While Wundt was no metaphysician, he also studied for most of his career a *Voelkerspsychologie* (collective and historical psychology) that was to be different from the natural science. This historical psychology was not the natural science (*Naturswissenschaft*) for which he is now known; it was to be closer to philosophy, which is exactly cultural and historical, in the spirit of "cultural science" (*Geisteswissenschaft*), empirical but mediated by langauge and neither experimental nor immediate. This work was never translated into English.

5. This is true insofar as science focuses on the object of our perception. At the same time, science can of course objectify the mind. To do so is to make the subject (the mind) into an object of our perception, appreciated by a part of the mind that is looking, and one that is never looked at without the looker retreating to yet another vantage point, which itself, in turn, can only be objectified by yet another distantiation. The always-present residual looker continues to create a philosophical, indeed a metaphysical, indeed a dualistic, problem. Wundt, of course, must have disputed this point. Thus, the reduction of the study of the mind to what then constituted science was a reduction from studying the mind's unique nature to a study of some of its elements and functions. It is hard today to assess the relative importance of such various issues, and even today such a reduction is totally lost from view.

6. Wundt's psychology was shaped in important ways by the fact that, in Germany, special technological institutes not connected to universities shaped the practice of psychology independent of what in the United States was decisive: the role of students. The setting of psychology in American schools of education, engineering, and business also gave the American development a practical turn that was often seen in Germany as merely another example of American materialism. G. Stanley Hall, Edward Thorndike, and John Dewey all mixed their psychology with scientific pedagogy; Hall's early journal was, in fact, called *Scientific Pedagogy*.

7. There is a way that the cognitive psychology of the second half of the twentieth century operates upon this principle. Again, it is important to note that this reduction to science is a reduction from concerns about the nature of the mind to concerns with some of its functions, a concern more amenable to practical questions than to theoretical ones.

8. For example, how can I know that? Is that knower free to know? If so, we don't know it the way we know an object. If not, then knowing is not true knowing at all.

9. Wundt was not a building-block elementarist as E. B. Titchener was, but Titchener failed to make clear how his psychology differed from Wundt's. Those early American psychologists who accepted Wundt's psychology accepted his *Naturswissenschaft* (natural science) over his *Geisteswissenschaft* (mental, cultural–historical science). In fact, Wundt's (1900–1920) enormously ambitious *Voelkerspsychologie* was never translated, and the American psychology that followed was never introduced to Wundt's historical and social analysis of mental life. American interest in the late 1960s in such analyses, such as those from the Frankfort School (e.g., Marcuse, 1966; Benjamin, 1969; Habermas, 1968; Horkheimer; 1972), never benefited from Wundt's work.

3

The Psychology of William James

THE LIFE OF WILLIAM JAMES (1842–1910)

William James's extraordinary career began at his birth into a wealthy and well-known family in New York in 1842. His father insisted on educating all his five children, including William, who also visited Europe extensively as a young man. In 1867 at the University of Berlin he attended lectures in physiology, remarking that it was "time for psychology to begin to be a science" (Schultz, 1975, p. 130). Plagued by digestive problems, insomnia, poor vision, a weak back, and chronic depression, James nevertheless took a medical degree in 1869 from Harvard and decided that he was free to believe in free will. Armed with this conclusion he set about to cure himself, and in 1875–1876 he taught his first course in psychology, "The Relations between Physiology and Psychology." In 1875 he established a small laboratory at Harvard with $300.

In 1878 he married and eventually had five children. Shortly after establishing himself in Cambridge, he contracted with Henry Holt and Company to write a psychology book. His anticipated two-year task took twelve years, during which time he became professor of philosophy in 1885 and professor of psychology in 1889. His *Principles of Psychology* appeared in 1890, and was surprisingly popular. James therefore produced his *Principles of Psychology: Briefer Course* in 1892. Nevertheless, his opinion of the work was that it was "a loathsome, distended, tumefied, bloated, dropsical mass, testifying to nothing but two facts: *1st*, that there is no such thing as a *science* of psychology, and *2nd*, that W. J. is an incapable" (quoted in Allen, 1967, pp. 314–315).

Convinced of his own conclusion about psychology, James, now a leading, if not the premier, psychologist in America, dedicated himself to philosophy, producing *Talks to Teachers* in 1899, *The Varieties of Religious Experience* in 1901–1902, and three other books. He retired in 1907 and died in 1910.

THE PLACE OF PSYCHOLOGY

In the first chapter of his *Psychology: Briefer Course* (1892), James states the relation of psychology, the natural science, to the rest of knowledge: "Most thinkers have a faith that at bottom there is but one Science of all things, and until all is known, no one thing can be completely known. Such a science, if realized, would be Philosophy" (p. 1). James knows this is not the best of all possible worlds: "Meanwhile it is far from being realized; and instead of it, we have a lot of beginnings of knowledge made in different places, and kept separate from each other merely for practical convenience sake, until with later growth they may run into one body of Truth" (p. 1). This optimistic development is already underway: "These provisional beginnings of learning we call 'the Sciences' in the plural. In order not to be unwieldy, every such science has to stick to its own arbitrarily-selected problems, and to ignore all others. Every science thus accepts certain data unquestioningly, leaving it to other parts of Philosophy to scrutinize their significance and truth" (pp. 1–2). A little later James adds, "The full truth about states of mind cannot be known until both theory of Knowledge and Rational Psychology have said their say. Meanwhile, an immense amount of provisional truth about them can be got together, which will work in with the larger truth and be interpreted by it when the proper time arrives" (pp. 2–3). Therefore, James concludes, "Such a provisional body of propositions about states of mind, and about cognitions which they enjoy, is what I mean by Psychology considered as a natural science" (p. 3).

As we read James's (1892) psychology, we find again and again that some crucial metaphysical question receives an equivocal answer. An example is the question whether, or in what sense, the mind is autonomous from the material lawfulness of the brain. On the one hand, the activity of the mind is "uniformly and absolutely a function of brain action, varying as the latter varies, and being to brain action as effect to cause" (p. 6). This "working hypothesis of this book," however, is not taken by James to be the final formulation of the truth, and in fact he later points out that "the whole feeling of reality, the whole sting and excitement of our voluntary life, depends on our sense that in it things are *really being decided* from one moment to another, and that it is not the dull rattling off of a chain that was forged innumerable ages ago" (pp. 237–238). Taking these reflections seriously, James concludes, "This appearance, which makes life and history tingle with such tragic zest, *may* not be an illusion" (p. 238).

And so psychology, as a natural science, must postulate complete determinism. At the same time, James suspects a psychology will have to incorporate phenomena we normally call "free will." In positing determinism, we certainly are not committing ourselves, in James's view, to anything more than a convenience. Such tentative conveniences will enable our psychology to proceed without having to answer all the questions at once. We see here something of Wundt's attitude, as indeed it was the attitude of a lot of people in the early days of psychology.[1]

James does not, however, refrain from arguing with the metaphysicians and philosophers when he believes he can do so from a scientific (i.e., empirical) point of view. This attitude has become a central tenet of all subsequent scientific psychology. With little hesitation, James will point to a view of Hume's or Kant's and call it "absurd" or "having no basis whatever." He is not, in these passages, engaging in metaphysics but in science. It will depend upon the larger truths of philosophy to interpret psychological findings, but when the philosophers offer us views of the mind that are patently wrong on empirical grounds, James feels at liberty to criticize them.[2] The empirical criterion for knowledge cannot answer all our human questions. But it can answer questions about a range of facts. What are the facts of mental life?

These questions are not the same as metaphysical issues, which go beyond the facts to propose formulations about the nature of thought, the mind, imagination, and so on. However, although James claims to be a scientist and to establish scientific truths, he cannot totally avoid being a metaphysician, for he does speculate about the nature of the mind throughout his book. And yet James must be counted as a scientist in *Principals of Psychology*, for he insists on an empirical basis for his descriptions, and when he speculated, as in his theory of emotion, his ordering of phenomena into more systematic views often follows the deterministic assumptions of natural science.[3]

James (1892) was not, however, an experimentalist, as were his German counterparts. Although he dutifully read the psychophysics of the day in German universities, he gives it brief space: "As absolutely nothing practical has come of it, it need receive no further notice here" (p. 22). He did not share the vision of an experimental determination of the relation between mind and matter, nor therefore was psychology for James the propaedeutic science. The mind that he pursued with relentless description and tried at every point to correlate with what was known of the brain was not the mind of the German universities. That mind appeared to most Americans, if not also to James, to be mysterious stuff or a transcendental entity. In contrast, James's "mind" was *the mind working*. Here are a few of James's chapter titles: Attention, Conception, Discrimination, Association, Memory, Imagination, Perceptions, Reasoning, Consciousness, and Self.

That list of topics, of the mind working, occupies a central part of James's *Principles* (1890). These topics are arranged, especially in his more compact *Briefer Course* (1892), between initial chapters on input, sensation, and sense organs, and concluding chapters on output, "the bodily activities"; namely, emotion, instinct, and will. Indeed, we have a general picture of the nervous system as a whole that diagrams the superstructure of James's entire psychology.

Coming in at the bottom right in Figure 3.1 are sensations (S), which either traverse the reflex arc (at C) and exit as motor action (M), or go through the upper loop, which includes the cerebral hemispheres (H), again eventuating as action, but considered action, rather than reflexive action. His vivid description of the behavior of decerebrated frogs makes it clear that their lack of the upper loop changes their behavior such that it is almost totally mechanical, while normal frogs ordinarily "look before they leap" and engage in what James (1890) calls "considerations." It is the "considerations," the central loop, that make up the central chapters in his psychology of human beings, including their consciousnesses and selves.

Figure 3.1
Reflex Arc, Including the Cortex

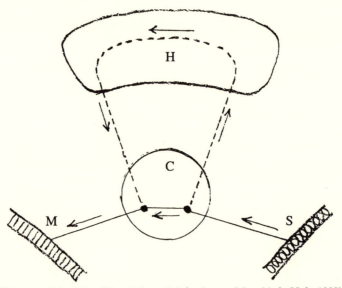

Source: W. James, *Principles of Psychology: Briefer Course* (New York: Holt, 1892), p. 98.

Various individual chapters in James's psychology are so remarkable that we will have occasion to remind ourselves of this superstructure of his theory. While there have been modifications and complications, it is not unfair to say that this general model remained in mainstream American psychology virtually untouched for well over half a century and is still explicit (or at least lies dormant) in most American psychological thinking.

THE SYSTEM

Suppose that you wanted to develop a science of smell. You would be aware that a number of odors are discriminable from one another, and are, in fact, also quite memorable to the population at large. Once one has smelled a skunk, one will forever recognize that odor and never confuse it with roses or tobacco. But the science of smell needs to describe the skunk odor, and the rose, and the tobacco, in such a way that these various phenomena are put into some systematic relation to one another. In order to do that, we would have to find some dimensions on which various properties of smells are more or less present, or categories of which various smells are or are not members. Whether we follow the dimensional (quantitative) or the categorical (qualitative) strategy, we will be making crucial decisions. We will be naming the phenomena, defining and describing them, according to some conceptual scheme.

Where ought that conceptual scheme come from? Where, in fact, did it come from in the development of psychology? If we look critically at James's (1890) *Principles* in terms of those decisions he made, we would be looking for the root metaphors in terms of which he wrote his psychology.[4] Further, we could do no better than to take the chapter, "Habit," and the chapter, "The Stream of Consciousness," to see the basic metaphors of his whole psychology.

Habit and Consciousness

Habit is based on a fundamental property of matter to retain the shape it has and yet to be subject to change its shape under pressure. Our lives are, in no small measure, like matter in this respect. Just as we might say the skunk's odor is penetrating and sharp, so might we say our lives are like the plasticity of matter: subject to change, but essentially stable. James (1890) is quite clear that this is what he means when describing habit as "in the first instance, a chapter in physics" (vol. I, p. 105).[5]

Consciousness, on the other hand, demands a different metaphor. What is consciousness *like*? James explains four characteristics of consciousness in great detail—that it is always mine, always changing, yet always continuous, and always selective—but the metaphor that sums these all up is the chapter title itself, "The Stream of Consciousness." Consciousness is like a stream.

The flowing instability of a stream is utterly unthinglike, and it contrasts sharply with the plasticity of matter that appeared in the habit chapter. The stability of matter and the fluidity of a stream: This pair of metaphors defines human nature for William James. The dignity of this pair should not be underestimated, for the two themes, of continuity and sameness versus discontinuity and changeability, have permeated every major thought system in the West since the pre-Socratics.

It is important, however, to note that James (1892) did not think of the plasticity of matter to be a mere metaphor, but, rather, he was in fact speaking about very particular matter indeed: our nervous system. Habit, considered psychologically, is of course only part of the story, but James develops the idea. Socially, habit is "the enormous fly-wheel of society, its most precious conservative agent" (p. 143), and physiologically, habit is "nothing but a new pathway of discharge formed in the brain" (p. 134). Psychological habit is thus the link between the material basis of human nature in the nervous system, on the one hand, and social stability, or even conservatism, on the other.

Being plastic, however, the nervous system is also subject to our shaping, and James (1892) offers us a number of maxims for shaping it to our advantage, to "make the nervous system our ally instead of our enemy" (p. 144). These maxims are advice about how to deal with our own material nature, how to make our bodies allies, how to engage for our own uses the plasticity of our nature. The maxims all require, of course, effort and attention. While James argues that effort is, in fact, none other than the disciplining of our attention, the real question is whether our attention itself is sufficiently independent of habit to bring the latter under control. On this point, James states, "To what brain processes [attention and effort] correspond, we do not know. The strongest reason for believing that they do depend on brain processes at all, and are not pure acts of the spirit, is just that fact, that they seem in some degree subject to the law of habit, which is a material law" (p. 149). And yet the maxims are offered as if we could, by attention and effort, follow them and improve ourselves. By what agency could this be possible?

If we therefore turn to consciousness, we find anything but an agency (like a soul) to answer this question. And so the question is put off until that extension of the consciousness chapter, James's famous chapter on the self. But what we do find in the consciousness chapter is a description of consciousness through the metaphor of a stream, and James no doubt feels this is the central chapter in his science of mental life. If psychology is to be the science of mental life, then just what mental life is like becomes crucial for the science, and James believes that previous descriptions have falsified the phenomenon (especially the bits of consciousness that appear in Hobbes and Locke as "ideas" and "sensations," and reappear in the later nineteenth-century Germans like Helmholz and Wundt, as well).

The "stream" may be divided between substantive and transitive phases, as a bird flits from twig to twig, never really staying in any one place, and yet, like a bird, having points of nonmotion and rest. The sensationists, from Locke to Herbart, proclaimed the substantive states to be all there is, with the ultimate absurdity in Hume's doctrine that we can never perceive relations between events at all. The intellectualists, on the other hand, most notably Kant, conclude that relations, while never perceived, are nevertheless known, and therefore they must be known a priori.

James (1892) insists that an unbiased look at what consciousness is really like will show that we ought to speak of "a feeling of *and*, a feeling of *if*, a feeling of *but*, and a feeling of *by*, quite as readily as we say a feeling of *blue* or a feeling of *cold*" (p. 162). Consciousness itself registers both the substantive and the transitive phases, and hence the science of mental life must reckon with both. Both are in our data; we need not turn to metaphysical conclusions or suppositions to explore images and sensations, on the one hand, or the relations between them in our mental life, on the other.

We will certainly not, therefore, find agency in the stream of consciousness, at least insofar as such an agency would require a metaphysical statement from James. And yet one of the features of consciousness itself, beside being always mine, always changing, and always continuous, is that it is always selective. Consciousness always selects, from an array of possibilities, one focus, moment by moment. James will not attribute to consciousness an agency that will require a metaphysical statement, but he certainly claims, with no ambiguity and on purely empirical grounds, that the events of mental life are selected and selective.

The Self

The chapter on the self, James (1892) states, is the "finer work" that follows "this first general sketch" (p. 175), of consciousness in general.[6] The self, for James, has already been implicated in his description of consciousness as always mine and as always selective. These two features of consciousness accordingly refer to two aspects of the self. That consciousness is always mine is a way of saying that it refers to the self I know, the "me." That consciousness is always selective is a way of saying that the self is not only known but is also a knower, an "I." The "me" and the "I," or "self as known" and "self as knower," make up the two parts to this rich and complex chapter.

The "me" that is "known" is divided by James (1892) into the *material me* (body, clothing, possessions), the *social me* (as seen by others), and the *spiritual me* (that sense I have that I am an agency, which I know as my "soul," or some such term). With respect to each, James then describes our feelings of self-regard, self-seeking, humiliation, pride, and other such issues. Self-esteem, he notes, is the quotient of success/pretensions, a concept somewhat better, I think, than the mass of research on self-esteem in the twentieth century. Amidst these various selves and our feelings about them one personally organizes his life, hierarchizing the selves by value and calculating the nearness to actuality for each envisioned potentiality. James's descriptions of the experience of oneself are as true as any in the entire literature of psychology.

The self as "knower," the "I," presents James (1892), and us, with a different task. James's goal here is to show (1) that the concept of a transcendental ego or soul is superfluous for psychology, and (2) that psychology without such a metaphysical construct is still perfectly able to explain its own data. The soul is usually considered a necessary explanatory construct, James says, because of such observed characteristics of consciousness as the unity of thought, the sense of personal identity, and the sameness of self as known and self as knower. Can we account for these features of consciousness without positing a soul?

If we take seriously the actual streamlike character of consciousness, where every thought is colored by its context, what James (1892) calls "the fringe," then any given thought need not be joined to the others by the agency of a soul, but rather already has within it, at the fringe, knowledge of previous thoughts that cohere into that pattern of experience we call self-identity. Whatever thought "owns the last self owns the self before the last, for what possesses the possessor possesses the possessed" (p. 205).

We need not, therefore, posit a soul, a "thinker" self that transcends what is apparent to us as we simply observe our own consciousness. "The thoughts themselves are the thinkers" (James, 1892, p. 216). This is not important to James, because he distrusts philosophers; indeed, we see he depends on them only to offer versions of the final significance to psychology the natural science. James believed that philosophers have nonetheless posited entities that "explain" phenomena in such a way as to close down further empirical, scientific investigation. The soul is one such concept, which, under the scrutiny of psychological discipline, misleads us and distracts us from the essential task at hand: the science of mental life.

Psychology as a Natural Science

As a natural science, psychology is obliged to correlate, at every possible point, the functioning of mind with the functioning of brain. A theory of a transcendental soul, which is not a function of the brain, thus also undermines the integrity of psychology as a natural science. However, the true believer in the soul may resist the notion that psychology can be a natural science, just as the true believer in science may resist the notion of the soul. Either way, we will have to cope with James's argument in order to sustain either view. And we will have to cope with the multitude of correlations between mind and brain James points out in subsequent chapters.

On the other hand, a look at these correlations reveals a pattern in James's (1892) thinking, of which the following passage is typical:

In subjective terms we say that *the prepotent items* [of a memory] *are those which appeal most to our* INTEREST.

Expressed in brain terms, the law of interest will be: Some one brain-process is always prepotent above its concomitants in arousing action elsewhere. (p. 262)

James begins with an experiential datum, that some items from a memory will force themselves into the forefront of that memory, and declares the datum to be an example of a principle of mental functioning he calls "interest." Interest, then, is also expressed as a law of neural functioning. Now of course if neural functioning follows laws, like the natural laws of motion, gravity, and so on, then this law would ipso facto be the explanation of the datum with which James started. However, this line of thought holds only as long as one presupposes a cause–effect relation between brain and mental activity. James (1892) is aware, and made us aware on the first page of his book, that presupposing our conceptual goal cannot be defended. On the other hand, to establish that concept would be to establish psychology as a natural science. But is this the only possible relationship between mind and brain consistent with science? James does not establish this fact. It remains only as a goal, a hypothetical premise, or a project for creating psychology as a natural science, not as a fact.

From a purely logical point of view, James begins with a datum, then infers a brain process correlated to it, which in turn explains the datum. This is patently circular and no more nor less so than if one inferred a soul that then was used to explain the datum. It seems, therefore, that more than pure logic enters in to the superstructure of James's (1890) *Principles of Psychology*. That something is precisely the bias of the times, the bias that must result when, with Wundt and James, we

set aside metaphysical questions in order to narrow our scope sufficiently that we can proceed to create a science.[7]

Let us not merely debunk with our word "bias," for such narrowing is
necessary in order to give birth to the new science at all. But let us also
not equate "scientific" automatically with "unbiased," an equation
James never made but that we, in the twentieth century and after, have
assumed more and more, the less proximity we have to James himself.

Emotion

We must, of course, deal with James's theory of emotion before we
abandon James again to the archives.[8] The singularity of the James
theory of emotion has often obscured the fact that this theory, along
with his theories of will and instinct, describe the "effector" (efferent)
side of the organism. This is in contrast to the earlier chapters on sensation (afferent) and the middle chapters on habit, consciousness, thinking, and so on (central) (see Figure 3.1). We must therefore see emotion
in the context of James's larger theory of action.

The emotion theory, apart from this context, can be simply stated.
James (1892) argues that our usual supposition about the order of
events in our emotional life is wrong. We ordinarily suppose that (1)
we see a ferocious bear in the woods, then (2) we feel fear, and then
the emotion that fear yields (3) our trembling and eventually our running. James reorders this sequence to read, (1) we see the bear, (2) we
tremble, even run, and (3) the emotion of fear follows the trembling.
Or even more to the point, our emotion of fear is the experience of our
bodily reaction, and that without this bodily experience, the fear, or
love, hate, or whatever emotion, would not in fact be an emotion at
all, but a flat and neutral cognition.

Rather extraordinary controversy has surrounded what looks to be
merely the assertion that emotions are emotional only insofar as they
include the sensation of bodily upset. Part of the controversy has come
from the fact that James (1892) was read as saying that the afferent
nerves from the viscera to the brain are the physiological mechanism
of emotional experience. And that reading is in fact not far from James's
own statement: "My theory . . . is that the bodily changes follow directly the perception of the exciting fact, and that our feeling of the
same changes as they occur *is* the emotion" (p. 375). James's main point,
of course, is to get at a "generative principle" for emotions that can
take us beyond the mere classification and phenomenal description
that had characterized "scientific psychology" (his quotation marks)
up to that time, an exercise that failed to help us understand our emotions one whit better than we did before we began.

However, the whole matter of emotion appears differently if we take the emotion theory in the context of James's (1892) instinct and will theories, these three being the postinput and postcentral "final or emergent operations, the bodily activities, and the forms of consciousness consequent thereupon" (p. 370)—in a word, James's theory of action.

Action

James's (1892) theory of action begins with the ideo-motor theory, that an idea is always translated into action, unless it is inhibited, and requires nothing more than the idea itself, no special power of will: "Movement is the natural immediate effect of the process of feeling, irrespective of what the quality of the feeling may be. It is so in reflex action, it is so in emotional expression, it is so in voluntary life" (p. 427).

The ideo-motor theory, then, is a general theory of all specific actions (will, emotion, instinct, habit) that says ideas or emotions or stimuli will lead naturally to action, unless they are inhibited. We need to remind ourselves at this point of James's (1892) diagram (see Figure 3.1), in which incoming currents either translate immediately into action via the reflex arc or are detoured through the cerebral hemispheres. Even when they are detoured through the hemispheres, they "naturally" lead to action unless they are inhibited, unless they become entangled in what James earlier called "considerations."

As it is for all these ideas, feelings, and stimuli, so it is with impulses that derive from instinct. "Every instinct is an impulse," more particularly, an impulse to act "in such a way as to produce certain ends, without foresight of the ends" (1892, p. 391). Now for human beings there is always foresight of the ends. Does that mean that human beings have no instinct? Most assuredly not; in vivid contrast to John Watson, who wrote a quarter of a century later, humans have not less equipment than animals, but more. Instinct is not subtracted. Added are more "considerations," the upper loop of the reflex diagram in Figure 3.1. Stereotyped instinctive action is all but missing in human behavior, but that is because the central processes are so complex. Actually, human beings have the most complex battery of instincts of any animals; human impulse life is more varied and rich than that of any other animal. But humans also inhibit the ideo-motor tendency to action in the most varied ways. Even animals are often given two contradictory instincts or impulses in any given situation, such as fight and flight. For humans, there eventually are an infinity of other possibilities because of reasoning, consciousness, self, and so on.

James's theory of action, therefore, is primarily a theory of the selection of action, of the various ways that actual bodily activity emerges from his psychology. Instincts and their impulses, sometimes multiple, are one action system. Volition is another, most highly developed in human beings, sending the incoming current through the most complex network of cerebral events—the upper loop—and enabling human behavior to be sorted out in foresight before it is enacted. We have traditionally called this sorting "decision making."

James's (1892) careful description of five kinds of decisions people make shows clearly that the "fiat," the effortful determination of a particular course of action, is a rare event indeed. "The immense majority of human decisions are decisions without effort" (pp. 433–434). James seems to be saying that the traditional "faculty of will" has been exaggerated; careful scrutiny of our mental life shows very few cases of the fiat, although one cannot dismiss it altogether, for it does occur. We need, therefore, as a part of the theory of action, a theory of volition. Of what does this fiat consist?

It does not consist of muscular effort. It is just as strenuous upon the will to hold still before a firing squad as it is to effortfully climb the stairs one more time in the face of fatigue. Indeed, the phenomenon of will has little to do directly with action, for actions naturally follow from ideas, impulses, perceptions of bears, and so on. The essential phenomenon of will is the effort of *attention*: "The strong willed man . . . is the man who hears the still small voice unflinchingly, and who, when the death-bringing consideration comes, looks at its face, consents to its presence, clings to it, affirms it and holds it fast, in spite of the host of exciting mental images which rise in revolt against it" (James, 1892, p. 452). Therefore, "the terminus of the psychological process in volition, the point to which the will is directly applied, is always an idea" (p. 455). As a part of the theory of action, therefore, the theory of volition is an attempt to describe part of the process of the selection of action, according to ideas and attention. All these occur in the upper loop of Figure 3.1.

The same must be said of the theory of instinct. Instincts are impulses and impulses lead automatically to action—unless they are inhibited. For human beings, they almost always are inhibited, at least in some degree. Not only has nature given us opposite impulses, but we can in our mentation (and often do) generate additional incompatible impulses spontaneously. Habit will also inhibit an impulse, or it will solidify an impulse into a pattern during a critical period (as in imprinting). And ideas as well, if we attend to them, affect the clicking off of instinctual impulses.

Finally, (and this is the major point) James's theory of emotion is also primarily an attempt to account for the selection of action. The action of emotion is almost entirely reflexive: the flushed face and the clenched fist. The reason for reordering the sequence from perception →

emotion → action to perception → action → emotion was not only to make an argument about the physiological mechanism of emotional experience. In addition, and perhaps more important for James's total theory, the reordering was necessary in order to show further how action is selected, in emotion as well as in instinct.

In the case of emotional action, the role of the upper loop and of subjective experience in the selection of action is relatively small. Emotion is unlike volition, which is often not as effortful as we may want to suppose, but which nevertheless is an effector system in which the upper loop and conscious experience is decisive. The conscious experience of emotion, on the other hand, has less to do with selecting action than does reflex. Conscious experience of emotion is almost wholly a by-product; it is a matter of our being conscious without the control that usually attends such conscious experiences as thinking, imagining, or willing. Our bodies control us, not only in that the reflex clicks off, admitting little interference from consciousness, but also in that consciousness itself, which does intervene in volition, is itself swamped by its bodily perceptions.

Such an interpretation of James's (1892) emotion theory is not the usual one, for the hypothesis about the physiological mechanism of emotional experience has been the easiest part of James theory to attack—and to understand. However, we must remember that James's science is of mental life; his theory of action (emotion, instinct, and will) is of "the bodily activities, and the forms of consciousness consequent thereupon." As one of the "more important classes of movement" (p. 373), the emotion theory states that as "bodily activity," emotional action is selected by the body, especially perhaps the viscera, and as a "form of consciousness consequent thereupon," emotional experience is filled with—preempted by—bodily sensations.

Not only does his formulation allow him to show that there are various degrees to which conscious experience determines action; his emotion theory also allows him to describe quite clearly the phenomena of emotions as experience, in contradistinction to other carefully described classes of events in mental life, such as reflexes, instinct, and will.

THE JAMESIAN LEGACY

It is not unfair to say that James left us with more psychology than we have been able to use. By the beginning of the twentieth century, American psychology was turning more and more to E. B. Titchener (Chapter 4), whose actual psychology is conceptually much simpler. Even with Watson's (Chapter 5) later overthrow of Titchener in the second decade, there was no rush back to James's highly refined descriptive work and carefully honed conceptual handling of the most complex processes of the mind.

For some reason, Watson had contempt for James, even though Watson took over James's reflex model almost lock, stock, and barrel. Today James is all but unread, at the great cost, one might say, to the quality of thinking in American psychology. Hardly a chapter in James's book does not have modern representatives, most of whom are not as conceptually or descriptively astute as James, but most of whom feel they invented their ideas in the creative flurry of their own decade's research efforts. Our thought about the Jamesian legacy therefore refers not only to the influence James has in fact had, but also to the as yet unmined psychological insight packed in his *Principles*.

First of all, James was systematic, and he demanded of his system that it included everything important to psychology. There are no developmental, nor social, nor abnormal chapters in James's book, although he mentioned such issues from time to time. But nearly every other conceivable angle of psychology is considered, often in its own chapter, and among the chapters exists a network of mutual implication and support one can only call a system. Even though the book was published in 1890, well before psychology was commonly taught in universities, James tells us more than most such courses, then or now, about human beings and their lives.

To call James's psychology incomplete or more than once inconsistent is to pronounce judgment from a standard no psychology has ever achieved. James's system nevertheless demonstrated the possibility of a coherent science whose parts have intelligible relations to one another, relations that can and were expressed as psychological theory. And this coherence has, in ensuing decades, largely disappeared.

And while James had none of the contempt for philosophy seen in later psychologists like Watson, he successfully held philosophy at bay and teased out a coherent field of study separate from philosophy. He did not explore the details of how the brain causes mental events, or how the mind causes physical events in the brain and elsewhere. He dealt with such issues when he had to by resorting to description and postponing explanation.

James was incapable of merely reporting an experimental fact without showing what it meant, without giving it some kind of interpretation that would make it relevant to other facts. Throughout, the empirical facts provide a guide to theory.

This sort of empiricism may be more than merely modest. James's empiricism is both factual and interpretive, with interpretations always conditioning one another. It could have set American psychology on a track appropriate to the historically revealed complexity of psychology. Just as James's philosophical pragmatism is open to increasingly complex questions depending on what one wants to understand, so also his psychology recognizes the practicality of letting any question be answered at various levels of complexity. The practical result tells one whether one needs to go deeper. Psychology needn't answer all the questions at once.

Second, James's psychology was simultaneously a science of mental life and a science of that science. Nothing in the system was irrelevant to the creator of the system itself. James did not study the mind as a mere object of study, but simultaneously studied himself. Psychology, in James's hands, was therefore obliged to account for itself as well as its so-called subject matter. This would not necessarily be required for any other science, and psychologists since James have often not felt it to be required of psychology, but James did so, as so he wrote with the complexity and subtlety that he did.

In order to appreciate the importance of this complexity, we need to look ahead briefly and see American psychology's considerable confusion on just this point, especially in the revolution provoked by John Watson. Watson may have been correct to see that aiming to solve the puzzles of traditional philsophical dualism offers psychology unlikely future success. Watson's solution, unwittingly like James', to escape philosophy by becoming scientific, however, failed to escape philosophy. By defining knowledge as that which is objectively verifiable, Watson thought he was avoiding metaphysics. He did not appreciate that metaphysical issues are inevitable, even in science. Nevertheless, he saw them as unscientific, and hence as akin to matters of religious faith. According to Watson, knowledge is either scientific in a positivist sense or indistinguishable from faith and opinion.

Thus, the separation of psychology from philosophy that we see in James's thought of the 1890s was simply not understood by his successors two or three decades later. If James looked into aspects of conscious experience, according to Watson he was being unscientific. Thus, Watson's revolution was the application of a rule, a principle, a narrow theory of what "knowledge" really is. It was a radical surgury that nearly killed the patient. It did indeed postpone American psychology's study of cognition in human beings until after mid-century. In the meantime, psychologists were obliged to be behavioristic.

This methodological straightjacket was strained but not broken by the intense curiosity of Tolman, who fully believed that rats have experiences, if not actual hypotheses. The methodological orthodoxy was cheerfully ignored by Piaget's studies of children in France, or Freud's studies of hysterics in Vienna, much of whose work, like James's psychology, was primarily descriptive and followed commonsense notions of what we can know and how we can know it. But the real point here is that James showed us a different approach from what psychology became after Watson, and it was one that can account for its own knowledge. Because psychology omitted the psyche for decades after Watson, the mental events of the scientist and the very possiblity that there is knowledge at all—instead of mere dumb entitites bumping into one another in the world—remained a mystery.

James did not tolerate this mystification in 1890, and it remains puzzling that American behaviorism more or less did so for so much of the twentieth century. All it took, by James and by many other nonbehaviorists since, was the practice of first describing one's data. Data are of the world, but also of our consciousness of the world, and therefore what we study, like ourselves, is sometimes more than dumb entities bumping into one another. Like ourselves, organisms that behave in the world are conscious. Not to the elaborate extent of human consciousness, perhaps, but data of their behavior nevertheless force us to account for their behavior in ways similar, in principle if not in detail, to our own as knowing psychologists.

Third, therefore, consciousness was the very center of James psychology, but consciousness described in its everyday, living, breathing complexity, not the atoms of German sensations or Austrian acts (neither Wundt nor Brentano). If one is to have a science of mental life, it is terribly important to have an accurate picture of the mental life you want to have a science of. James took the task more seriously, perhaps, than any psychologists before him or since.

Fourth, although James was not an active experimentalist, he believed in experimentation and, in his more speculative moments, grounded his thoughts in closely observed phenomena. Throughout his book the reader is simply asked whether this is true, to be tested against whatever personal or public data one might bring to the reading. James had no loyalties to previous theories, so his own theories could and did emerge freshly from thoughtful scrutiny of the phenomena at hand.

Fifth, and finally, James built a psychological theory out of description. His descriptions deal with whatever appears. Sometimes he focuses on overt behavior, which is objective and thus would be amenable to science. But with equal fervor he described subjective experiences. Positivists may not call this science, but James genuinely describes what appears, regardless of its metaphysical status as an event in the subjective flow, especially of human life. To be sure, he rejected a soul religiously conceived, but he certainly included a verifiable experience of self as a purely empirical datum.

James was a philosopher, especially later in his life. But even as a psychologist in 1890 he knew that either affirming a soul or denying it would embroil him in metaphysical questions he wanted to postpone.

But in addition, affirming a soul would be jumping to a conclusion before the descriptive data were in. It would be not only metaphysics, but metaphysics poorly done. Thus, his descriptive psychology, and his pragmatic philosophy, were not unrelated. Human understanding is human understanding. When all the knowledge from all the sciences is in, he said, we shall call it "philosophy."

William James was able to enter into the possibilities of psychology without becoming entangled in philosophical dualism. This required a strategy that was available to, but not taken by, mainstream psychology in the twentieth century. The path offered by James is perhaps easier to see today than it was in 1910, when Watson began to become impatient with everything that was not scientific, particularly philosophy and religion. Psychologists will not, however, see it clearly even today without seeing James, and how we failed for most of the twentieth century to hear what he had to say.

NOTES

1. Hilgard (1987) describes the contributions of these two, Wundt and James, as complementary. Wundt's forte was laboratory founding and laboratory instruction, whereas James's influence came in his propagation of ideas, primarily through his enormously popular writing.

2. This attitude, which allows psychology to at once depend on science and yet to recognize that scientific facts do not speak for themselves, has become less obvious in later psychologies. We clearly can employ a deterministic framework in psychology and yet live our lives and interpret our experience as if there is free will. This issue points to questions that are not always handled well by psychologists, especially those who feel that science offers the "real truth," as opposed to philosophy and other prior efforts that have simply been superseded. In fact, we have no choice but to accept James's view here, given the fact that the intellectual framework inherited from the history of Western thought simply contains two noncongruent frames of reference, that of mechanical causality and that of human freedom and morality. I have tried to deal with this neglected fact and its even more frequently neglected implications for psychology in Keen (2000a; 2000c).

3. Common sense (which assumes a limited free will) says that I, as a consciousness, decide to get angry or am provoked to do so, which causes bodily reactions like adrenal activity. James's theory of emotion makes the conscious mind much more passive. My anger does not originate in my consciousness, thus leading to adrenal activity, but rather the causal relations in my body follow from an external stimulus that causes adrenal activity, which I, in turn, experience as anger.

4. The notion of "root metaphor" is a metatheoretical concept clarified by Sarbin (1977, 1993), to whom all of psychology is indebted for this and other metatheoretical contributions.

5. See James (1890, vol. I, p. 105). This comment extends James's commitment to science, in the sense of physics, somewhat further, and it extends his theory of human being to its physical nature somewhat further as well. Note that while James sees humanity as descriptively like matter, especially in its bodily (nervous system) presence, this does not commit him to reductionism. However applicable are the laws of matter to persons, they are not necessarily the whole truth about humanity.

6. It is interesting to note that if the chapter on the stream of consciousness describes some kind of whole, half of which is described in further detail in the chapter on the self, there is a missing half of the whole James did not include in his psychology. This would be a description of the world in mental life; that is, of the world as experienced. Might we suggest that modern phenomenological psychology is, in some measure, completing James's psychology a century later?

7. The term "bias" here is not meant to say "error." Literally, a bias is an angle. The bias here is simply an angle of vision.

8. It is instructive, if discouraging, to read the history of American psychologists' effort to study emotion after James. Hilgard (1987) uses terms like "neglect," "preoccupation," "partial," " and "one-sidedness" in a few paragraphs introducing the topic in his historical treatise. While the names Leeper (1948), P. T. Young (1943, 1949), Tomkins (1962, 1980), Candland et al. (1977), and Plutchik (1980) come to mind, the effort of psychologists even to come up with simply a list of emotions appears to be futile. It is fair to say that the psychological study of emotion in twentieth-century American psychology is like studying rain by studying water drops without a context of temperature, humidity, and other trappings of meteorology. Every feature of every emotion varies with its psychological context. Hilgard (1987) notes, "A dynamic supplement is required to take account of the sequence of happenings in which the motives and personal values may be of greater significance than the named emotion" (p. 345). This comment suggests the importance of a recent trend to understand human psychology in terms of the concept of "narrative" (Sundararajan, 2000b; Sarbin, 2000; Keen, 2000b; Ginsburg, 2000).

4

The Psychology of E. B. Titchener

THE LIFE OF EDWARD BRADFORD TITCHENER
(1867–1927)

Edward Bradford Titchener was an Englishman whose work with Wundt left him imitating Wundt's German academic formality and assuming Germanic, professorial dignity.[1] He produced dramatic academic rituals in his lectures at Cornell, where he taught for thirty-five years. Titchener never doubted that Wundt's psychology was the correct one, though it was no longer the only psychology after James and others. His early years at Oxford focused on philosophy and classics for four years, and physiology for a fifth year. But his two years in Wundt's laboratory in Leipzig (1890–1892) shaped his entire teaching career at Cornell, including the Germanic formality—and his personal generosity to colleagues and to some students. He granted fifty doctorates in psychology at Cornell, each no doubt intended to extend the light of Wundt's new science to America. Roback (1961) states, "Titchener . . . engaged a voluminous work on systematic psychology. He was a conscientious and eager translator. Wundt owed much to him in that respect, and his own textbooks enjoyed wide popularity through translations into half a dozen European languages" (p. 184).

After 1909 he lectured only on Monday evenings in the spring semester of each year, spending most of his time in his study at home, managing to persuade Cornell junior faculty to wash his car and put up his window screens "not on command, but out of respect and admiration," according to Schultz (1975). He was elected by the charter members of the American Psychological Association (APA) to membership in 1892 at the age of twenty-five, but he resigned shortly thereafter "because the association would not expel a member he accused of plagiarism. It is said that a friend paid Titcherer's dues for a number of years so that his name might be listed" (Schultz, 1975, p. 86).

While William James announced matter of factly that his psychology would be a natural science, E. B. Titchener announced it with flourishes of inspirational rhetoric. He portrayed the severe dedication science entails, as well as the richness of rewards that can ensue. For psychology to be a natural science was not, for Titchener, a possibility among possibilities. It was inherent in the notion of psychology itself, and yet it had to be driven home with the most elaborate of arguments.

James was hardly casual about either science in general or psychology in particular, but Titchener was several times over the more anxious to claim the mantle of science. Psychology is all serious business, the sacrifices great, the stakes high, and the temptations manifold. Just as Wundt had broken new ground in Germany by introspective techniques of scientific measurement of the mind, Titchener was a representative of this important intellectual challenge in the United States. Titchener's scientific psychology held as much prestige as any course of study at Cornell in the first decade of the century.

Titchener's psychology was a simplification and a rigidification of Wundt's psychology, dating from before James and imported in the person of Titchener to Cornell a few years after James wrote. Although he wanted a science of mental life, the "mental life" studied by Titchener was not James's stream of consciousness, weaving through a myriad of behavioral, neurological, and biologically adaptive contingencies. Titchener's version of the mind was anything but what the man in the street, who may well enjoy James's book, would understand. Psychology, first and foremost for Titchener, had to be absolutely and categorically distinguished from common sense.[2]

"Science deals, not with values, but with facts" (Titchener, 1929, p. 1). Common sense, on the other hand, is trapped in a network of values: practical goals, personal preferences, problems to be solved, and hopes, fears, and desires. All these values interfere with the science of psychology, whose goal is merely to observe unflinchingly and testify courageously to the facts of mental life. In order for this rigorous standard of scientific work to be met, very strict methodological rules had to be followed, rules for how to observe, to analyze, and to experiment. But if all these values had to be excluded, what in mental life is left? Exactly the structure and processes of consciousness, which are as they are regardless of the commonsense uses to which they are usually put.[3]

These processes and this structure exist, according to Titchener, independent of meanings, for meanings are merely the vehicle for commonsense values. In the first chapter of Titchener's *A Beginner's Psychology* (1915), he offers many versions of the argument that the structure and processes of consciousness are not inherently meaningful. Meaning is added only later, when the mind is in commonsense use. The bare, meaningless fact is the stuff of science. While others (he called them mere technologists) may put their knowledge to work in a commonsense, practical setting, the scientist is and must be totally disinterested in such matters.

As with Wundt and James, the mind is for Titchener nothing beyond its phenomena; no metaphysical attributions are permitted. Somewhat different than James, however, Titchener comes to define the actual subject matter of psychological study as "the world with man left in," as opposed to physics, which studies the world with man abstracted out. That is, the phenomena of the mind are not its various functions, as in James; the phenomena of the mind are its perceptual content as it looks at the world, appreciating exactly the fact that the mind is looking. Titchener's science of the mind requires experience of something external to itself.

At the same time, this world as experienced must be sharply distinguished from the meaningful world of everyday common sense. The psychological proviso, "as experienced," means to Titchener (but not to others, e.g., phenomenologists) as experienced in a carefully controlled and measured way, under specifiable and repeatable conditions, and totally devoid of meaning, either personal or semantic. The facts of mental structure and process are the goal, not their value, their meaning, their usefulness, or anything else about them.

Much more elaborately than James, Titchener worked out the place of psychology in relation to her two sister sciences, biology and physics. In his *Systematic Psychology: A Prolegomena* (1929), his last (in fact, posthumous) book, Titchener describes this place first in terms of point of view, and second, in terms of subject matter. The first is the more systematic and Titchener's preferred formulation. Its very elaborateness suggests the extent to which psychologists felt they needed, early in the twentieth century, to strive for scientific status.

Psychology is the study of the variables of the world as experienced, considered against the constant of biology, or dependent upon biology, or more precisely, upon the nervous system. Only a normal and fully functioning brain can offer data for psychology. Biology, in turn, is the study of the variables of life considered against the constant of physics, or dependent upon the physical world, or more precisely, upon the environment. Only a normal or fully functioning physical world can offer biology its data. Physics, then, in its turn, is the study of the variables of the physical world that are not dependent upon any other constant, but are, in Titchener's ambiguous phrase, "interdependent."

This formulation, elaborated in great detail, is far from clear decades later, but like the positivisms of the day it states that the physical world is "what it is" absolutely; its facts interact with one another whether a consciousness is there or not. Thus, physics is to study the base of a highly systematic hierarchy within the sciences, such that each science has a precise relation to each other one. The fact that it looks neither familiar nor particularly suggestive of how these sciences stand today suggests that this degree of the positivistic redefinition of knowledge has faded, at least as Titchener understood it. Titchener was so intent on establishing psychology as a natural science among natural sciences that his conceptual work here is merely schematic and tends to neglect the true nature of these sciences.

One could not pronounce that opinion about his view of psychology, for psychology was, in fact, for years just as he said it was, and just because he said it was—at least in those universities that most emulated the Germans. What has now happened, of course, is that the science has been redefined since Titchener, so it is very difficult even to appreciate what Titchener was up to, let alone to agree with him. Perhaps a closer look at the psychology itself may help us to see what Titchener indeed meant.

THE SYSTEM

A look at the table of contents of any of Titchener's many books shows immediately the character of his psychology. Chapter headings for his *A Beginner's Psychology* (1915) are typical:

1. Psychology: What It Is and What It Does
2. Sensation
3. Simple Image and Feeling
4. Attention
5. Perception and Idea
6. Association
7. Memory and Imagination
8. Instinct and Emotion
9. Action
10. Thought
11. Sentiment
12. Self and Consciousness

While it has not survived with the dignity of James's psychology, Titchener's concept was very central for many psychologists, some of

whom like Titchener had trained with Wundt in Leipzig and who therefore believed that Wundt had it right. In contrast to the input–brain–
output organization of James's text, which describes the mind at work,
the logic of Titchener's chapters is a unilinear progression from simple
to complex. Each chapter follows the one before not because it is later
in a functional sequence but because it is conceived to be more complex, made up of the simpler elements described in the chapters before. We thus have a picture of mind that is indebted not to the data of
mind at work as much as to the mind in the laboratory: Elements combine to make compounds, which in turn combine to make more complex compounds, culminating in consciousness in general and the self,
the most complex compound of all.

There are complications to this general rule. Chapters 2 and 3 describe the basic elements of consciousness, the fundamental project.
Both of these are distinguished from simple feelings in that feelings
cannot be made the object of study. Once one tries to focus on the
pleasant–unpleasant aspect of an experience, its pleasantness or un-
pleasantness disappears. It is not, of course, clear today, nor was it to
other psychologists who disagreed with Titchener, just why these
three—sensations, simple images, and simple feelings—are the irreducible elements of which all else is built.[4] Titchener's reasons seem to
stem from his complicated experimental findings, whose method we
shall presently examine. If one were to disagree with that method,
and many did at one time or another, then the entire edifice of Titchener's psychology becomes more than precarious.

Chapter 4, on attention, begins the investigation of processes, not of
elements, after elements are described in Chapters 2 and 3. Processes
are also presented with the simplest first, culminating in the most complex. Unlike James, the process of attention is not, for Titchener, related to volition. We attend to whatever sensation is the most vivid.
The notion that one can attend to whatever one wants to is one of
those commonsense ideas that science must replace with experimental observation. Titchener's laboratory always showed that attention
is merely a by-product of the vividness of sensation. Does that mean
that effortful attention—so important for James's psychology—does
not exist? No, it exists, but scientific analysis shows that attention is
merely a combination of sensations with kinesthetic sensations and
simple feelings. Volition, or effort, in contrast, is a commonsense idea.
Science shows us the elements of volition, and hence science clarifies
the imprecision of everyday conceptions with the analytically astute,
experimentally demonstrable facts of mental life.

In the next chapter, on perception and idea, a similar analysis is
performed. As experienced, perceptions are only apparently simple;
under scientific scrutiny their complexity reveals itself, again as spe-

cial combinations of the basic building blocks of consciousness: sensations, images, and simple feelings.

As these analyses are carried out, Titchener (1915) maintains a more or less constant reference to the nervous system as well: "If we can analyze the perception or idea, nucleus and surroundings both, into its mental elements; if we can say what nervous processes are correlated with these elementary mental processes" (p. 117). And finally, "If we can further establish the nature of the guiding and shaping nerve-forces; then our psychological account will be, in strictness, complete" (p. 117). Here we see Titchener aiming to resolve the mind–body problem by observations of what mental process correlated to what brain process. After this is done, metaphysical dualism will no longer be a problem.[5]

In some cases, however, the nervous system is more than a correlated and parallel chain of events. In the perception of space, for example, Titchener (1915) could not reduce this mental event to particular sensations, images, and feelings, even after the most complex experimental isolation and varying of elements. Therefore, the nervous system is brought into the discussion as follows: "We cannot help perceiving it *as* deep and solid; and this pressure is laid upon us by what we have called racial heritage, an inherited disposition of the nervous system; the brain meets the impression halfway" (pp. 129–130). Here the particular character of the inherited nervous system determines the flavor of subjective experience.

The metaphysical conclusion to this line of thought would have been to see the brain as cause and mental experience as effect—a psychophysical interaction. In Titchener's mind, however, such metaphysical formulae were entirely beside the point of psychology. His vision of the mind–brain relationship is almost always stated as a matter of parallel events. The nervous system sets the limits on the possibilities of experience, such as our inability to perceive ultraviolet light. The larger philosophical question is regarded by Titchener to be precisely the kind of problem from which we are liberated by the introduction of scientific methods and the scientific dedication to pure fact, cleansed of metaphysical speculation and strictly dependent upon experimental data. Titchener's intention to replace metaphysics with science was hardly esoteric at the time.

Methodological considerations, therefore, loom large in Titchener's psychology, and his general concept, following Wundtian psychology in Germany, was to extend those methods to mental life that were so successful first in the physical and chemical sciences, then in the biological and physiological sciences. It was a small move, for Titchener, from inspection to introspection, and both were contrasted with the older philosophical methods of rational argument and speculation.

Introspection, however, like all scientific observation, also had to be sharply distinguished from the casual observation of everyday life.

If I see a book lying three feet from me on a table, my common sense interprets the data as a book, assumes that it is rectangular in shape, and so on. These interpretations and assumptions are "the stimulus error," taking what is known of the object from other contexts and reading that knowledge into the current experience of the object. Scientifically, the current experience is not of a book but of a patch of red, and it is not rectangular. Parallel to the bent-stick appearance of a stick in water, the introspective report should say trapezoidal. Inspection of the stick in the world may show that it is straight, but that is not psychology. *Intro*spection here looks in the mind for accurate mental data, just as *in*spection uses accurate data of the worldly stick in worldly water. Of course, considerable discipline is required to do introspective labor well—truly scientifically—cleansed of both philosophical speculation and such commonsense intrusions that tell us what everyone knows, that the stick is straight or the book is rectangular.

The key methodological routine that can assure a scientific status to one's observations is, of course, the experiment. In fact, experimental psychology was, in Titchener's (1915) mind, the exact equivalent of his own, and not others' work, and it constituted the only true "psychology" in the sense he used that term: "An experiment is an observation that can be repeated, isolated, and varied. The more frequently you can repeat an observation, the more likely are you to see clearly what is there and to describe accurately what you have seen" (p. 20). This sense of discipline continues: "The more strictly you can isolate an observation, the easier does your task of observation become, and the less danger there is of your being led astray by irrelevant circumstances, or of placing emphasis on the wrong point" (p. 20). The purpose of all this strenuous rigor is as follows:

The more widely you can vary an observation, the more clearly will the uniformity of experience stand out, and the better is your chance of discovering laws. All experimental appliances, all laboratories and instruments, are provided and devised with this one end in view; that the student shall be able to repeat, isolate, and vary his observations. (p. 20)

What then, was the day-to-day work of psychology as it dominated not only Cornell but many universities across the land at, and right after, the beginning of the twentieth century? To repeat, the science of mental life in Titchener's hands aimed at a thorough description of experience in terms of its fundamental elements—sensations, images, and simple feelings—ultimately to be correlated to the workings of the nervous system, but not at this point beholden to what was known and not known about the nervous system. For years, students flocked to Titchener's psychology courses at Cornell; his psychology was the center of avant garde science and it generated the greatest excitement. What did they do in those courses?

Consulting his *Manual* (1901–1905), which Heidbreder (1933) rightly notes, "rarely takes a chance on the reader's intelligence" (p. 118), we find every point of theoretical argument and experimental procedure specified to the finest detail, showing "sheer lack of pedagogical tact" (p. 119). In the chapter on attention, Titchener (1901–1905) asserts that "attention is not a faculty, or an activity, but rather is a *state* of consciousness," whose "principal laws" include "the process attended to becomes more clear and more distinct than the rest of consciousness," and also "more intense," "more durable," and so on (quoted in Heidbreder, 1933).

To call attention a "state" rather than an activity, faculty, or power of consciousness is necessary to maintain the loyalty of description to the data of introspection, which includes only processes (simple and complex), attributes of processes, states of processes, and modes of connection of processes.

But Titchener (1901–1905) does not ask his reader to accept, on his authority, that attention is a state of consciousness. Rather, elaborate experiments are described in which two students work together, one being the observer (O) and the other the experimenter (E), following directions such as the following:

O settles his head in the head-rest, and lays his hand comfortably on the table, the fore and middle finders resting upon the bulb. His eyes are closed. E starts the mixer. At the "now" or the bell-ring, O fixates the outermost gray ring of the disc, i.e., the outermost gray patch that he can perceive upon the white surface. (vol. 1, p. 112)

As for the actual data that come from this routine, "As the gray fades or drops out of view, he presses the bulb: gently if the gray fades slowly, sharply if it jerks out of sight. As (or when) the gray returns, he relaxes the pressure. The curve of fluctuation is thus written, above the time, upon the smoked paper of the kymograph" (p. 112). Each piece of apparatus, and its arrangement, is described before these instructions. As soon as the drum has rotated once and O has left his record, he also writes immediately his introspective report of the fading and returning of attention. "At least ten such experiments should be made" in order then for both O and E to write out in their notebooks answers to such questions as "What is the average duration of a complete wave (rise to rise or fall to fall) of attention? What is its mean variation? What were the extreme (longest and shortest) times found?" (1915, vol. 1, p. 112). In addition to the quantity, duration is examined: "What is the relation of the periods of disappearance to the periods of appearance of the gray? Why do we choose this minimal stimulus difference for observation instead of looking for the functions in intensive stimuli which would naturally hold the attention?" (p. 112). Finally, some reflections on the data gathering are asked: "What are the chief sources of error in the experiment? What further experiments can you suggest?" (p. 113).

Thinking this routine over, one might wonder whether the experimental questions and the theoretical questions appeared to Titchener in the same way his students saw them. That is, the important theoretical question is whether there is in consciousness anything beyond what introspection claims—processes, attributes, states, and modes of connection of processes—that is, sensations, images, and simple feelings. Is there, for example, something like an activity or a power of concentration to be observed? The experimental questions, on the other hand, are about the laws, the quantitative relations between separable variables.

We might wonder if Titchener and his students had some sense, as we do today when we see this psychology, that the important theoretical questions were not submitted to experimental test but were laid down by fiat. Did anyone then believe that the elaborate experimental procedures were about matters relatively trivial, compared to Titchener's theoretical insistence that consciousness is the structural facts and the process facts introspection examines?

At stake here is the character of consciousness, the mind, or mental life, of which psychology is the science. Titchener never seemed to take seriously the possibility that that which psychology should study is made up of acts, as Brentano argued against Wundt; or a stream of meaningful events, as James argued; imageless thoughts, as Wuerzburg psychologists maintained; and so on. Titchener was a visionary: He envisioned the future of psychology, and he was certain that future would include exactly the facts as revealed by introspection—and he excluded everything else. Titchener's vision is not difficult to understand as an extension of scientific methods to the mind. But he imported from physics and chemistry more than methods and more than a loyalty to the truth. He did not see a variety of possibilities for naming and describing that which psychology was to study. Titchener seems instead to have decided that Wundt's conception of mind, or rather what he thought made up Wundt's conception, was the center of the new science.

Titchener did not apparently take Wundt's *Voelkerpsychologie* seriously, and he focused on mental content—sensations, images, and feelings—assuming that everything else, including attention, emotion, and even the overt action in reaction-time experiments, are all ultimately understandable in terms of this content.

THE TITCHENERIAN LEGACY

Both Edna Heidbreder and E. G. Boring, two of our best historians of psychology, lead us to believe that Titchener's main contribution to American psychology was to establish a psychology against which our later psychologies have all rebelled, to have given behaviorism, Gestalt psychology, and the rest a "negative identity" reference point. They all were not Titchener. Boring went so far as to say, in 1927, after Titchener's death,

The death of no other psychologist could so alter the psychological picture in America.... He was the cardinal point in the national systematic orientation. . . . The opposition is between behaviorism and Titchener, mental tests and Titchener, or applied psychology and Titchener. His death thus . . . [produces] classificatory chaos in American systematic psychology. (pp. 489–506)

Heidbreder (1933), who calls Titchener's psychology "a gallant and enlightening failure" (p. 115), adds that Titchener had the additional virtue of giving Wundtian psychology a sustained and spirited tryout.

I believe we have the right, if not the obligation, to try to understand, to speculate, if you will, about this failure. Much of the rebellion against Titchener has been superficial or outright wrong, such as the accusation that he was not scientific or that he was too metaphysical. Such epitaphs are mere mudslinging, using the terms "scientific" and "metaphysical" as fancy words for "good" and "evil," understanding neither science, nor metaphysics, nor, for that matter, Titchener. Nor was the failure due to Titchener's Germanic style, or at least this was not completely the explanation.

We shall argue in the next chapter that American consciousness was significantly different from the scientific awareness of nineteenth-century Germany, but in fact the Wundt–Titchener psychology also did not survive in Germany in the twentieth century. While political and military events may have deprived Wundtian psychology of a fair test, perhaps, it is clear that Wuerzburg (*Akt*) and Gestalt detractors left Wundt behind as decisively as Titchener was left behind in this country.

We must recall the big picture. Nineteenth-century German physiology brought the enlightenment of physical science to the study of the body and most especially the nervous system. It seemed the logical next step, in Germany and in America, to extend this method to the study of the mind. This was the essential vision behind Wundt and Titchener, and behind James as well, although it comes out differently, in the writing and in historical effect, for James. We need to ask whether, in general, psychology, the science of the mind, is a workable idea at all.

There is the troublesome question, first clarified perhaps by Kant, whether human consciousness, which so successfully observes and formulates about the world, can successfully observe and formulate about itself. Titchener's psychology leaves us a crucial legacy in beginning to explore this issue. Nothing less than the possibility of a science of the mind is at stake.

We have several options in considering this very central issue. Our first option is to argue that consciousness can investigate itself. James's psychology is vivid testimony, in a way. Perhaps, however, we are driven to a second option, that human consciousness can do this only indirectly, by observing another, which means observing the externalization of consciousness in speech and behavior, rather than consciousness observing consciousness itself. Or perhaps there is a third option, that human consciousness cannot be observed at all, in which case psychology, in the literal sense of a "science of the mind," is impossible, and we all ought really be biologists, as later behaviorists seemed to say, studying only behavior and forgetting the mind altogether.

Against the first option, which points to James as a living demonstration that a science of mental life is possible, it could be pointed out that James's brilliant descriptions are exactly descriptions of consciousness in its various modes. It can also be noted that whenever James goes beyond mere description toward an explanation in causal terms, he turns indeed to biology, the nervous system or the exigencies of adaptation.

Some experimentalists say James's psychology ceases to move but merely sits there as accurate description, leading nowhere. This argument, however, would lead us to believe that James's descriptive work tells us nothing new, that it does not effectively argue against erroneous ideas of the past. That is not true. Or this argument would lead us to believe that James's method, which is merely empirical and not experimental—asking us to consult our own experience to confirm or disconfirm his finding—is not a method that works to produce ever more penetrating self-understanding by the inquiring science. I believe this is also untrue of James's psychology.

However, I believe we should leave the issue of whether a direct, introspective science of the mind is possible somewhat in doubt. Certainly, Titchener's case should lead us at least to wonder whether such a science can be an experimental science. Of course, the example of Ebbinghaus (1913), who pioneered the study of human memory, produced quite sound scientific results early in the twentieth century.

However, memory, at least when it is accurate, presents a scientist with relatively little conceptual work to do. Considerable ingenuity is required to ask good questions, but they are usually small ones. Large questions, like those approached by Freud, again cast doubt on whether we can have very much of a rigorous science of the mind. Phenomenology (see Chapter 16) offers something at this point.

Considering the second option, which says that a science of the mind can work only if the observed mind is someone else's, and hence must proceed indirectly, one would argue that if this state of affairs were true, it would follow that everything each of us knows of "how the mind works" is only an inference from watching our fellows. That certainly appears untrue.

Considering the third option, which says that the mind is in principle not subject to scientific knowledge, we find ourselves limiting science to the observable functional relations between conditions and behavior, a limitation that clinches the argument that the mind is unavailable to science, just as Watson thought he had demonstrated. But if that is as good as psychology can do, we must permanently rule out psychology literally understood as a science of the psyche. Furthermore, other social sciences such as sociology, cultural anthropology, and much of economics and political science, use and depend on the consciousness of actors in order to understand their actions. Are all these disciplines simply humanities?

These considerations, in a way, are psychology, or at least they are a critical part of all social sciences. A critical look at various approaches in all these disciplines is essential to thinking about what, as psychologists, we are doing.

This is the Titchenerian legacy: these questions, these doubts, and these considerations. Titchener never doubted that there could be a science of mental life; he constructed that science as experimental and he limited mental life to the elements and processes of conscious contents. Perhaps his mistake was to insist on being experimental, for his experimental routines did not address the most important theoretical questions, such as whether the elements and processes of mental contents, as he conceived them, are in fact as he conceived them. Perhaps Titchener was, paradoxically, experimental without being sufficiently empirical in the sense that Brentano and James were empirical.

Is it possible to be "excessively" experimental without being "sufficiently" empirical? Such a science would be a science that answered those questions generated by the experimental method without sufficient reference to the lives of persons. Such a science misses the forest for the trees. If that was Titchener's problem, in how many subsequent psychologists can we see the same problem? Most of the immediate successor psychologies developed as anti-Titchenerian. Watson is a splendid example. It would be a curious irony if the anti-Titchenerians imitated his crucial error (say, indulging an expermental criterion of what is good psychology) while correcting his superficial error (such as, say, exclusively engaging experiments about mental but not behavioral life). That issue requires further study of the history of psychology.

NOTES

1. Of Wundt's students whom are known in the Unitied States, only Titchener, a non-European (an Englishman) retained a touch of the German culture of educational prestige. Cattell, Judd, Scott, and even Munsterburg all eventually became more like James than Wundt, even though their primary training had been with Wundt. William James was thus an enduring influence on American psychology, but also, and, Hilgard (1987) suggests, more important, was the simple fact of American culture: "Wundt's laboratory won out over James's dislike of experiementation; James's pragmatism, or practicalism, as one once called it, won out over the exclusive basic science emphasis and the lingering German idealism of Wundt's theoretical system" (p. 65).

2. It is a noteworthy irony that Titchener, eventually maligned in American psychology, was an enthusiastic follower of Ernst Mach, the German physicist and later philosopher of science, whose positivism inspired Watson and his supporters in riding Titchener out of town. Like all ironies, to understand this one is to deepen our grasp. Mach knew that all scientific data begin in the consciousness of the scientist, and the path from there to codified knowledge was the arena of concern in his positivism. Watson's treatment of the consciousness of the scientist was brief at best, for dwelling on it would detract from his focus on behavior. It is as if he assumed that a scientific experiment, because it is controlled and objective, guaranteed that the results speak for themselves, independent of anyone's consciousness. Titchener, in contrast to Watson, sought to have a science of mental life because, like Mach, he appreciated that knowledge *is* consciousness, and in this sense he took Mach much more seriously than did the positivist opinion that inspired and supported behaviorists' defiling of consciousness and pronouncing it unworthy of study.

3. This definition by Titchener is quite telling. Consciousness to Titchener was much more transparent than James said it was, much freer of all those complications—personal, social, emotional, and bodily—that made James's psychology relevant to people's lives. Titchener, so roundly condemned by scientific psychologists since Watson, actually manifested the virtues recommended by these same scientific critics: knowledge based on pure observation of the data of the laboratory, independent and insulated from the messy human concerns of real life.

4. In fact, these elements seem to have been taken from British philosophers of the seventeenth century, such as Hobbes and Locke.

5. Titchener never doubted that consciousness and brain must be related, as is of course currently believed as well. Dualism for Titchener did not name two kinds of realtiy; it named a philosophical doctrine that lacked the scientific findings that would redefine "realities," mental, physiological, and physi-

cal, into an interlocking body of scientific knowledge. He saw his work as moving toward an elimination of dualism and all metaphysics by science. His science of psychology was eventually to clarify its dependence on physiology, just as physiology would clarify its dependence on physics, in an organized hierarchy of knowledge. He may well have believed that metaphysics is nothing but a prescientific approximation of what the sciences will finally clarify. The differences among sciences, then, were merely different levels of analysis, having no metaphysical significance. Insofar as this psychology fails (and it does so vividly), what could remain of the science ("ology") of mental ("psyche") life? What could remain of psychology? It is clear there were other approaches, but it was finally behaviorism that most obviously gave psychologists something to do. Without experiencing the depth of struggle with dualism and the intensity of the hope for science, the collapse of Titchener's psychology seems a minor event. It was not. And yet there remained cultural support for psychology even in the face of Titchener's, and others', frustrations. Human curiosity does not give up.

5

American Psychology in 1910

OTHER THEORISTS

Between 1890, when James's *Principles* was published, and 1910, when Titchener's stature was its greatest, a good deal more was going on than the development of these two theoretical points of view. Laboratories were established at Yale, Princeton, Johns Hopkins, Wellesley, Columbia, Chicago, Clark, University of California, University of Michigan, University of Wisconson, and Vassar, to name a few, and studies of animals appeared. Freud, Jung, and Jones all published in the *American Journal of Psychology*, the systematic study of children got underway led by G. Stanley Hall, learning as a special topic appeared under the leadership of Edward Thorndike, and Pearson published his early papers on correlational statistics. The American Psychological Association was established by Hall in 1892. A score of journals were established, mental tests became important research tools, and American college students were offered and eagerly took up the new science with an enthusiasm that has not let up since.

In spite of Titchener's hegemony in the early decades of the century, American psychology was also growing according to another, more native, and more American ground plan. The journals of these decades mixed Titchenerian psychology of mental contents with a multitude of other concerns that characterized American thinking and simply did not fit into the tight and rigorous German mold of what was known of Wundt and especially of Titchener. These concerns eventually found a unifying theoretical theme in "functionalism," which we shall discuss later.

Although John Watson's (1930) *Behaviorism* gave Titchener's "Germanic Experimental Psychology" its coup de grace, the functionalist temper of American thought was plainly visible already in William James's psychology. It was destined to dominate American psychology, a dominance so complete that nearly every American psychologist today is a functionalist and practically none of them openly identify themselves as such. So assumed has functionalism become in American psychology that it passes for common sense, or science in general, and rarely is even an issue.

The bearers of this American consciousness eventually outweighed Titchener in sheer quantity of energy and talent. No single psychologist could contain "psychology" to any predefined system and method against the aggressive brilliance of G. Stanley Hall, J. Mark Baldwin, James McKeen Cattell, and Edward Thorndike, not to mention William James and John Dewey.

Two very early psychologists will be discussed in this section, G. Stanley Hall and James Mark Baldwin. Along with James and Titchener, these psychologists captured the theoretical scene in America between 1890 and 1910. The group of James, Hall, and Baldwin clearly also represent early forms of functionalism, discussed in the next section, as opposed to the structuralism of Titchener.

It was Titchener himself who established this terminology and therewith the sloganish labels that eventually isolated him in American psychology. Titchener's argument was characteristic. Biology is divided between structure (what is), function (what it is for), and ontogeny (how it got that way). Psychology, he thought, could follow the same divisions, but the first (propaedentic) order of business had to be structure, what is. The rest can be studied only after structure, and furthermore, to study function and ontogeny without having established the structural facts leads science to be corrupted by "values." Titchener believed that the commonsense and problem-oriented "psychology" of the man in the street ran the risk of compromising the newly won scientific status of psychology.

James Mark Baldwin (1861–1934) clashed with Titchener in the 1890s in one of those amazing controversies in which there was little that was incomparable between the stated positions of the two men, but behind these statements lay reasons both understood, and *there* lay an irreconcilable difference. These statements were as follows: Titchener said that muscular reaction time is shorter than sensory reaction time; Baldwin said that sensory reaction time is, in some persons, shorter than muscular reaction time. They had the same data at hand. If you tell the subject to concentrate on the stimulus, you are measuring sensory reaction time, and if you tell the subject to concentrate on his or her response, you are measuring muscular reaction time. Both men also knew that Titchener used only highly trained introspectionists as subjects, while Baldwin used naïve subjects.

Hence the issue would seem to be which subjects, Baldwin's naive ones or Titchener's highly trained ones, tell us "the truth" about this issue. That question, however, hinges on a deeper, unspoken issue that really separated Titchener and Baldwin, namely, the purpose of psychology, or the *nature* of "the mind" that psychology studies.[1] Baldwin maintained that "human nature is unpracticed and psychology should study human nature" (p. 532), to use Boring's (1950) concise formulation, while Titchener assumed that "the mind" is that meaning-free, value-free substrate of factually present structure and process that is only muddied and obscured by studying it in naïve subjects.

Titchener's position would say that Baldwin may as well ask the man on the street about his neural pathways and call these naïve data reliable science. But Baldwin's approach was riding the speedier train of Darwinian evolutionary thought, within which it is exactly subjects who are more naive, and more natural, who tell us more truly the nature of the human mind.

Like James and many others, Baldwin, would say that Titchener isn't investigating the mind as it is, but only as it is assumed to be by the introspectionists. The difference made by Darwinian thought was often unspoken, even when Boring recapitulated the argument in 1929. The issue was temporarily settled by Angell and Moore (1896), who said both men were right—not really settling the issue behind the issue at all. These deeper issues are often settled, as this one was, only by history itself.

The Baldwin of this controversy was profoundly Darwinian, and his view thus represented all the functionalists who opposed Titchener. In addition, Baldwin himself was an untiring worker. He established laboratories at Princeton and Toronto and hence, like Hall, James, and Titchener, was one of the first generation of founders of American psychology. With Cattell he established the *Psychological Review* and its various spinoffs, the *Psychological Index*, the *Psychological Monographs*, and the *Psychological Bulletin*, and published influential books, including *Senses and Intellect* (1889), *Feeling and Will* (1891), *Mental Development in the Child and Race* (1895), and *Social and Ethical Interpretation of Mental Development* (1897), to mention only his psychological works. He also published in philosophy and international relations, having an active interest in both Mexico and France.

Of particular interest for this chapter is Baldwin's (1913) *History of Psychology*, for it tells us how he understood the past, and hence himself and his fellow psychologists of the time. Hardly alone, Baldwin imitated Darwin's developmentalism. He saw three great epochs in human history: the prelogical epoch of primitive peoples, the spontaneous epoch of the ancient Greeks, and the reflective epoch of the modern, post-Cartesian period. Also not uniquely, Baldwin saw a direct parallel between these historical epochs and the ontogenetic development of thinking in the individual.

This parallel was more than an analogy to Baldwin, for both cultural and personal developmental processes engage the selection of ideas from the struggles of time, not unlike Darwinian selection. In both developments one can see an inherent directionality. Both personal and historical development, Baldwin thought, manifests a directionality through stages of divided loyalties, such as self versus world, then self versus others, mind versus body and man versus God, to a final realization of the individual self.

The specifics of the analogy between human history and human development need not concern us until we come to modern psychology in historical time, and its analogical correlate, refined maturity in individual development. At this point, Baldwin (1913) does not simply affirm the finality of science as, say, the French sociologist Comte before him had done. Rather, the final stage contains later and more refined representatives of each of the three epochs:

Modern psychology reflects the alternatives which philosophy has worked out in its varied systems. . . . We see the early alternatives reproduced . . . in the modern period. . . . [These three,] positivism, rationalism, and immediatism—science, philosophy, and faith broadly understood—*are* the modern alternatives. (p. 160)

After articulating this historical theory, Baldwin states,

As in modern culture, so also in individual thought, the choice among them is largely a matter of temperament.

In conclusion we may say, in view of the confirmation that our study has given of the parallelism between individual and racial thought of the Self, that in the history of psychology we discern the great profile which the race has drawn on the pages of time. (p. 160)

Baldwin (1913) is not being a racist in the modern sense here. In the context of the time, these are more biological than sociological statements. Primitive men were like children. These thoughts speak Darwin's sense of science. In fact, functionalist psychology is definitely embodied, and engaged biologically with the environment. He goes on, "On closer inspection it [cultural evolution] appears to be made up of a great number of smaller profiles, placed on end, coming down the line. Each of these in turn . . . contributes something to the larger picture which is the portrait the race . . . is making of the human Self" (pp. 160–161).

What we see here is, first, Baldwin's creation for psychology, and hence for his own work, of an historical context. Simultaneously, it is, second, a creation for the historical process of a psychology in history. This is an implicit or explicit facet of every modern psychology. Every psychologist a century ago explicitly knew his or her "place" in history. When Darwin still had to be argued in intellectual circles, a psychology had to be created in developmental-historical terms. We no longer need to argue for Darwin, and thus we are not as historically self-conscious as we were a century ago, but the task of historical self-consciousness, not unlike my own—and perhaps yours in taking up this book—is to see psychology's presence in an historical context.[2]

This creation differs notably from that of Titchener, for whom science is simply the basic obligation and task of human intelligence. Baldwin also differs in centering on self. Note his questions about the personal self and its historical process. How does the self emerge from one historical and evolutionary process into personal developmental time? And how does that process contribute to another development over historical time? To take these questions seriously is to be curious more ambitiously than psychologists are today.

Even more energetic than Baldwin was G. Stanley Hall, who founded the American Psychological Association in 1892 and became its first president, and founded the *American Journal of Psychology*, *Pedagogical Seminary* (later called the *Journal of Genetic Psychology*), the *Journal of Religious Psychology*, and the *Journal of Applied Psychology*. He spearheaded the use of questionnaires and mental tests in educational psychology and in 1904 published his influential *Adolescence: Its Psychology, and Its Relations to Physiology, Anthropology, Sociology, Sex, Crime, Religion, and Education*.

While president of Clark University, he remained an active teacher and promoter of psychology, and he invited Freud and Jung for Clark's bicentennial celebration in 1909, Freud's only visit to America. He established psychological laboratories at Clark and Johns Hopkins and in both places trained many of the next generation of leaders in American psychology. After his retirement, he characteristically wrote a book on *Senescence* (1922).

Psychology could have asked for no more enthusiastic advocate than Hall (1904), who outstripped even Titchener in his optimistic confidence that psychology would solve the world's problems. He said that psychology "embodies a new idea of profound practical and scientific importance which has a great and assured future" (vol. 2, p. 40), namely, "psychic evolution." Of course, "psychic is even more upsetting than biological evolution, for it lies nearer to all human and practical interests" (p. 55).

And yet the development of psychology, Hall (1904) believed, would bring a "new and higher monism and an evolutionism more evolved" (vol. 2, p. 40). The opponents psychology had to struggle with were several in number: philosophy, Christianity, and traditional prejudices. But they all shared the nondevelopmental view, which saw the mind as eternal and outside of nature. It was Spencer, Hall points out, who finally saw mental life in developmental time. Whatever may be true about innate ideas, "from Aristotle's ten to Kant's twelve . . . although *a priori* and innate in the individual, were acquired by the race" (p. 41).

Hall's (1904) psychology was imperialistic; psychic evolution would explain the history of Western thought: "Plato and Kant showed genetic progress *despite* the rigor of their reasoning" (vol. 2, p. 51, emphasis added), and idealism as a philosophy was dismissed as "premature excessive development of associative activities over those of the projection system which mediates sensation and motion" (p. 45). Most of all, Hall's psychology would make "plain how gross have been the errors in both conceiving and practically training the soul" (p. 41). According to Hall's vision, psychology "prefers a long program of hard work yet to be done to a sense of complacency in any present finalities. It appeals to the really young, and would appreciate and meet adolescent needs rather than deal in sad sights which belong only to senescence, whether normal or precocious" (p. 55). What sounds sentimental is not: "It believes youth the golden age of life, the child the consummate flower of creation, and most of all things worthy of love, reverence, and study. It regards education as man's chief problem, and the home, school, church, and state valuable exactly in proportion as they serve it" (p. 55).

The practical nature of the work of psychology is typical among scientists at the beginning of the twentieth century. We can also clearly see how Darwinists framed their tasks. These features are comparable to the enthusiasm of Titchener's message. Both claim that the science of mental life is answering an almost sacred call.

THE FUNCTIONALISTS

Aside from Baldwin and Hall, we must count George T. Ladd and William James among the first generation of American functionalists. Chicago produced another nucleus of functionalist psychology, primarily in the work of John Dewey and James R. Angell (John Watson also came from Chicago). Columbia University produced yet another nucleus in James McKeen Cattell, Edward Thorndike, and, later, the remarkable Robert S. Woodworth, whose career extended into the 1940s.

G. T. Ladd (1887) probably offered the original definition of functionalism in his pre-James psychology text, *Elements of Physiological Psychology*. Although a clergyman who eventually turned to focus on philosophy and religion (William James, James Baldwin, and G. Stanley

Hall did the same thing late in their careers), his early formulations allowed an almost systematic set of postulates that underlay function-alist psychology.[3] Boring (1950) articulates them as follows: (1) At the center of psychology is a self, which (2) actively initiates action in the task of adapting to the environment, thus (3) harboring and imple-menting teleological motives, which when studied will (4) yield a sci-ence that is practical for the concrete business of living. These early postulates were hardly unique to Ladd, as we know from studying James, nor were they all equally relevant to later statements from the Chicago and Columbia schools. But they certainly set up the contrast with both Wundt and Titchener.

In 1906 James Angell of Chicago, a close colleague of John Dewey, was president of the APA and entitled his presidential address, "The Province of Functional Psychology," published in the *Psychological Review* (Angell, 1907). In accord with the militantly nondogmatic pos-ture of functionalism (a somewhat self-consciously calculated contrast to Titchener, perhaps), Angell offered three definitions of functional-ism and let the listener take his or her choice. First, he contrasted the study of "mental operations" to the structuralist study of mental ele-ments. This contrast is not quite fair to either Wundt or Titchener, who spoke of processes and struggled hard against the tendency to crys-talize elements into isolated bits—a struggle that was not, however, always successful.

Second, Angell (1907) said that functional psychology is the "psy-chology of the fundamental utilities of consciousness," whereby the mind is "primarily engaged in mediating between the environment and the needs of the organism." The Darwinian and Jamesian flavor of this definition vividly contrasts with Titchener and Wundt.

Third, functionalist psychology engages the entire organism, men-tal and bodily, in its unified, wholist adaptive enterprise. This defini-tion contrasts with Titchener's limitation of psychology to mental life, where the only relevant bodily facts are cerebral and their only rel-evance is as parallelistically conceived conditions of mental activity. This comparison is at once massive and subtle. For Titchener, the en-vironment supplies the content for conscious life, but not the other end of an adversary, adaptive process. For Titchener, the body is the condition of mentation but not the coactor in an adaptive negotiation with the environment.

The Columbia version of functionalism is perhaps best represented by Thorndike, although Cattell's development of mental tests and Woodworth's later (1920s) formulations of "dynamic psychology" could equally serve us. Thorndike must be seen, perhaps along with Pavlov, as the cornerstone of what later became, in the late 1930s and 1940s, the central study of learning in American psychology.

Learning itself, of course, is a purely functionalist focus for psychological study. Only someone interested in the adaptive process would single learning out as the key phenomenon for psychologists to study. Without the hearty dose of evolutionary thought in American functionalism, learning is secondary to the basic elements and processes of consciousness that Titchener conceives as the target of psychology. We now see learning as the origin, in fact, of the "meanings" and "values" that Titchener said must be bypassed in order to study the mind "factually."

Wundt, whose psychology was much larger than Titchener's, would have looked more favorably upon the study of learning as a part of the higher mental processes (HMP) that must be studied to produce the propaedeutic science. He took it up, however, primarily in his never-translated *Voelkerspsychologie* (1900–1920), which studied the history and culture of man, the necessary context of meanings and values in the HMP.

Turning to Thorndike, we see the continuing influence of Darwin. First were Thorndike's animal studies, including his famous puzzle boxes which cats learned to solve and escape from. Second, he focused on education, producing his *Educational Psychology* in 1903 and his *Introduction to the Theory of Mental and Social Measurement* in 1904. It is noteworthy that John Dewey, originally with Angell at Chicago, moved to Columbia in 1904, and so we must see that Dewey, the redoubtable philosopher–educator, had more of a role in the development of American functionalism than is immediately apparent. Of course, he is most vividly associated with the later William James and the American Pragmatist movement in philosophy.

Now what exactly is going on in American psychological theory in all these functionalist developments? It is a profound modification of the European idea of psychology. Nearly every psychologist mentioned in this chapter studied for a semester or a year or two in Germany. Germany was where the "new psychology," the "physiological psychology," meaning the "scientific psychology," was happening. James, Titchener, Baldwin, Hall, Scripture, Cattell, and Angell each made his pilgrimage; Ladd studied Wundt carefully before he wrote; and Thorndike knew the German literature. Only Titchener was not a native of America (he was English), and only he resisted this profound change, the Americanization of psychology.

The change we are seeing in the development of functionalism is a profound result of the enormous impact of Darwin's theory of natural selection. Functionism may also be seen in a larger context of "naturalization," first conceived in the Renaissance vision of nature as humanly and rationally comprehensible. This break with pre-Renaissance thinking may be seen as a return to the Hellenic idea, and so on. Naturalization is not only a demystification and a secularization of the world into a "nature" that will yield to human intelligence, it is also the development of a definite evolutionary worldview that characterized Western thought, more or less, but progressively, since Descartes.[4]

First the solar system, then the world's objects, then the body of man in early nineteenth-century physiology, then—his mind? Well, mind seemed the next step to the German founders, but we now see the matter differently. The next step seems historically to have been not the mind as Germany's scientists conceived it, but the whole person as American scientists conceived it. Once one takes Darwin seriously, then extends Darwin to social process as Herbert Spencer and William Graham Sumner did, one begins to see the evolutionary struggle as involving the individual, the whole person, and this person becomes the unit of analysis, a natural phenomenon of which the body is only a part, the mind is only a part, and the parts matter less than the whole.

The whole person, as a natural object, is caught up in the same network of forces that characterize all of nature. The mind might be analyzable scientifically, but American psychologists did not think that was important apart from the organism–environment relations that determine what the organism will do.

Wundt secured psychology for science (as against metaphysics) by working out of a relationship to physiology. His version of an actual relation between the physiological brain and the psychological mind was a convenient doctrine of psychophysical parallelism that did not claim to be important as a metaphysical doctrine, nor did Wundt allow that a metaphysical position was important for his science. Mind–body parallelism was a stopgap formula that allowed the analogy to precede. The mind was conceived of as just as natural an object as the brain, and the methods were to be equally scientific.

We saw that in the hands of James this situation came out differently. Psychology, as a natural science, was incomplete, James was clear, without its philosophical context, but he proceeded nonetheless. James offered a different kind of naturalization, not of the mind by analogy, but of the person by the tentativity that characterizes all the sciences. James's position allowed the continued naturalization of the person without the rather forced analogy of mind to body that was built into the views of Baldwin, Hall, Angell, Cattell, and Thorndike. Dualism was, for these theorists, one of minimal difference, a psychophysical parallelism. This was also true of Wundt's and Titchener's view. It allowed a fuller integration of the Darwinian notion of organismic adaptation, and placed the center of the action between the organism and the environment instead of between the mind and the body.

This reorientation allows one to proceed with the business of psychology without becoming preoccupied, or concerned at all, with the metaphysical question of the relation between mind and body—to proceed without that perpetual sense of discomfort about the parallelist stopgap that always hovers around the German program. The Darwinian polarity of organism and environment liberated psychology from metaphysics more completely than did Wundt and Titchener.

Concretely, functionalism allows one to study human development, animal behavior, individual differences, learning, and abnormal syndromes, and to develop psychological tests for humans and puzzle boxes (later mazes) for animals. Throughout all these kinds of research, one need not worry about the relation of mind to body, for it is the adaptation of the whole organism that is at stake. Consciousness is nothing special, but merely one of the pieces of adaptive equipment of the organism, important not in its metaphysical status but only in its functional—adaptive—significance.

For James, who saw these possibilities for the new science, it was all nevertheless based on a fundamental tentativity. The philosophical issues that had to be ignored, the philosophical positions that had to be assumed, were temporary working assumptions, not a kind of truth legimated by the label "science." This tentativity, so important to James, was easily lost as enthusiasm for the possibilities of the new science grew. The new science may have been forgetful of its unpaid debt to metaphysics, but it was supported by an unspoken sense that functional psychology had historical legitimacy as the next step in the naturalization process that supported and implemented the scientific worldview. It was seen as the next step in scientific progress.

THE PSYCHOLOGY OF THIS HISTORY

We may see American psychology in the two or three decades before 1910 as psychology within American life, taking American life as the context, or ground, and psychology as the figure. From this perspective, psychology played into the American scene as a part of Americans' reaffirmation of faith in scientific progress, apparently resolving the tense polarities of nineteenth-century romanticism and science in terms of the unflinching optimism of Social Darwinism. Psychology fit in as yet another plank in the platform of scientific progress, straining to forget any doubts by forgetting the doubters: the poets, philosophers, and religionists.

We may also look at American psychology in this period by looking at what Americans did to psychology, by taking psychology as the context and American versions of it as the figure. From this perspective, we have seen that the Darwinian sense of "function" permitted

American psychology to zoom ahead of its European fathers. By 1910 all psychology was already dominated by American psychology.

American psychologists were aware of themselves in both of these ways. They were bringing to America further reason for confidence in the scientific achievements of the new century to come, and they were bringing to psychology that perspective which would enable psychology to flourish as a science without the nagging doubts about unresolved philosophical issues. The psychology of this history must therefore be a psychology of this optimism, of this sense of American uniqueness, if not superiority, and of great enthusiasm.

Whenever a group of scholars discover themselves and one another as united under a label like "psychology"—and that label had every bit as much punch as "space program" did in the 1960s—and when they make this discovery within a sense of optimism and superiority, the resulting enthusiasm will yield predictable results. Psychology recruited brilliant minds and ambitious men (fewer women were allowed to be ambitious, of course), whose sense of their work was the sense of glory itself: pioneers, no longer in the service of geographical expansion, but now in the service of scientific progress, erasing ignorance and superstition and discovering scientific mastery of the last holdout against the scientific worldview, the human mind itself.

The ambitiousness and brilliance was bound to become highly competitive, and the development of factions and schools was practically inevitable. On the competitive surface, the game was rough and tumble, but beneath this competitive surface lay a sense of common mission that led Baldwin to respect Titchener in spite of their difference, which was, after all, a profound one. G. Stanley Hall seemed genuinely open-minded, Angell was a truly tolerant man, and even James's late remarks about psychology, the "dirty little science," were somehow good-natured and good-willed. Watson's contemptuousness of his predecessors in the next decade may not have been entirely new, but its harshness was indeed out of tune with a sort of Golden Age in which the brilliance and ambition of the principal actors was channelled by a shared sense of ushering in an assured future.

NOTES

1. This issue of the nature of the mind was already taken up in detail by James (1890), but it was only with the popularity of Gestalt psychology (see Chapter 7) that Americans fully appreciated such a question. Until then, James's descriptions had rarely provoked a challenge to the passive and atomistic character of the mind that Titchener and others had unconsciousness inherited from British empiricism of the seventeenth and eighteenth centuries.

2. The developmentalism of Darwin is decisive here, of course, but we

should also remember that Darwin himself could not have recast biology (and the rest of culture) into the developmental pattern without the prior work in Europe by Hegel and the Hegelians.

3. Why did Ladd, James, Baldwin, and Hall all turn from psychology to philosophy and religion a hundred years ago? Part of the answer lies in the ambitiousness of their vision, which clearly outstripped any single lifetime of scientific effort. Thus, the scientific route, however trusted, did not seem to promise satisfaction quickly enough. Perhaps a better answer can be found in appreciating the depth of their curiosity, and perhaps the intensity of their hopes, which sustained them all (as it did Titchener) through difficult years in the development of psychology. Beyond that lies the explanation that the élan of the American culture itself made it happen, a culture whose reputation we know but whose current state, after a twentieth century of vicious wars and images of nuclear doom, is in notable disrepair.

4. This change in the status of the body in the psychology of the early decades of the twentieth century signals both the influence of Darwin and at the same time a serious effort to modify the tendency of psychological theory to be dualistic. Titchener, explicitly a dualist, makes the body irrelevant except as a cerebral parallel to mental life. James, never clearly a dualist nor overcoming the problem, proves in retrospect to have engaged the body in a larger role in mental life than Titchener allowed. In part, James was forced by the tradition of syntax to speak of emotion as a perception of bodily events, as if they were separate or separable. In later functionalism we see the body as an actor no less than the mind, an idea limited in James to his emphasis on physical reflex as preceding and occasioning an emotion. In functionalist thought, the effort is more concertedly to establish the idea that organism–environment relations constitute the focus of investigation. Further analysis into the separate parts of bodily movement and conscious perception is avoided as far as possible. We shall return to these issues when we discuss the "cognitive revolution" of the 1960s.

6

The Psychology of John Watson

THE LIFE OF JOHN B. WATSON (1879–1958)

Like Wundt before him, Watson set out to establish an entirely new school of thought in psychology. Schultz (1975) points out that Pavlov, Angell, and Thorndike supplied much of the raw material for the advent of behaviorism. But Watson became so famous and popular that he must be reckoned with.

His move from Chicago to Johns Hopkins in 1908, where he was offered a full professorship and an opportunity to direct the laboratory there, began twelve enormously productive years as a psychologist, after which he was forced to resign because of highly sensationalized divorce proceedings. Somewhat ironically, Titchener was of more help to him than Angell, according to Schultz (1975). In 1921 he left academic psychology to become an advertising executive, where his characteristic hard work earned him a vice presidency by 1924.

Even though he never returned to academic psychology, he remained an influence with the public by publishing in *Harper's, Cosmopolitan, McCalls, Colliers,* and *The Nation*. His lectures at the New School for Social Research led to the popular book, *Behaviorism,* which he revised in 1930 at the age of fifty-two. In 1957, just before his death, the American Psychological Association honored him with a citation that praised his work as "one of the vital determinants of the form and substance of modern psychology . . . the point of departure for continuing lines of fruitful research" (Schultz, 1975, p. 198).

While his seminal ideas date from 1913, it is plausible that acceptance of his psychology in America, especially by the general public, benefited from his own energy, and charm, which built upon his reputation for the last three or so decades of his life. He retired to a farm in Connecticut, where "he did things in great style and loved to show a display of power" (Larson and Sullivan, 1965, p. 165).

THE PLACE OF PSYCHOLOGY

In 1930, Watson wrote, "The raw fact that you, as a psychologist, if you are to remain scientific, must describe the behavior of man in no other terms than those you would use in describing the behavior of the ox you slaughter, drove and still drives many timid souls away from behaviorism" (p. v). If Watson had had a crystal ball that enabled him to see into the future some four or five decades, he would have seen the relevance of his statement for later, as well as the earlier times he had in mind. Psychology both has and has not followed, and recovered, from Watson.

Those earlier times began in 1912, with his lecture series at Columbia (Watson taught at Johns Hopkins), followed by an important *Psychological Review* article in 1913, and in 1914 his *Behavior: An Introduction to Comparative Psychology*. In 1919 he published *Psychology from the Standpoint of a Behaviorist*. The quote in the previous paragraph about the ox is from *Behaviorism* (1930), a revised edition of his 1925 book.

Watson's vision was not merely the obvious Darwinian idea, for functionalists were all certified Darwinians. Beyond the functionalist liberation from Wundt and Titchener, Watson insisted that consciousness can have no role at all in a scientific psychology. Angell and Woodworth had assigned consciousness a role in the adaptive processes of organisms, but this practice, Watson (1930) insisted, was to perpetuate metaphysical notions of the mind, religious notions of the soul, and other superstitions—"heritages of a timid savage past" (p. 3)— which would prevent psychology from occupying its rightful place among the natural sciences. In Watson's hands, the naturalization of man extended to claiming that whatever is not objectively observable in a laboratory is supernatural and, hence, is the mortal enemy of science.[1]

Watson's combativeness is hardly the first in the history of science, and it led to predictable polarizations in which very real differences between American functionalists like Angell and James and Germanic structuralists like Wundt and Titchener were obscured. Watson could not discriminate them because they all had dealings with the magical folklore that consciousness is worthy of scientific study. Since psychology must be cleansed of such "old wives' tales," the best strategy was to claim the rapidly developing methods of animal experimentation as the only legitimate method for scientific psychology—and to point out, as a theoretical correlate, that humans are not, after all, different in principle from their evolutionary ancestors.

Watson's challenge is therefore a double challenge, claiming a methodological breakthrough to genuine science, and a theoretical breakthrough to the final laying to rest of the ghosts of prescientific thought. In both arenas, methodological and theoretical, the key term is behavior. According to behaviorism, if it's not behavior that can be studied by animal-experimental techniques, it's not the subject matter of psychology, and further, it's not important to investigate. Watson's vision is a genuine revolution in science, fundamentally changing the definition of the science itself, the questions it asks, and what qualifies as answers. If ever psychology underwent a "paradigm shift," it was between 1915 and 1930, during which every Titchenerian in the country experienced the fall from top rank to old fashioned.

Functionalism, of course, was not slain as Titchener was. Indeed, behaviorism was the impetuous and radical little brother of functionalism. But functionalist and therefore American psychology was permanently modified methodologically. The behaviorist methodological tenets (largely simply positivism) still hold sway in psychology today, while the theoretical exclusion of consciousness and its phenomena from psychology does not. These methodological tenets were stated by Watson as follows: "It is the business of behavioristic psychology to be able to predict and control human activity. To do this it must gather scientific data by experimental methods" (1930, p. 18). "Methods" did not include, of course, Titchenerian introspection or Wundtian psychophysics, for both of these presuppose that (1) there are mental events—itself an unprovable assumption, Watson points out—and (2) that psychology is studying them. Reaction-time experiments, in contrast, were objective and legitimate, as long as they didn't lead to speculations about mental events.

Watson's success is due in part to the actual power of this methodology. Much of the older subject matter could be redefined in behavioral terms. Sensation, for example, an old topic of Germanic origin, could be explored by conditioning techniques. That is, older methods required that subjects report, verbally, whether they saw (as a part of their conscious experience) a light of a certain color. Newer methods of conditioning light and shock could lead to a conditioned reflex. Thus, one could discover whether a stimulus caused a "sensation" by seeing whether it produced the conditioned reflex. The liberation from introspection and its accompanying interminable arguments about mental life seemed genuinely within the grasp of the behaviorist.

But why would one study sensations if the new subject matter of psychology was to be behavior? Is not Watson admitting, with this example, that consciousness exists and matters? Not at all, Watson could reply. Sense organs are a part of our behavioral equipment, and their limits bear on predicting and controlling behavior. The nub of the issue is what one means by the word "sensation." For scientific purposes, that word can and should be entirely divorced from its mentalistic connotations and defined as present when it leads to the response and absent when it does not. The important thing is that sensations now mean the working of sense organs and not mental events.

THE SYSTEM

Central to the eventual systematic theory was Pavlov's work on conditioning. Watson generalized Pavlov's rather more limited reflexology to a principle underlying all human development and hence all human behavior. His 1930 book, therefore, is populated primarily by the notions of "stimulus" and "response." To predict and control are therefore further specified by Watson as to "predict, given the stimulus, what reaction will take place; or, given the reaction, state what the situation or stimulus is that caused the reaction" (p. 11). This general formula states the essence of the scientific program for psychology as Watson envisioned it.

What psychological phenomena can be dealt with by this formula? According to Watson, all of them. Overt behavioral skills, of the kind Thorndike's cats acquired in escaping his puzzle boxes, could be reinterpreted in terms of stimulus and response. Thorndike's law of effect (which we now call "reinforcement"), which postulates "pleasure" as stamping the response in, is pronounced by Watson (1930) to be a belief that "habit formation is implanted by kind fairies" (p. 206). Manual habits in general are understood in terms of stimulus substitution or response substitution, both understood in terms of Pavlovian principles, while complex activities are simply "a second stage of conditioning," in which the "muscular stimuli coming from movements of the muscles themselves are all we need to keep our manual responses occurring in proper sequence" (p. 219).

Memory, of course, cannot refer to a mental phenomenon for Watson, but there is a behavioral analogue: the retention of manual habits. Such retention itself, be it long or short, cannot actually be explained by psychology. Watson (1930) thought, like Titchener, that physiology is ultimately required to explain the causal details, but "fortunately we can continue our work in behavior without awaiting the true explanation of these biological phenomena couched in physico-chemical terms" (p. 210).

What about our memory of thinking, or thinking itself? When "rightly understood," the relation between thinking and talking will "go far in breaking down the fiction that there is such a thing as 'mental' life" (Watson, 1930, p. 224). First, Watson argues, talking "is in the beginning a very simple type of behavior" (p. 225), entirely analogous to . . . "the establishment of simple conditioned motor reflexes" (p. 230). Of course, language behavior shows conditioning at "second, third and succeeding orders . . . formed with very great rapidity" (p. 231), but, in principle, talking can also be understood in terms of stimulus and response.

The explanation by principles of conditioning is also adequate to explain how language behavior in turn comes to be an "equivalence for reaction" (Watson, 1930, p. 233), vastly economizing on muscular expenditure for humans with language. The trials and errors in learning by Thorndike's cats is even simpler. Furthermore, "Soon the human has a verbal substitute within himself theoretically for every object in the world. *Thereafter he carries the world around with him by means of this organization*" (p. 234). Watson extends his conclusion, suggesting finally that he even explains human thought, "and he can manipulate this word world in the privacy of his room or when he lies down on his bed in the dark. Many of our discoveries come largely through this ability to manipulate a world of objects not actually present to our senses" (p. 234). We can see that Watson understands that thinking, from a behaviorist viewpoint, "is in short nothing but talking to ourselves" (p. 238).

But has not Watson thereby admitted the "mental" into his psychology after all? The question really hinges on whether thinking is mental in the usual sense, and Watson proposes the bold hypothesis that it is not mental at all, but indeed is behavior, laryngeal, subvocal behavior.[2] The external invisibility of laryngeal behavior may create a methodological complication, but, in principle, behavior, not mental events, is what the term "thinking" should refer to—if, that is, we want a scientific and not a religious definition of thinking. Even meaning, that final claim of the antibehaviorist, is a shorthand of one's way of reacting to an object. My reaction to it is its meaning to me. Nothing mental is necessary to explain even meaning.

Our manual habits and our thinking have now been brought under the systematic account of behaviorism. Only emotions remain, and emotions are, in a way, the easiest of all, if we only see that mentalistic definitions of emotion, including even James's theory, will lead us away from scientific progress. Emotional reactions are, in a word, conditioned visceral responses. As a matter of fact, James's introduction of the body into the study of emotion, in the face of the faculty psychologists and Germanic psychologists who consider emotions to be purely mental, makes James's theory much closer to Watson than Watson's more immediate predecessors. James stood against exactly the introspective approach to emotion in favor of a causal analysis that made the body crucial.

Watson, however, insists on misunderstanding James. James does describe our sensing of bodily reactions as conscious. And Watson's (1930) remarks are harsh: "He saddled upon the study of emotions a condition from which it can scarcely recover" (p. 142), and "No sane person can ever again use the old introspective method with which James and his immediate followers came so near to wrecking this most thrilling part of psychology" (p. 195). James's sin was to have defined emotion as the perception of bodily events rather than as the bodily events themselves. Perception takes place in consciousness and makes emotions into a phenomenon for the subject as well as for the psychological observer. This definition was to Watson simply unforgivable.

However we might feel about Watson's treatment of James, his use of the Pavlovian model led him to crucial observations and experiments that corrected many popular beliefs about children's emotions and their development. As always, the Pavlovian formula led Watson to hypothesize that only minimal reflexive equipment exists at birth and that the usual array of emotions with which we are familiar all develop according to conditioning. This hypothesis has been generally confirmed. It also forced Watson to specify exactly what reflexive equipment exists at birth, and Watson said that "love," "fear," and "rage" are the unconditioned responses with which we are born. He did not mean these terms, of course, to refer to their everyday common-sense meanings, but only to patterns of behavior. Psychological language, here as elsewhere for Watson (1930), is a mere labelling: "We should probably not call these reactions fear, rage, and love, but rather reactions X, Y, and Z" (p. 158).

Watson's theory here is a Pavlovian specification of James's approach as much as the radical break Watson envisioned. Looking back on these remarks, it is as if by the 1920s it was enough to call James an introspectionist in order to justify rejecting him. The departure from James was, of course, radical in terms of methodology and the advance of operational thinking, and the severing of psychological language from the natural language is begun and nearly completed in the psychology of Watson. This severing was decisive in the history of American psychology, making psychological research distinct from everyday life. This separation does call us to question whether this increased precision of research itself is bought at the expense of relevance to everyday life. We shall see this problem again later with Skinner, in whose hands it has been transformed.

Watson's (1930) research, however, established stimulus generalization in the famous account of little Albert, who was conditioned at age eleven-and-a-half months by pairing the presentation of a wooly rabbit with the striking of a steel bar behind Albert's head. Before conditioning, Albert liked rabbits and feared loud noises. Afterward, he feared rabbits—and, by generalization, cotton wool: "Surely this proof of the conditioned *origin* of a fear response puts us on natural science grounds in our study of emotional behavior. It is a far more prolific goose for laying golden eggs than is James's barren verbal formulation" (p. 161). Watson concludes triumphantly, "It yields an explanatory principle that will account for the enormous complexity in the emotional behavior of adults. We no longer in accounting for such behavior have to fall back on heredity" (p. 161). Later, Watson demonstrated reconditioning as a cure for unwanted emotional responses, antedating modern behavior-modification techniques by four decades and provoking the heuristic question for us why it was four decades before Watson's idea entered the practical application of psychology in the clinic.

Manual habits, thinking, and emotions have now each been brought under the behaviorist purview. It is significant that while Watson introduced something radically new in each case, his selection of categories for his radically new perspective are very old. They mirror exactly conation, cognition, and affection, the most common of the faculties in nineteenth-century (and ancient Greek) faculty psychology.

While these are separable "forms of organization" of habits, Watson was very clear by 1925 that these three systems function simultaneously and are constantly interacting in complex human behavior. Like Titchener's atomistic thought and analytic procedures, Watson insisted on breaking complex phenomena down to their basic elements, in this case the single S–R bond, but he also went further in suggesting the way they are integrated into manifest complexities. Every S has, he noted, not only an R that becomes an S for the next R, but also every S has actually three Rs, a manual (skeletal), a verbal (laryngeal), and an emotional (visceral) R. Any of these Rs may be the crucial S for successive elements in complex behavioral chains.

Since, for humans at least, much of our psychological processes are not obviously overt and tend to get called "thinking," Watson merely points out that if thinking is what we call it, then thinking is done by the whole body, through the interaction of laryngeal, skeletal, and visceral responses. The locus, indeed, of the whole of Watson's psychology is the body. By shifting the locus from mind to body, Watson not only forced himself into the rather awkward hypothesis that all thinking is laryngeal; he also brought to bear the Rs and Ss of the rest of the body, visceral and skeletal, to augment the larynx as the locus of thinking. This appreciation of the whole body as a functioning unit strengthens the general behaviorist approach immeasurably.

It is a short step to describing human personality as the sum total of habits, laryngeal, manual, and visceral, that have developed since one's birth. An "overbearing personality" must be described in terms of concrete, behavioral patterns; impressionistic adjectives like "overbearing" lack the precision of science, but their translation—or better, their operational definition—into behavior makes a science of personality possible. One can, if one wants, interview a patient, a job applicant, or whomever, but the information one gets from an interview is not what he or she says. That is mere mental content and predictive of very little. That he or she says it and how he or she says it, on the other hand, are not mental but behavioral. These are behavior, what one does, and we can predict, within limits, from behavior.

This notion has the advantage of hardheaded predictive rigor, uncompromised by the persuasiveness of the other's supposed mental content. The crucial issue in personality assessment is always what the individual will do, not the content of his or her consciousness. Behavior is, according to the behaviorist, the beginning and the end of psychology, even the psychology of the self.

It is also historically noteworthy that Watson, in 1925, saw Freud as significant enough an adversary to combat. He wanted, of course, to remove "a lot of mystery in psychology," saying that his theory of bodily thinking "throws most of Freud's psychology out of court (but not his *facts* nor his *therapy*)" (Watson, 1930, p. 260).

THE WATSONIAN LEGACY

No one can deny that American functionalism was bound to survive German structuralism, in this country in any case. But Watson's work has been decisive for the development of American psychology. His greatest strength was also his greatest weakness. The absolute and uncompromising injunction against everything mental, and the corresponding impetus to the development of a psychology of the physical body and its movement, go hand in hand.

The latter has not only yielded many aspects of contemporary psychology, it secured human psychology firmly within the physical relations of the natural world. However much we may, in later times, resist the reduction of man and self to a natural object, "an assembled organic machine ready to run" (Watson, 1930, p. 269), we cannot deny that this perspective on human behavior speaks at least part of the truth, and certainly a part we dare not ignore.

At the same time we must recognize that Watson's intolerance amounts to a metaphysical proclamation, and more important, a metaphysical proclamation that pretends to be science and free of metaphysics. The out-of-hand equation of the material with the real and the mental with the unreal was not proposed by Watson as the metaphysical position it actually is. Rather, it was proposed as a necessary corollary to natural science. Watson's view was that the only scientific view of the nature of man was that the essence of man is the body. To be "scientific," for Watson, was to commit oneself to being materialistic, mechanistic, and deterministic. That view may be seen as not a liberation from metaphysics but rather as a dogmatic metaphysical stand.

We should understand that Watson was not a trained philosopher and so he did not understand it this way. That is surely a forgivable blindness, especially in light of the provocative and heuristic results of his psychology. We must also understand that innocence of any philosophical knowledge was not a kind of ignorance in Watson's day. It was indeed a sign that one was a certifiable scientist. Watson was caught up in the antimetaphysical attitude actually begun by Wundt in his concerted effort to establish psychology as a science.

The cost of this innocence, however, should not be underestimated. The possibilities for bias that we noted earlier, whenever one must assume a metaphysical position in order to precede with the science at all, comes to full fruition in Watson's psychology and in the conviction, for decades—even to today, but with decreasing frequency—that human beings are not conscious, or if they are, it doesn't matter. That remarkable view can only be seen as a bias, and one that retarded the development of a fuller and more complete psychology. We say, therefore, that Watson's greatest strength was also his greatest weakness.

And his greatest weakness was also his greatest strength, for his bias enabled something important to develop. This leads us to inquire whether this is always the case, whether one of the prerequisites of really decisive contributions to the development of a science is to close off certain questions and pronounce a bias dogmatically, perhaps even equating it with science itself, as Watson did. That is a serious question for the historian of psychology and, therefore, for every psychologist, and for all of us. That question is, I would say, part of Watson's legacy to us.

Certainly also central to Watson's legacy is what his psychology did to the consciousness of the general population. James and Titchener excited some generations of students with their avant garde science, but Watson brought psychology directly into the grasp of the mass media and their consumers, the general population. Anyone can understand conditioning, and while popular views may well have oversimplified Watson's psychology, they did so only in omitting his sense of the complexity of behavior, a sense that was not as highlighted in Watson's own work as was the simplicity.

Furthermore, Watson's psychology brought to the population an apparently scientific confirmation of some traditional and then popular American ideological tenets. His strong stand against instinct, which is most apparent only in his 1925 book after Kuo's 1921 *Psychological Review* article condemning the concept in general, is only a part of a more general distaste for innate psychological factors, genetic differences, and inborn talents, including intelligence. This overwhelmingly environmentalist view was bound to be popular in a culture that traditionally saw itself as rebelling against European aristocracy and affirming the notion that "all men are created equal." The view also corresponded to the then popular optimism and meliorism, the notion that human beings are perfectable through the application of human intelligence; that is, modern science. There is, in Watson's (1930) thought, no small amount of social vision: "I should like to go one step further now and say, 'Give me a dozen healthy infants, well-formed, and my own specified world to bring them up in and I'll guarantee to take any one at random and train him to become any type of specialist I might select'" (p. 104). Watson sees no limits; the creation of a doctor, lawyer, artist, merchant chief, and, yes, even beggarman and thief is possible, "regardless of his talents, penchants, tendencies, abilities, vocations, and race of his ancestors. I am going beyond my facts and I admit it, but so have the advocates of the contrary and they have been doing it for many thousands of years" (p. 104).

His enthusiasm for this optimistic view extended to replacing the current legal system with a behavioristic one, producing an "experimental ethics" and promoting a new "behavioristic freedom," a concept not entirely clear in light of Watson's strict determinism. But as we have said, Watson was not a philosopher, and these sentiments, while historically important for their popular appeal, are nothing more than the spillover of Watson's enthusiasm into sociological and philosophical fields. Both fields seemed to Watson reducable to behavioristic science, and that reduction had the popular appeal of a "scientific breakthrough" in the most perplexing of human problems.

Within psychology itself, I believe we must point to two additional aspects of the Watsonian legacy: methodology and theory. On the methodological front, Watson's views have been so decisive that we could almost say that whatever was in fact scientifically accomplished in American psychology during the middle third of the twentieth century was accomplished within the Watsonian, positivistic definition of knowledge. This leaves open the question of whether we accomplished very much, or could have accomplished more some other way, but we can say for certain that whatever facts were established were secured according to the definition of facts offered by Waston: facts grounded in quantifiable, behavioral events in objective space and time.[3]

Theoretically, Watson has lasted less well. We now have multiple branches of psychology that deal explicitly with the events of consciousness and experience. It remains important that research in these areas, such as later twentieth-century studies in cognition, methodologically engage overt behavioral events. However, these fields of research are about that which Watson banned from the subject matter of psychology. There is, therefore, an important theoretical legacy, and that is the issue with which we began this chapter. Is the human being describable in exactly the same terms we employ to describe the ox we slaughter? Or must it be? Current behaviorists may still insist, as Watson insisted, "yes" on both counts. And the controversies surrounding their stands are not dissimilar to some of the early objections to Watson.[4]

This question of the uniqueness of human consciousness persists presumably because it is not simply a scientific question; it is somehow prescientific, somehow engaged at the level of science before data are collected, that theoretical level that determines what data to look at. No one disputes the facts behaviorist psychology has given us. But we do not quite believe, as Watson did, that if knowledge is not behavioristic it is not psychology, or even knowledge. Many will, however, say that if it is not behavioristic it is not science, thus allowing that there is something called "psychology" that is not positivistic science.

This claim today, however, has changed with changing definitions of science. Certainly behavioristic psychology has less and less to do with the frontiers of science that envision possiblities for knowledge not yet actual, and it is less interested in the social implementation of this knowledge. Skinner, who we will get to eventually, is, of course, an exception to this statement. But the positivism that defines both Watson's and Skinner's behaviorisms as "real science" is less and less important in the cultural battle against superstition and religion. The secularization of the twentieth century makes religion less a threat to the vastly expanded dependency we all know we have upon science. Religion is no longer the whipping boy it was in the days of the Scopes trial. And finally, when in the twenty-first century we read Watson's declaration of the 1920s that he knows absolutely no scientific evidence that consciousness exists, we smile indulgently.

The implications of that indulgent smile are not always clear, however. Watson was pronouncing that consciousness is not a reality. Only physical phenomena are real, not mental ones. Watson was pronouncing that dualism is dead. Like other such pronouncements, this one was "premature." There were many protesters against Watson's pronouncements in the 1920s, and Gestalt psychologists (Chapter 7) were among the most learned, the most scientific, and the most fearless detractors of behaviorism. They insisted that consciousness matters, but they did not insist that dualism does.

NOTES

1. Watson was hardly the first to try to cleanse science of subjective elements. Hilgard (1987) offers Beer, Bethe, and von Uxkuell (1899) and Loeb

(1889), who had been Watson's teacher at Chicago and published a mechanistic interpretation of behavior before Watson (Loeb, 1918). There was also, of course, Pavlov (1904, 1927) in Russia, and Max Meyer, a German immigrant to the University of Missouri, who published *The Fundamental Laws of Human Behavior* (1911) and *Psychology of the Other One* (1921), referring to the observed and not the observing psychologist. A. P. Weiss (1879–1931), also a German immigrant, develped a biological theory that was another version of what Watson called "behaviorism" (Weiss, 1925). That Watson has come to be seen as the single spokesman, or even sturdy pioneer, in the development of behaviorism testifies to his ability to write well. But Watson's popularity also indicates an academic resonance in the laboratories of psychology across the land, as well as a cultural resonance that creates psychology as a kind of consumer good, with dynamics independent of scientific originality.

2. To support the notion that thinking is not mental, Watson felt obliged to play with some of the radical implications of his own idea. In his 1928 book on child care, he stated, "With the behavioristic point of view now becoming dominant, it is hard to find a place for what has been called philosophy. Philosophy is passing—has all but passed, and unless new issues arise which will give a new foundation for philosophy, the world has seen its last great philosopher" (p. 14). Reading this, it is hard to find an explanation for the popularity of Watson's books, except in the antiintellectual, misanthropic, and adolescent conformity that produces mass sales of hula hoops and hood ornaments that sometimes overtakes any population.

3. Watson's blanket rejection of consciousness as a part of psychology stems from the fact that it was not observable in a behavioristic laboratory. Prior introspectionist laboratories of course observed it, but Watson rejected all this work. Consciousness, thus, was equated with belief in magic, voodoo, and Mary Baker Eddy (see Watson, 1930, p. 2). It is as if Watson equated consciousness with "soul." His psychology then proceeded as if consciousness does not matter. We must see this as an extraordinary path for a psychologist. He denies there is any evidence that consciousness exists. Perhaps more important, such a path entirely excludes from psychology any consideration of the scientist. How can anyone be a scientist without being conscious? I have pondered this position perhaps more than one should; many great thinkers have said foolish things. But such pronouncements are not randon. They tell us something. There are several possibilities in understanding how Watson could take such a position. First, it might simply be the case that Watson knew he was being absurd, but thought that the absurdity would make sense to those who understood that he was talking about the psychological laboratory, and not about the rest of the world. If this is the case, it certainly does not hold for the rest of his examples, which deal with child rearing and school settings. Second, it might be the case that Watson here simply misspoke: His attention-getting agenda got out of hand; he should have edited his own book more carefully. Third, there is the possibility that he was simply talking about experimental psychology and its scope, not about that which is basic to human existence. It is indeed exactly philosophy that he does not want to talk about. If this is true, then questions of what is basic to human existence are to be avoided. Fourth, Watson did and said what he did "in role," and the role was

that of a scientist who is supposed to doubt everything. Rigor was defined by skepticism. It is possible that he accepted the role and enacted it without understanding that there are limits to role taking, even if the role is that of rigorous scientist. But a fifth and more extreme interpretation is hard to escape: Watson seems actually to have believed that sources, or kinds, or approaches to knowledge other than his own had no place at all in psychology. If there is a meaningful place to apply the word "arrogance" in the history of psychology, this must be it. Watson was proud, he was dogmatic, and he was arrogant. Beware of prophets who have no self-doubts. And I confess to another, a sixth possiblity. Watson perhaps never took himself or his work seriously. After being a psychologist, he worked in advertising. What makes him different from other psychologists, and other scientists of all kinds, is perhaps that he was merely an opportunist, not really committed to anything. However we understand Watson's decision, we should be impressed with (1) the extraordinary prestige of positivism (see Radnitzky, 1970), and (2) its tendency to lead to the conclusion that scientific methodology guarantees truth. Watson simply had no self-doubts about the correctness of knowledge acquired scientifically, nor any sense that knowledge beyond science is of any consequence for psychology.

4. This radical "scientification" of psychology is certainly difficult to judge simply. We must first recognize the impetus to knowledge getting that it created. That effect came from wedding the prestige of science to the study of behavior, a fusion well underway, but hardly as focused and aggressive as it became after Watson. Second, the limitations enforced by behaviorist psychology delayed the other approaches to psychological questions, such as psychology's contribution to the psychiatric care of "mental patients." This delay was overcome by Freud's popularity and by the intellectual force of Freud's thought only slowly and partially. Therefore, third, the limitations placed on popular psychologizing along Freudian lines discouraged, perhaps, the more sensation-seeking purveyers and customers of self-absorbed, "quick-fix" fads. Thus, genuine psychoanalytic therapy was allowed to develop. Indeed, an entire generation of scientifically fraudulent charlatans may have been discouraged by Watson's rigid scientism. We will never know if there was, nonetheless, gold in those behavioristically forbidden hills, but if there was, and if it had been allowed to flourish, the sifting of the wheat from the chaff would have perhaps taken much longer.

7

Koehler's Gestalt Psychology

THE LIFE OF WOLFGANG KOEHLER (1887–1967)

Along with Max Wertheimer (1880–1943) and Kurt Koffka (1886–1941), Wolfgang Koehler invented and developed Gestalt psychology in Germany between the two world wars of the twentieth century. All three were harsh critics of Hitler's leadership, and all three were forced to leave Germany, but not before their journal, *Psychologische Forschung*, published twenty-two volumes. Hitler abolished it in 1938.

Koehler's background in physics is obvious in his effort to see patterns common to the mind and to the physical world. In fact, the Gestalt vision extended from the dynamics of human subjective experience, to apparently random social groupings, through patterns of standing water and electrical fields, to the solar system itself.

After teaching at Clark and at Harvard, including the William James lectures of 1935, Koehler left Germany for good and taught at Swarthmore College until his retirement. In 1956 the American Psychological Association gave him the Distinguished Contribution Award, and he was elected president of the APA in 1959. Of all the Gestalt psychologists, Koehler's books are the clearest, most popular, and most persuasive, but the movement has had notable American advocates as well since its inception, such as Hans Wallach (Koehler & Wallach, 1944). Gestalt psychology has appeared in every introductory psychology textbook since before the middle of the twentieth century.

German psychology did not cease with Wilhelm Wundt. Nor did Wundt prove more permanent in Germany than Titchener did in America.

Despite the political and military upheavals in Europe in the early decades of this century, Germanic (including Austrian) psychology was producing its own reaction to the Wundt–Titchener psychology of content. Brentano (1874/1960), whose act psychology opposed Wundt from the very beginning, was a very influential teacher whose students at Vienna eventually populated Southern German and Austrian universities. Their psychology was sensitive both to aspects of content that could not be reduced to elements, such as form qualities (square, circle), and to the active nature of perception and therefore the active nature of the mind itself. If the mind is active, if the mind *is* its acts, then Wundtian elements are mere content and Wundtian psychology is not a science of the mind at all. The followers of Brentano therefore had in mind as different a conception from Wundt and Titchener as did Watson in this country. But, of course, their alternative had none of the American Watsonian flavor. This German "revolution" eventuated in Gestalt psychology.

Koehler's book, *Gestalt Psychology* (1929/1947), is more accessible than either Koffka (1935) or Wertheimer (1959), although the English translations of these books add considerable depth and detail to Koehler's translated work, which contains equal criticism of the Wundt–Titchener psychology and of Watsonian behaviorism. The Gestalt critique of Wundtian elements made little impression on Americans, who had already banned them by 1925. Furthermore, Gestalt psychologists did not throw consciousness out of psychology, and so Gestalt psychology often appeared, to a Watsonian continent, indistinguishable from the introspective routines so recently replaced by behavioral experiments.

While Watsonians were cleansing psychology of consciousness and retaining the experimental method and a theory as atomistic as that of Titchener, Gestalt psychologists were rejecting the experimental method and the atomism of Wundt and retaining consciousness as the subject matter of psychology. Therefore, the importation of the Germanic "revolution" to America, where psychologists had just completed their own very different "revolution," was not an instant success.

In spite of this appearance, there is nothing essentially antiexperimental about Gestalt psychology, except insofar as "experimental" meant, with Wundt and Titcher, the creation of those artificialities so obvious in the routines of introspection. Gestalt psychologists, in their later clash with Hull and other behaviorists, performed many experiments, predicting different results and often getting them (see Koehler, 1959, for a summary). But the early work was strongly focused on experience as it happens for everyone every day, including the meanings and what Titchener call "stimulus errors."

A stimulus error, according to Titchener, was a perception that integrates a stimulus with associated content not actually in the stimulus itself. Titchener worked very hard to avoid such errors in order to investigate mental life in its basic elements. Gestalt handled this matter differently. Rather than seeing these complexities as interfering with the experimental revelation of the true structure of the mind, Gestalt psychologists insisted that these patterns and values themselves revealed the nature of the mind. The mind is such that it organizes stimuli into patterns and values. The Titchenerian effort to avoid them, Gestaltists argued, was an avoiding of the data, as given, of the mind.

Gestalt psychologists were, therefore, in the Brentano tradition, strictly empirical without being experimental. Theoretically, of course, the notion that the mind works according to patterns is an emphasis on works as well as patterns. That is, acts (as Brentano would have it)—what the mind does, as opposed to merely the content it contains—are crucial to psychology.

However, the more salient Gestalt objection against both Wundt–Titchener and Watson was their atomism. Whether one breaks the data down into Titchenerian elements or Watsonian S–R bonds did not matter to Gestalt psychologists. The fact that both were breaking the data down instead of taking them as they were given was a crucial error. And they are grouped according to units larger than such analytic elements. Further, these groupings are naturally occurring patterns that show us the inherent nature of the mind, in terms of what it does. It organizes, segregates, and makes meaningful.

The Gestalt theory therefore gave the mind inherent tendencies. This tended to run counter to the extreme environmentalism of Watson, which fit so well with American ideology, in which environment rather than heredity was seen as crucial. Gestalt, in contrast, was more "nativistic"; it assumed that the inherent equipment in the mind itself constitutes an active organizing agent. This idea ran counter to the passivity of the mind portrayed in associationism, a tradition of thought going back to John Locke, clear in Wundt and Titchener, and apparent even in Watson's portrait of behavior as always a response, a reaction, something caused from outside. And it is to be seen in his failure to envision complex motivations for behavior.

As for the mind, the Englishman John Locke's doctrine of *Tabula Rasa* stated that there is nothing in the mind that is not first in the senses. Leibnitz, a German contemporary of Locke, is reputed to have answered with a reference to the fact that the mind doesn't just contain content; it shapes and organizes it. Leibnitz's answer therefore was, "Nothing except the mind itself!" It was, however, Kant, of course, who a century later really formulated in detail this nativistic alternative, that the mind has inherent properties that shape experience.

The more passive, Lockean view underlay British associationistic theory and extended to the psychologists, Titchener and Pavlov. The difference was not, as some psychologists said, that Leibnitz, Kant, and Gestalt were "philosophical" while associationism was "scientific." These all were merely different theories of the nature of the mind; they were all different philosophies in this sense. But the philosophical debts of psychologists have often gone unacknowledged, especially since Watson's adamant antiphilosophical stand.

Therefore, Gestalt psychology was not at first taken seriously by many American psychologists because it was clearly out of joint with so many of the trends in the second, third, and fourth decades in American psychology. It insisted, first, on consciousness as crucial for psychology. Second, it appealed to empirical demonstrations from everyday life rather than controlled experiments. Third, it rejected the analytic tendency to seek elemental units of which complex patterns were mere composites. Fourth, it postulated the mind as active rather than passive, thus engaging what seemed to many American psychologists to be the wrong philosophical assumptions. Little wonder that many American psychologists could reject Gestalt psychology with their greatest post-Watsonian insult: "too metaphysical."

It is important to add, however, lest the impression is left that Gestalt psychology simply fell on deaf ears in this country, that much of the Gestalt idea is currently taken for granted, at least on a superficial level. The hypotheses that can be experimentally verified, beginning perhaps with Koehler's observations of apes (detailed in Koehler, 1917/1925), and later experimental verifications of transposition, size, and color constancy—all verifiable in animal-learning tasks—were accepted in good scientific conscience.

The theoretical implications of these data, however, have never been quite clear in American psychology, primarily because they speak to the question of the nature of the mind. Gestalt psychologists considered these implications to be crucial for the future of psychology. Americans under the influence of Watson considered them (perhaps rightly) to be primarily philosophical questions and therefore (and certainly wrongly) to have little bearing on the science of psychology.

In American universities, like universities everywhere, once an enthusiasm such as that for experimental facts becomes institutionalized into criteria for Ph.D. dissertations and professional advancement, the more reflective theoretical task gets short shrift. In light of the profound and exciting nature of Gestalt theoretical constructions, this negligence seems a pity on aesthetic grounds, if not on the grounds of the requirements of good science itself.

THE SYSTEM

The nature of the mind must be considered, according to Gestalt psychology, along with the nature of nature itself. These are not really separable issues, for the mind is a part of nature and follows its laws. The question raised by Gestalt psychologists are eventually questions about the kind of order that exists in nature itself.

What are the laws of nature? What kind of order does it manifest? Since the mind is a part of nature and follows its laws, Gestalt psychologists saw in the mind, especially in perception, patterns of nature. And they found that both the mind and nature have the order not of a machine, but of an entirely different kind: an order of the *dynamics of a field*.

Field dynamics are observable in a pool of water. On a level surface it will be round; the degree of its spread will be equally moved by gravity at every point on its perimeter and equally resisted by the viscosity of water. An even more impressive example is that of a soap bubble. The air pressure inside the bubble pushing out is exactly equal to that of air pushing in, and it is equally distributed, both inside and outside, across the entire expanse of the bubble. This pattern makes bubbles round at the base and semispherical. The distribution of viscous soapy water is determined by these forces in a dynamic field of forces.

Such an order is immediately demonstrable in the phenomena of experience as well, such as in the spontaneous organization of experiential elements into wholes, and in seeing coherent patterns instead of individual parts. A parking lot appears as rows, not just cars; we see a blue spruce as conical, not as branches, and even up close we do not focus on individual needles unless we intervene with a purpose. The resulting pattern is an entirely different phenomenon than the elements. Gestalt psychologists demonstrated an active, organizing mind by noting that we make a figure stand out from its background and that we perceive in terms of "good form" and "closure," by distorting perception toward symmetry and balance, and so on. Every elementary textbook has figures demonstrating this kind of order and these laws, the laws of the dynamics of a field.

In psychology, the importance of these demonstrations was that they refuted what Koehler called the "constancy hypothesis," the notion that there is a point-for-point correspondence between physical events on the surface of the retina and the experiential events of consciousness. Of course, we'd known since the nineteenth century that the mind was not a perfect photographic instrument, but Fechner's psychophysical experiments in the 1880s merely measured the difference along certain dimensions; they did not lead to a description of the order inherent in experience itself, an order that can be seen only by seeing a stimulus in the context of its experiential field. Experience itself is organized into segregated wholes according to the laws of field dynamics.

This phenomenon bears on psychology, and on the issue of how we conceive the psychophysical relationship. It says that conscious experience itself ("psycho-") is a level of organization that is not strictly beholden to the physiology of the sense organs ("-physics"). But this phenomenon also bears on the nature of nature itself. It suggests that the pattern of forces manifest in a system of planets rotating around a sun tells us more about how nature is organized than our conceptions of linear causality, such as one billiard ball hitting another. A field of forces is always in play in nature, unless the forces are artificially constrained, as they are in the creation of machines. The piston of a steam engine follows a topology convenient for harnessing power for human use, but it makes a poor model for understanding nature.

Nature is organized the way a magnetic field spontaneously organizes itself, not the way electricity drives an electric motor. Furthermore, our concept of the forces of nature have traditionally stated that uncontrolled by human intervention these forces would be chaotic and destructive. Gestalt theorists challenge this silent but powerful presupposition of much technology. The machine is not only an implicit model for us; it is a symbol of our mastery of nature and our bringing order where before there was, we mistakenly believed, mere chaos.

It is at this point—the respect for the natural order and a willingness to see it instead of fearfully feeling we must control it—that we can see the connections among disparate things: Gestalt psychology as an academic theory, Gestalt therapy as applied psychology, the nonrandom distribution of people at a party, and the symmetries of nature. Even the environmental movement in late twentieth-century America was delayed as long as it was because of some similar disrespect for the natural order.

In summary, then, the laws of nature include the laws of field dynamics. Field dynamics are the order manifest in an organism's behavior in its environment, in any environment's relation to the larger ecosystem (to use a term unavailable to Kohler), in any ecosystem's relation to the world, and in the world's relation to the cosmos. Field dynamics can be seen at every level. Gestalt theory is thus a theory of cosmic dimensions.

Gestalt psychology is primarily, however, a psychology. What does all this mean if we are interested in the behavior of organisms? The Gestalt psychologists provoke us to ask, How do organisms move around their environment? Not according to specific stimuli or specific causes, but always within and according to the laws of field dynamics. Furthermore, organisms do this differently than iron filings in a magnetic field. They do it according to their sensitivity to the dynamics of the field, because they are in touch with their environment in a way iron filings are not, through perception and awareness. In a word, organisms are conscious. Gestalt psychologists call being conscious "having insight."

The notion of "insight" has frequently been portrayed as the kind of one-trial or sudden learning manifested by Koehler's (1917/1925) apes when they discovered that joining two sticks enabled them to reach a banana that was out of reach using the sticks singly. This example distorts Koehler's concept, which is perhaps understandable in light of the fact that American psychologists were simply not prepared, aptitudinally or conceptually, to take such large natural patterns seriously, or, for that matter, to take conscious awareness seriously.

Koehler's concept of insight is really a statement that organisms are aware of their environment, and that this awareness matters. Organisms move out of the cold into a warmer place because they know, in some sense, where they want to go and why, and that going there will be better. They know this not because they have "learned," through trial and error, nor because they have habits or S–R bonds that make it happen. They know it because they are sensitive to and responsive to, and have insight into, the field of dynamic forces (including the attraction of heat) in their environment.

This insight of organisms is of course most highly developed in the complex consciousness of human beings, who also move within, and are responsive to, the dynamics of the field in which they are embedded. This sensitivity extends, for humans, to the field dynamics of social situations, such as the clusters that form at a cocktail party. Further, the field may be temporal as well as spatial: rhythms in music, or "good timing" in radio announcing, for example.

What, then, are the implications of this view for the relation between consciousness and the brain? The nervous system is a physical and natural system, and it also follows the laws of dynamics within its own field. Again we see that Koehler argues that the switchboard model is not as good as the "mass action" conclusions of Karl Lashley in the late 1920s. Furthermore, Koehler speculated that there is an "isomorphism" between the patterns of events in the brain and the field of forces in the experience of the organism. This isomorphism cannot, however, be demonstrated, and unlike much Gestalt theory, isomorphism is rarely accepted.

Nevertheless, field dynamics are ubiquitous. Gestalt theory is merely a statement that patterns in nature follow the same laws that can be seen in a field of physical forces like a soap bubble or those in an experiential field of conscious experience. The Gestalt of these patterns (form, shape, character) is not always the same. Different fields may have different dynamics. Howerever, there is a similarity of dynamics across the great variety of nature.

THE GESTALT LEGACY

The legacy of the Gestalt theory is almost totally confined to psychology. Koehler, Koffka, and Wertheimer had practically no visible impact upon American culture. Heidbreder (1933) has said, comparing the popular impact of Watson and Gestalt, "The man in the street understands at once what it means to regard the human being as a machine, and what it means to make it a better machine by a better adjustment of its parts. He needs only to use the habits of thought already in his possession, after discarding those which deal with consciousness" (p. 345). In contrast, Heidbreder notes, "Gestalt psychology can resort to no such simple measures. Though it calls psychology back to ordinary experience, to the plain observations of everyday life, it immediately begins inquiring why that experience is what it is, and thus steps out of the plane of common sense in its attempt to comprehend and explain it" (p. 345).

Within psychology, therefore, Gestalt psychology leaves an unusually rich legacy to the psychologist thoughtful enough to pick it up. In terms of two traditional theoretical battles between polar points of view, Gestalt has managed to find and establish a heretofore unrecognized third alternative. Consider the polarity of heredity versus learning from the environment; and consider vitalism versus mechanism.

The nature–nurture question has historically polarized at two levels, the question of the nature of the mind (Locke's *Tabula Rasa* equals empiricism versus Kant's transcendental categories equals nativism), and the question of the determinants of behavior (Watson's environmentalism versus instinct, talent, and native intelligence theories of individual differences). Gestalt psychology has often been hastily plopped on the nativistic side, but this is appropriate only at the level of the question of the nature of the mind. At the level of the determinants of behavior, Koehler considers both inherited mechanisms (such as talents) and learned mechanisms (such as habits) and shows that there is a great deal of behavior that neither can account for. Both are, in fact, versions of what Koehler called "the constancy hypothesis," or "machine theory."

Behavior is sufficiently varied that we "must try to find," he says, "a kind of function which is orderly and yet not entirely constrained by either inherited or acquired characteristics" (Koehler 1929/1947, p. 117). That principle of order is exactly the contemporaneous field dynamics in the organism's environment. By shifting root metaphors, Koehler is suggesting, we no longer need to decide between these determinants, nor leave a large error term when we somehow add the two of them together.

The vitalism versus mechanism polarity is still alive and well in American psychology and accounts, in part, for the inability to have settled whether psychology shall be as Watson said it should be. Perhaps because the issue is old, perhaps because it is philosophical, psychologists rarely let this question of the root metaphor of our science emerge for explicit consideration. The nineteenth-century roots are the inherent energy and vitalism of Johannas Mueller versus the mechanism of Herman von Helmholtz. Actually, however, the issue dates back at least to Descartes, who "settled" it by saying, in effect, that human beings are part machine and part transcendent of mechanics and of natural science: his body–mind dualism.

There is, in Gestalt psychology, a clear reintroduction of the mind into the mechanics of learning described by Watson. Insofar as we take both seriously (as it seems we must), we can see that nineteenth-century mind–body dualism has not been overcome by scientific psychology but reappears there quite vividly. But, of course, a difference between Gestalt mentalism and behaviorist physicalism has not been seen as a perpetuation of a historical metaphysical issue. Scientists, and especially psychologists, are proud of having made dualism, if not all philosophy, irrelevant if not obsolete.

The Gestalt psychologists are in the unique position of describing behavior in a way that does not choose one option, either heredity or environment, or vitalism or mechanism. Nor does their theory merely jam them together into metaphysical dualism. Instead, Gestalt changes the issue entirely. Agreeing with the mechanists that the mind is indeed a part of nature and therefore orderly, they nevertheless reject the machine model as a description of that order. Agreeing with the vitalists that behavior is not mechanical in the sense of linear causality, they nevertheless reject the notion that principles of life, or mind, transcend the order of nature and hence cannot be grasped scientifically. Such theoretical breakthroughs as this one can go unnoticed only with a studied ignoring of the questions themselves, a tendency one can certainly see in American psychology, especially after Watson.

Gestalt reinstated consciousness in psychology. This reinstatement was slow and partial, but certainly undeniable by the 1950s. Their version of consciousness is not a radical view of consciousness as transcendent of nature (or as that by virtue of which we can say the word "nature" at all, as Kant would have it), but rather is a naturalized consciousness, a consciousness no more mysterious than nature itself, since, indeed, it is decidedly a part of nature. This legacy of Gestalt psychology keeps alive the original hope for psychology, for a "psyche"-"ology," a science of the mind. The mind here is neither Wundt's rarefied laboratory specimen nor Angell's functional part of the organism's adaptive equipment. It is perhaps most similar to James's implicit sense of the mind, functional and Darwinian but of interest in itself as well, rather than merely a part of the adaptive equipment of the organism. James, it seems, is indeed one of the few American psychologists whom we could have counted on to have seen and met head on the profundity of the Gestalt challenge. Unfortunately, he didn't live to see it.

Another clear legacy of Gestalt psychology was the field theory of Kurt Lewin (1935, 1938), who also extended Gestalt principles to social problems (Lewin, 1948). Like Gestalt theory itself, Lewin's theory was often acknowledged without being appreciated in its more radical implications; for example, that behavior must be understood from the vantage point of the behaving organism. But Lewin carried field theory into social psychology and initiated what later was known as "group dynamics," the study of small groups as a field of forces, and later still the use of such groups as quasitherapeutic experiences, so-called encounter groups. Lewin has also "been forgotten" for his creative attempt to mathematize all field theory (Lewin, 1936). Perhaps this exercise was one of the brilliant failures of American psychology, like Titchener and MacDougall. Perhaps it was merely ahead of its time.

I believe we must say, finally, that like James (1890), the full legacy of Gestalt psychology is yet to be appreciated. Gestalt facts that are experimentally verifiable were accepted, and these have made a noticeable difference to Tolman (1948), Hebb (1949), and others. The later presence of Gestalt theory is much more implicit, as is the continuing distinction between body and mind. More than the Gestalt facts have proved important, it seems, in later American psychology. One can see the ideas everywhere, but the idea nowhere. There remain few self-identified Gestalt psychologists. And yet, as I look at American psychology in the 1950s or the 1980s or the twenty-first century, it is somehow unimaginable that it could have become what it did had Gestalt psychology never happened.

Part II

CLINIC AND LABORATORY
From Freud to Skinner

8

Completing the First Century

IS DUALISM A PROBLEM IN PSYCHOLOGY?

We shall see that much of the psychology in the second period relegated the mind–body problem to a position of irrelevance in psychology. This irrelevance is both true and not true. One can explore features of behavior, mental life, personality, or social organization without taking seriously that dualism remains an unresolved problem. To do so is to create real and useful knowledge. But it is also to postpone a complete understanding, an understanding that takes into account what we all know to be an intertwined and mutually dependent presence of physical and mental events in every life. These phenomena nevertheless seem in many ways to be separate realities.

It is as if, at some level, we really think mind and body are separate, or at least conceptually separable. Why might this be so? We can reduce the mind to the brain, or we can say that what we call "mind," "memory," or "ideas" and "ideologies" are really nouns that manifest misplaced concreteness. "Beauty" is not a thing, but an abstraction reified into a noun for everyday speaking, and it is one that suggests it has reality, when it is really nothing more than common attributes of objects of art that we like.

But there is more to the difference between mind and body than merely our thinking of them as different, and more than a casually accepted and historically given reification. There is the fact that they refer to separate spheres, at least separate in human experience; namely, the world of objects and the world of human experiences. Intellectually, we treat these two differently, and have done so for millennia. "The mind" belongs in a vocabulary and in a world of morality, where what happens is chosen by an actor. Objects are not like this. The mind occupies no space, but is that by virtue of which there is space as we know it at all.

On the other hand, "matter" belongs in a vocabulary and in a world of causality, where what happens can be understood as being no one's choice, but rather as the outcome of mechanically conceived causal relations in the world of things. Matter also occupies space, which mind does not, and space provides a template within which we reckon things, which is not true of ideas. (I have expanded considerably on this idea and its relation to psychotherapy in Keen, 2000a.)

Without taking seriously the relation of the mind to the brain, or the mind to the physical objects it knows, from which it abstracts ideas, information, and so on, we will never have a complete understanding of either mental or physical realities. Of course, science has understood much of the world, often to our benefit, without successfully understanding the mental facility (or the faculty) to do so. Our knowledge of physics can be independent of psychology and still be useful. And yet in psychology this independence obviously does not exist as it does in physics. A science of the mind cannot be about the mind in the way that physics is about the material world.

Our knowledge in both psychology and physics is of course incomplete, but our understanding of our "mental" grasp of "material" reality need not be complete for our physics to be good science, our productive capacity to soar, our astronomical sophistication to become acute, and so on. Yet the incompleteness of our grasp of life remains an outstanding feature of the modern world. We still must improve our understanding of mental events like "knowing." We do not know how to make others know what we think they must know in order to create, say, a peaceful world.

Behaviorism applied the scientific methods of physics to psychology and created a science of behavior. Perhaps, however, the agreement by psychologists to settle for behaviorism as a kind of physics of behavior is not ambitious enough. Cognitive psychology, central to mid-century American psychology, still methodologically confirms its knowledge by methods that imitate physics as well. This is true even though our research ideas must connect to our experience, and our theories of cognition must account for our experience. It is as if our understanding of cognitive psychology, at least, is very different from our understanding of physics.

Our understanding of cognitive psychology, research questions, theory, and findings is quite coherent without correlating mental events to physical ones in the brain. Perhaps cognitive psychology will eventually also connect to physiology and to neurology, and perhaps such a connection will add something to our understanding of cognition. But our cognitive psychology hardly depends on this correlation for its coherence. Mental life has a coherence of its own, and it is quite independent of the coherence currently seen in neurology, or any other theories or facts about the physical organ of the brain. We have become quite familiar, even happy with our dualism.

And yet we are not. Psychologists have put this problem on the agenda, and we have continually postponed it, reassured by the slogan that dualism is merely a philosophical problem, of no real interest to psychologists. This division of labor with philosophy is more than handy; many psychologists believe that they are the scientific ones and the important ones. Philosophy can struggle with dualism if it likes, but psychology can ignore dualism. Is or is not dualism a problem for psychology?

WHAT DID WE SEE IN PART I?

In Part I, we saw the first of three stages in the struggle with the dualism inherited from well before the nineteenth century. Each of these steps, from William James to Wolfgang Koehler, appears exciting, even adequate for many psychologists to establish psychology as an independent science that can neglect philosophy and become adequate even to answer scientifically what had been metaphysical questions. The first attempts related mental and physical events empirically, in a discipline called, appropriately, "psychophysics." This effort may or may not have run out of gas on its own, but it is clear that the Watsonian shock disrupted that program dramatically and redefined psychology without the psyche. Psychology became behaviorism. Perhaps settling for behaviorism was not ambitious enough.

By limiting the subject matter of psychology to the objective world, and by reducing that world to an S–R format, Watson became enormously important in defining psychology. The popularity of his work was partly because it had immediate practical application. But it also had tremendous theoretical appeal, because dualism, and in fact all of philosophy, not to mention religion, could really be forgotten in the face of behaviorism, or so it seemed. It was believed that a future behaviorist psychology needn't be bothered by its prescientific beginnings any more than medicine is bothered by earlier humoral or other superstitious practices.

This enthusiastic abandon was true in the heyday of behaviorism in the early decades of the century. During the 1930s, for example, the attempt to continue the mental science of Ebbinghaus on memory, or Dewey on education, had followers, but they remained on the fringe of the American psychology that was behavioristic. In American psychological theory, this meant an S–R psychology of learning, and in American psychological methodology it meant a positivist definition of scientific knowledge, thus ruling out any data that were not quantifiably behavioral. Various tests were devised to bridge the gap between science and reality; for example, to correlate scientific I. Q. scores or measurements of "interest" with human realities of age, education, and so on.

All this changed when it became clear in this country that Gestalt psychologists in Germany had reintroduced consciousness into psychology, and that they had expanded the reach of science partly by expanding the methods and vision of science. As long as we had wanted nothing but a science of behavior, Gestalt psychology offered us little. Insofar as we still want only to predict and control behavior, Gestalt psychology offers us rather little. But Gestalt in fact broke through the behavioristic hegemony to envision new methods, new phenomena, and new ways of understanding scientific law.

In general, the Gestalt hope was for laws that are psychological, laws that apply to psychic events but nevertheless are congruent with physical laws. Between the two realms no longer lies a no man's land of dualism, an unbridgeable gulf between mind and body, but rather an underlying structure of field dynamics that applies equally in both realms.

Three very different kinds of data obey laws of field dynamics. First, the distribution of organisms in a field. People at a cocktail party will distribute themselves in the room in clusters that themselves are equal distances from one another and from the walls. Within such groups, people will face into a circle that gives everyone a view of everyone else. This might seem to have nothing to do with field dynamics, except that predatory birds will distribute themselves equally over a field of prey, and fish within a field of food, perhaps clustering (but equally distant from one another), thus obeying the same dynamics as humans.

Second, human consciousness organizes a random perceptual field into groupings. We see neighborhoods as rows of houses, perhaps organized around a center, not just as random houses; we see flowers as round and trees as symmetrical. We spontaneously see patterns, in fact, not individual houses, petals, or leaves, nor do we then, as a second mental act, see rows, roundness, and symmetry.

Third is the soap bubble, a demonstration from physics, that the laws of symmetry, created by the forces of a gravitational field and a uniform viscosity of soapy water, produce again the same field dynamics as the distribution of animals in a field of prey, and of objects in a field of vision.

In each case, a field of forces is at work, and can even be described mathematically. But more crucial for psychology, this appears not only in mental, subjective–experiential life, but also in organismic survival patterns, and in physics. The mind–body split might leave us forever facing two different worlds as far as our linguistic representation and formulation about possibilities is concerned, but science may be able, Gestalt psychology seemed to say, to find an order more basic than the particulars of mental and physical phenomena.

LOOKING FORWARD TO PART II

As we move into Part II of this account of our history as psychologists, we move into a period in which psychologists began to think of themselves differently. Until after World War II, the American Psychological Association, begun in 1892, did not include so-called clinical psychologists. Only in 1948 did the counseling and clinical psychologists, who had had their own association, the American Association of Applied Psychology (AAAP), join the APA, adding several divisions to APA and swelling its numbers.

This marriage of clinical and experimental psychologists in the newly shaped APA did not change the perception, among all psychologists, that the group as a whole consolidated around two rather different activities: the experimental acquisition of scientific knowledge from the laboratory and the therapeutic helping of people in the clinic. This polarity ceased to be represented in organizational terms insofar as the AAAP brought its divisions into the APA in 1948, but this polarity did not disappear from how psychologists thought of their field. Psychologists consciously knew which of these two groups they identified with, and rather few embraced both or neither.

What was not conscious, however, and seemed to have less and less relevance, was mind–body dualism, or, for that matter, any such struggles with philosophy or religion. The mid-century split between experimentalists and clinicians seemed to be about the kind of work one wanted to do, not about a philosophical issue at all. And that appearance is hardly wrong. But the historical processes of that appearance also engage less explicit attitudes than the work one wants to do. Such motives themselves are matters of temperament, or worldview, or who one's intellectual friends are, or other such variables that are still under the influence of deeper issues. All these are shaped by historical tendencies and trends established in earlier ideas.

A polarity as ancient as dualism in fact reappeared in psychology without the earlier dualistic labels of "mental" science and "biological" science, but in this history we can now see that mentalistic psychologists became clinical and biological psychologists became experimental. The manifest content of this duality seemed to be a matter of interest or occupation, but the latent content of mind and body can be missed only by intentionally looking the other way, by refusing to understand what is obvious to all nonpsychologists; namely, that mental science and biological science have not really overcome the dualism. The metaphysical distinction, so vehemently ridiculed in the behavioristic hope of leaving philosophy behind, has moved from an explicit theoretical issue to an implicit one, but one that nevertheless appears as a matter of occupational interest. Philosophy was forgotten, and remembered only inexplicitly—in how we grouped ourselves.

No one seems to have seen it this way, nor do we typically see it this way now. There are few examples of what Irving Janis (1982) has called "groupthink" that have captured so many people for so long as those examples that exist so vividly in the history of psychology.

ENTER FREUD

Even before the creation of Gestalt psychology, there was a growing population of mentalistic psychologists, those who did counseling or, imitating medicine, "clinical work," and there were also those theorists who inspired it, such as Freud. Meanwhile, an older tradition of physiological psychologists, originally dedicated to exploring the relation of brain to mind, came to focus on the relation of brain to behavior. The label "behavioral" was officially designed to cover both experimental and clinical work by 1940, but that solution could not hold. The behaviorism of Watson had declared mental life to be distinctly not a part of psychology. This fact drove those disposed to explore mental life either into the "mentalism" of Gestalt or, more frequent, into the clinical task most typified by a prior population of school counselors, and even psychiatrists, who eventually embraced Freud.

The vivid polarity, then, between clinicians and experimentalists that bifurcated psychology at mid-century has a latent content. Whatever motivated mentalistic psychologists toward Gestalt or early efforts at "mental testing" came to focus on "mental illness." That is where one found like-minded colleagues. By the same token, whatever motivated biological psychologists toward physiological research, or the psychology of Pavlovian conditioning, came to focus on "behavioral science." That is where they found like-minded colleagues.

In the first case, we see a perseveration of interest in the mind, and in the second, a perseveration of interest in "prediction and control," an attitude developed most fully in the physical (and biological) sciences. Both found themselves part of the "science of psychology," and yet these two groups heard distinctly different drummers.

The psychology of learning, championed originally by educational psychologists and researchers like Dewey (1922) and Thorndike (1936), split into a behaviorist camp, begun by Guthrie (1935), and a mentalist camp, of which Gordon Allport (1938/1960) is an excellent example. It was Guthrie's work that catapulted the psychology of learning into the very center of American behaviorism, and Allport's that spearheaded the study of personality, an explicitly nonbehaviorist concern, and a concern for which mental life was as central as it was absent from the behavioristic psychology of learning.

In Part II, we first see Freud's psychoanalysis (Chapter 9), imported largely by psychiatry from Europe in the early decades of the century. Freud's theory became the dominant theory of personality by mid-century. Freud was also a vivid champion of the study of the mind, as opposed to the body, which he included in his psychology only as a source of problems the mind has to cope with. This "clinical-personality" focus must be compared to an "experimental-learning" focus such as that of Guthrie (1935) and Hull (1943). Hull's intervening variables between S and R, between input of stimuli and output of responses, were purely logical and mathematical constructs. Mind is missing; behavior—that is, physical movement in physical space and time as understood by physics—is everything.

Of course, behaviorists knew that organisms have something like what we think of as "minds," and Hull's work was extended by Dollard and Miller (1950) into the study of conflict and neurosis, while maintaining much of Hull's approach and obeying the now dominant requirement that everything must have a behavioral index to be included in the science of psychology. Dollard and Miller brought an epistemology of the animal laboratory to the study of persons.

Even more impressive, perhaps, was the work of Tolman (Chapter 10), who brought a psychology of persons into the animal laboratory. His subjects were all rats, but his theory was distinctly mental, whereas for Dollard and Miller (1950) the subjects are all persons, but the methods were still behavioristic. And as welcome and energetic as were Dollard and Miller and Tolman in their efforts to keep vital a link between mental life and physical methodologies, the latent content of body–mind dualism was never resolved, the two separate realms of discourse as they shape our spontaneous understanding were never really integrated. Dualism lived on, recognized less than ever before because of the vehemence of Watson's rejection of philosophy and the acceptance by American psychology of Watson's positivist epistemology and methodology, the price paid to be counted among "the sciences."

MID-CENTURY

We can see other culturally shaped features of American psychology after World War II. America had even more decisively declared its independence from, and even domination over, European passions that had for half a century caused so much political and military trouble. The truly American science of the psychology of learning was one response. Another was our inspired effort to understand the war, a scientific challenge beyond the reach of laboratory-based learning psychologists.

This task was not, however, beyond an Americanized Freudian psychology, if the latter was combined with some "mental measurements" of peoples' "attitudes and values." These all are visible in a notable study, *The Authoritarian Personality* (Adorno, Frenkl-Brunswik, Levinson, and Sanford, 1950), done in America by psychologists, many of whom maintained roots in Europe, and who thus drew both on Freudian theory for hypotheses and on mental testing and detailed interviews for scientific data that could verify them.

American psychology of the 1950s therefore had elements of Watson and Gestalt from before the war; learning theory, which began before the war but became popular after; postwar survey and interview techniques; and clinical theory from Freud, who died in England in 1939, in flight from the Nazis in Vienna. *The Authoritarian Personality* meshed all of these trends, which now are so specialized and thus disparate that they were hardly ever again to be combined. The combination of psychoanalysis and cultural anthropology also flourished briefly after the latter had been popularized by Ruth Benedict (1938) and Margaret Mead (1949). Much of that ethological work had been done before the war.

Carl Rogers, the premier clinician, and Clark Hull, the premier behaviorist at mid-century, are explicitly compared and contrasted in Chapter 11. While Rogers is the purest mentalist of all, Hull's theory avoids mental construction with studied thoroughness. And yet we see, in Chapter 11, some remarkable similarities. Carl Rogers, like Freud, dealt with phenomena of the clinic. Roger's humanistic good will and lucid simplicity in doing therapy made him enormously popular with clinical psychologists, none of whom dwelled on the fact that they were mentalists in a metaphysical sense. Most clinical psychologists simply ignored the brain and thus obscured the dualistic rift, as if a return to the larger problem was for a later generation. None returned explicitly to the dualistic latent content of psychology, even if they knew this problem was there.

Much of this studied neglect of dualism is equally true of Hull. No one offered American psychologists more hope that experimental psychology would replace philosophy. Both thus reinforced a focus on either clinical or laboratory problems, which had by then become ends in themselves. It is as if dualism had become so institutionalized that it appeared in the setting of their work, or the character of their goals, as scientist or as therapist, but not in the content of their thought.

At mid-century, Hebb (1949) (Chapter 12) offered yet another attempt, and of course not the only serious one, to deal with dualism. Freud saw the body only through the lens of the mind, and Tolman saw the mind only through the lens of bodily behavior, but Hebb explicitly tried to connect mind to brain, to continue a program of psychology to explicate and specify what we already know—that the brain is the physical organ of the mind, and that there must be a comprehensible connection between them.[1] Hebb was the only one to keep the dualistic latent content of psychology explicitly in view, to see and discuss the philosophical root, the big picture within which psychology came to exist. And he attacked it directly by trying to dissolve dualism with science.

Adding Piaget (Chapter 13), a Swiss explorer of children's minds, we see such intensity of focus that he, like Freud, seems to have abandoned any larger perspective within which the dualistic history still echoes. He did, however, spend much time in philosophical work. In fact, like Freud's agenda, his work is really larger than exploring mental life. Piaget saw himself as an epistemologist, which is an effort to make lucid the human penchant for knowledge, a philosophical ambition as great as Freud's hope to redefine human beings in such a way that human residency in a body can be lucidly understood, rather than anxiously parlayed into neurotic symptoms.

Skinner (Chapter 14) propelled experimental psychology to new heights after the war, and by 1980 had written enough, both in the scientific and popular veins, to have made the fusion of humanistic concerns with scientific ones again impossible. His argument, we shall see, was that if we take science seriously it will lead us into the understanding necessary to satisfy the most ambitious of social engineers.

All these psychologists were twentieth-century citizens; the mark of modernity is conspicuous in their work.[2] Their own part in the historical process portrayed here was rarely explicit in their own motives, and it is perhaps only in retrospect that we see that the script from which they were reading their various versions of truth has roots in modern, indeed even in ancient, philosophy.

NOTES

1. On sorting out a comprehensible relation between mind and brain, note the pessimistic quip, "If the brain were simple enough to understand, we wouldn't be able to."

2. Hilgard's (1987) exhaustive historical treatise describes eight schools of psychology by 1940, and argues that they account for not more than half the psychologists by mid-century. Woodworth (1931) thought less than half, fifty-six years earlier. The remainder, unaligned psychologists, were seen by both

as crucial to the future. Perhaps this confidence in the unaligned comes from the fact that Hilgard (1987) distinguishes a "school" from a "system." A school involves social influences while a system involves intellectual ties. Schools, thus, like all social products, are temporary in their relevance. On the other hand, systems are primarily intellectual products, which may be temporary as well. But systems are ideas, and ideas do accumulate as the history of psychology, a part of our common history as a profession and a society. Insofar as one's ideas, traditional and individual, professional and personal, supply the backdrop against which we reckon the meaning of all we perceive, there is an impressive staying power in ideas as well. Systems can be distinguished from professions, which currently organize many psychologists, and professions have replaced systems, it seems, in how many psychologists think about themselves, their knowledge, and their lives. In spite of these changes, the deeper tradition of dualism seems, upon lifting some veils, to live silently on.

9

Sigmund Freud's Psychoanalysis

THE LIFE OF SIGMUND FREUD (1856–1939)

Freud's influence worldwide is inestimable, and a fascination with his theory began in this country shortly after Freud's groundbreaking *The Interpretation of Dreams* in 1900. Born into an orthodox Jewish family, he lived amidst European anti-Semitism his whole life. Nevertheless, Freud finished doctor's training in the 1890s, only to discover that many of his patients had symptoms unrelated to physical disease. After considerable struggle with his clinical data, Freud came to beleive that these symptoms were metaphoric expressions of emotional motives, often expressing thoughts and feelings that the suffering person himself or herself would reject. Strange as it seemed at the time, Freud imagined a symptom stating such a thought as, "I'll show my mother who can be really helpless!"

Through many revisions, Freud's vision of the dynamic and largely unconscious character of the effects of childhood on adult life developed steadily for over four decades. Thus, Freud first practiced late nineteenth-century medicine, only to find it often irrelevant, and so he then invented psychoanalysis. His invention involved a long and laborious process that nevertheless made sense of seemingly senseless paralyses and other physical symptoms. In addition, psychological symptoms like obsessions, compulsions, and phobias became comprehensible. Some of these, at the time, were barely recognized at all as psychological symptoms, but were dismissed as unexplainable quirks of character.

The English translation of Freud's complete works is twenty-four volumes, and modern psychiatry simply could not be what it is today without Freud's pioneering explorations, hypotheses, and rigorous scrutiny of the data his patients offered him. Most psychiatrists are not, in fact, psychoanalysts, but their training cannot bypass Freud's work, even in the age of psychopharmacology. In addition, Freud published several provocative book-length essays on culture, society, and religion, the most famous of which is *Civilization and Its Discontents* (1961/1930), which is required reading for any person who calls himself or herself educated in the Western world.

The presence of Freud in American psychology was, and remains, both powerful and problematic. By the 1930s Freud had already had a greater impact on American culture and popular consciousness than any other psychologist, although he was accepted into the fold of academic psychology with even more hesitancy than Gestalt. Experimental attempts to verify or refute Freud have always been trivial compared to the historic importance of his ideas, an importance that ranks him with Darwin and Galileo. Whether the experimental failures have been embarrassments to Freud or to the experimentalists still depends on who you ask. But for some decades, and still today in some quarters, these experimental failures were and are taken as reasons to ignore Freud, or even to disclaim him as a psychologist. Indeed, to call Freud a psychologist is a little like calling Bertrand Russell a logician. The importance of neither can be described within the confines of a single discipline.

Freud did not enter the psychological scene through the regular channels. Between his physiological training with Bruecke and Helmholtz in the 1880s and his appearance in American academic psychology in the 1920s, he had been in this country only once, invited by G. Stanley Hall to lecture at Clark University in 1909. After that visit, Freud simply returned to Vienna and continued his work within the Viennese tradition of psychiatry.

This identification can hardly explain his influence, and, in fact, his medical allegiance has made him a foreigner in academic psychology. On the other hand, hearty American advocates, such as Hall and Lindsay (1957) in their *Theories of Personality*, made psychoanalysis available to thousands of American undergraduates. This volume was the first book of its now commonplace kind.

The great problem with Freud, however, is what he said. Watson could go along with Freud's emphasis on childhood, but hardly on "the unconscious mind." This notion is exactly not consciousness, and yet Freud's treatment looks mystical enough to a Watsonian to reject it out of hand. Koehler could go along with Freud's talk of consciousness but could hardly accept Freud's emphasis on childhood. Could

Hullian learning theory be fused with psychoanalysis? Dollard and Miller tried, but, as with other experimental programs, never captured Freud's depth of incisiveness. Functionalists functionalized Freud, but his thought stubbornly refused to be reduced to functionalism.

All these reasons to not take Freud seriously are countered by the massive fact that Freud is, among other things, undeniably a psychologist, and a brilliant one. As late as Hall and Lindsay's (1957) description in the 1950s, a clear grasp of Freud's concepts was a new experience for many who liked to think of themselves as "Freudians."

I believe we can begin to understand the perplexity with which we still confront Freud if we recognize the difference between kinds of psychological theory. Let us distinguish—somewhat artificially—between predictive and interpretive theory. Freud's psychology is not, and was never meant to be, predictive. Prediction is important to psychologists for two reasons: because it is practical in the application of psychology, and because its success of failure is a criterion of truth. No one can seriously deny these relevancies of prediction to psychological science, and yet prediction is not the only practicality, and predictive truth is not the only truth. In thinking about Freud we must recognize that his was a different kind of practicality and a different kind of truth from how these things had come to be understood in most American academic psychology.

Predictive practicality places the psychologist outside the practical situation as a temporary presence, and asks him or her to make an intervention the consequences of which he or she knows ahead of time. The psychologist is, in this kind of practical situation, a good psychologist if and only if he or she knows what effects will follow these causal inputs. The criterion of success is achieving a specified goal by intervening in an efficient manner. Freudian practicality is entirely different. Goals are never quite specified nor speciable; the efficiency of intervention is therefore never measurable. Freud confronted patients— persons, not problems—to solve or goals to achieve. The application of his psychology was to interpret, not to predict. He succeeded not when he could predict the effects of his causal inputs, but when a patient could say, "That's right! I now see! I now understand what I'm doing," and when that understanding made possible (but did not cause) alternative ways of being who they were.

But Freud claimed more than practicality, even taking into account the fact that practicality for Freud went far beyond prediction. Beyond all that, Freud claimed to be speaking the truth. Since Freud rarely made predictions and offered only interpretations of events already past—post-dictions, if you will—we are confronted with the question of whether prediction is the only criterion of truth, or better, whether predictive truth is the only kind of truth. Predictive statements tell us what events will occur under certain conditions. Interpretive statements tell us what events, already past, mean. Predictive truth can be tested in a laboratory. Interpretive truth cannot.

What sort of psychology is it that cannot say what future events will occur but can and does say what past events mean? Surely this is not psychology the science at all. It is philosophy, or even religion. However, before we equate science with prediction, let us see if that equation may not be too narrow a definition of science. Think of Darwin, surely a scientist, who made no predictions at all but offered us, exactly, an interpretation. An interpretation is an ordering of facts in such a way that they are coherent and refer to something about which a human observer can say, "I see; now I understand."

Every psychology is interpretive, whether it is predictive or not. Watson is important not only because he led us to predictions, but, more crucial, he offered us a way to understand ourselves and one another. Titchener's ultrascientific psychology foundered on precisely the point that he never questioned his interpretation of the nature of the mind (as essentially composed of elements, an interpretation). He merely assumed it.

Surely an interpretation is better if it can be put to empirical test. But not all interpretations can. That one's personality "is but the end product of our habit systems" (Watson, 1930, p. 274) is no more testable by predictive means than Titchener's view of the nature of the mind or Freud's view of personality. There simply are, in psychology, preexperimental, interpretive stages of our work that tell us what data to look at. They define the nature of the mind, of man, or of life. What then is the criterion of truth of interpretative statements?

Darwin was a "good" scientist because he allowed us to see a coherence in a mass of previously unrelated, or incoherently related, data. He allowed us to say, "I see. I understand." What he did for the mass of anatomical data at his disposal Freud can do for the mass of personal data from a life history. The coherence itself creates and is created by a framework that allows us to see what any single historical event means. It puts the event into a context within which it becomes intelligible, perhaps for the first time, perhaps replacing an older strained or vague intelligibility with a clear and coherent one. This kind of truth, interpretive truth, relates directly, of course, to Freud's kind of practicality, the practicality of understanding oneself and thereby of seeing possibilities for being oneself that were formerly invisible.

Little wonder it is, I think, that psychologists who try to assimilate Freud's truth and Freud's practicality to prediction reject him. Perhaps the paradox of this rejection, like saying that Bertrand Russell is not a logician, becomes clear in light of these considerations. Freud was a scientist, Watson's positivism notwithstanding, as was Darwin.

But we must meet them both at the theoretical level at which they come to us, or we entirely miss their point.

THE SYSTEM

Freud was, broadly speaking, a rationalist. He insisted on rational theory and believed that human rationality was the only hope to improve the human lot. He did not believe, however, that human rationality is all of human nature, and, in fact, the most crucial part of his interpretation of persons' lives was about our irrationality. Not only does this fact point to the theory of the unconscious, that part of our mind that escapes rational abilities, but it points to the wellsprings of human motivation in the instincts (*die Triebe*, equally well translated as "drives").

A convinced Darwinian, Freud understood the instincts to be our heritage from our prehuman ancestry. The instinct theory underwent many modifications in Freud's career, but they are nearly always related to sex (for the preservation of the species) and aggression (for the preservation of the individual organism). The instinct theory not only defined man in Darwinian terms, it also enabled Freud to focus his attention on the body, its erogenous zones (oral, anal, genital), and the partial instincts associated with them. Most important, however, the instinct theory enabled Freud to speak in terms of energy, his concept of "psychic energy," which he thought was derived from biological energy, and which he usually called "libido."

Libido drives everything we do, our behavior, our fantasies, our dreams, and our symptoms. Grounded in our biological heritage, libido has sexual and aggressive directionality, but it is obviously modified in thousands of ways before it surfaces in the behavior or experience of human beings. These modifications emerge from the fact that, in addition to our instincts, we have acquired, in our personal life histories, taboos and inhibitions that are in direct conflict with raw libidinal expression. These taboos and inhibitions are learned very early in life, before our verbal intelligence is developed sufficiently to understand them. And so they, like the instincts, are largely unconscious, and the conflicts that occur throughout our daily lives are also therefore largely unconscious.

In his most developed statement of the structure of personality, the instincts are called the *id* (Latin for the "it," an impersonal, biological force) and the taboos are called the *superego* (the "over-I," or, in everyday terms, conscience). Both are parts of every personality; therefore every person's conscious life is an arena in which the large forces of unconscious biological drives and imperfectly conscious social–moral constraints play out their conflict. The human situation itself is therefore inherently conflictual: internal id and internal superego are personal representations of contradictory forces into which each of us, as conscious person, is thrown. Forces of biology (id), culturally defined morality (superego), and, of course, real-life contingencies of reality are the three often conflicting parties with which all of us must make peace.

From the resulting conflicts emerge the modified expressions of libido in everyday motives and activities. Everyday motives and activities are, therefore, never quite as simple as they seem to the conscious mind. Built into every conscious motive are disguised biological desires and compromised moral injunctions and taboos. Everything we do moves our lives into directions we do not know we want, and away from paths we do not know we fear.

Freud's theory of dreams, his first big conceptual breakthrough, shows this compromise between desire and morality quite clearly. The manifest content of a dream, which we remember, is a distorted expression of latent content. That latent content is made up of infantile wishes, driven by instincts, and moral taboos, learned in our ealiest family relationships. The "dream work" allows a manifest content that expresses symbolically the unconscious psychodynamics, where the conflict is played out while we sleep.

Similary, when awake, our conscious intentions only partly account for our behavior. Intentional actions as well, including our neurotic symptoms, have a latent content, an unconscious meaning. What becomes dreamt, and consciously recalled, needs to be interpreted in order that our personal unconscious contents, wishes and taboos, can become clear to us. And this interpretation elucidates the meanings of neurotic symptoms.

Especially in the presence of neurotic symptoms, much that we do needs to be intepreted in light of these complex psychodynamics. The particulars of your or my psychodynamics, in turn, are most easily seen in dreams. Dream interpretation is therefore central to therapy. It is a laborious and time-consuming process, carried out mostly by the patient as he or she tries to unravel the distortions of the dream work, and to see his or her own basic conflicts as clearly as he or she can. These conflicts illuminate what puzzles us about our actions. Laborious as it is, dream interpretation remains a central part of psychoanalytic therapy. Mysterious as they may seem, neurotic symptoms also make sense.

Freud's third and final part of personality is the *ego*, which is largely conscious, but there are also unconscious ego functions, such as the repression of instincts, protection of self-esteem, and other so-called defense mechanisms. If the *id* represents the biological and the *superego* the moral components of man, the *ego*, with all its defensive work to do, is a crowded and busy locus of rationality. No wonder, then, that the most crucial function of the ego, judging reality accurately, is so often compromised by psychodynamics. There is the additional complication that personal psychodynamics contain hearty doses of a culture's moral content, so that even conflicts between cultures can be elucidated by psychoanalysis (Freud, 1962/1915, 1962/1932).

To the extent that the ego can run our lives, that our conscious motives are our real motives, that they are not wholly preempted by cultural values or personal desires, and that they are calculated within a more or less rational assessment of reality, we are able to live realistically. But the ego is caught between three masters, each of which makes demands on our conscious self that conflict with the demands of each of the others: (1) the id, striving for energy discharge and instinctual expression, (2) the superego, striving for moral purity and threatening guilt, and (3) reality, that intransigent network of factors of the real world, ignored only at our greatest risk.

Neurosis is the failure of the ego to mediate these contradictory demands successfully. Neurosis is a compromise of our untainted perception of reality. Compromises with unconscious wishes (biological id), or family taboos (personal superego), or cultural biases (cultural superego), lead us to see others wrongly, to decide a course of action that will lead us into trouble, to behave unrealistically or irrationally. Classical neurotic symptoms, such as hysterical body maladies, obsessions, phobias, and anxiety attacks, all emerge because the ego's task of guiding us rationally through the complex mazes of life is compromised by the unconscious conflicts in ourselves.

Since biological desires and moral constraints simply do conflict, and since unconscious conflicts are inevitable for everyone, it follows that neurosis is always a matter of degree. Unconscious conflicts are always ongoing, even though they began in childhood experiences, when the styles, trends, and patterns of our psychic functioning were taking shape.

Growing up is inevitably a conflictual process. The desire, say, to vacuate our bowels—an inherently pleasurable activity, especially for the pre-tabooed infant—must meet the resistance and eventually capitulate to the cultural forces of socialization. In the process of toilet training, crucial issues are settled and built into our personalities, issues such as whether I control my body or my body controls me, and whether I control my body or my parents do. By the time we are adults, the specific events of these conflicts are forgotten (that is, repressed), and the elaborate fantasies of conflicts with parents no longer remain conscious. What does remain is the fact that we all experience the enjoyment, a partial gratification, in dirty jokes—or we are disgusted by them, depending on whether the desires or the taboos are stronger. No human being, we see, is neutral; no one has no emotional response to the four-letter words for such dirtiness.

Most crucial of all in childhood are the conflicts of the Oedipus complex, which settles, in the late preschool years, issues of love and hate in the primary family. Of course, the distribution of love and hate in relation to one's parents has had a profound effect on how we now experience love and hate. Of course, the same is true for how we see and feel about lovers and haters, and for how we feel about our own feelings and about the feelings of others.

This conflictual situation is always more complex than simply loving the cross-gendered parent and hating the like-gendered parent, but such a pattern is a general outline within which everyone's childhood, with its unique characteristics, is originally played out. The intrusion of Oedipal themes into our everyday dealings with reality are serious compromises of the ego's rational and realistic coping. And they are inevitable, even though they do not always appear in later symptoms.

A symptom, then—a bona fide neurosis—is merely an exaggeration of such an intrusion. What intrudes may be the infantile wishes (id) or the moral taboos (superego)—or, most common, some unconscious amalgam of both—and we recognize them as irrational. Their puzzlement to us comes from the fact that their connection to our personal histories of conflict is unclear.

The goal of psychoanalytic therapy is to make the connections clear—not simply intellectually clear but, more important, emotionally clear, clear in terms of our feelings, both contemporaneous and infantile. Such clarity is achieved only through the most strenuous explorations of the unconscious. These explorations, in memory, actually relive the old conflicts in order to both elucidate and correct what currently is being expressed in our irrational symptoms.

While these are the core elements of Freud's theory of personality, they hardly exhaust Freud's writing, which, in its twenty-four volumes, covers topics in art and literature, group psychology, religion, anthropology, biology, sociology, and—although Freud would not quite admit it—philosophy. Freud *is* a philosopher, as well as a psychologist. He does psychology at its most basic level: What is the nature of man, of the mind? What is involved in being a human being? For all these and like issues, Freud has his answers. There is little in human behavior that cannot be understood in Freudian terms—and that has not already been so understood by Freud himself.

We see here a monumental interpretation of human psychology. It is not a particularly cheery one, for the tragedies of conflict and guilt are built in. It is also not clear how one could test the truth of the notion that the human situation is inherently contradictory and that the price of civilization is guilt. But testable or not, everyone has some view of the human situation, its inevitabilities and its possibilities. The more one reads Freud, the more one sees that Freud has his reasons, and if we have reasons for disagreeing with him, either personally or as a basis for a science of personality, these reasons have to be grounded in as hard-headed and unsentimental a scrutiny of the data as Freud's.

Of course, the nature of Freud's data is indeed peculiar. For four decades or more, Freud had a full schedule of psychoanalytic patients. No one knows how many people that includes, but the psychoanalytic process is one in which the analyst exposes himself or herself to the innermost secrets of human beings, facets of persons so secret that they themselves did not initially know about them. His patients, of course, included persons no more neurotic than you or I, and a key source of data for Freud was also always himself, Freud's lifelong self-analysis. In addition, Freud dealt with adults. His entire developmental theory, which is central, is retrospective, grounded in what is remembered and what is forgotten—only to be remembered again in the analytic process.

There can be no doubt that this kind of data gathering puts a certain slant on things that may well look different from other perspectives. It is also difficult in working with these data for the self-correcting routines of science to be guaranteed. After coming to believe that the Oedipus complex is universal, can we really expect Freud to note a very different pattern even if it's there? Perhaps not, and perhaps, therefore, the lack of predictive checks in interpretive science is very costly.

Freud himself, however, never thought of his work as anything but science. Science did not mean then, as it sometimes does today, only experimentation. It meant an attitude of dispassionate observation and vigorous scrutiny of one's own biases—as inherent obligations—and it meant a willingness to throw common sense, tradition, and cultural verities out if they did not conform to what one saw. And it meant, in contrast most vividly to Jung, a belief in the possibility of rational human intelligence to uncover the essential coordinates of nature, including human nature. These are, perhaps, not unworkable methodological guidelines for that region of our science that is interpretive and not subject to predictive checks.

THE FREUDIAN LEGACY

One must mention first the fact that Freud's name became a household word by 1930, and remains one today, although without the racy flavor it had in the 1930s. Indeed, popular culture has taken over sexuality, partly under the influence of Freud, so that sex, by the turn of the millenium, was simply less intensely laced with the thrill of the forbidden. The man in the street in our culture now believes, as thoroughly as our ancestors believed in God, that there is a region of our psychic functioning we are unaware of, that childhood is decisive for adult character, and that sexuality remains a critical part of human misery and human happiness. In manifestly simplified form, Freudian thought became a part of Americans' definitions of themselves and one another during the twentieth century.

However, Freud also began a tradition, a line of scholarship from Jung (1960–1979) and Anna Freud (1937) (his daughter) to "post-Freudians" such as Harry Stack Sullivan (1947), Karen Horney (1937), and Erik Erikson (1950), to name only the most famous of them. Not all these scholars were mere psychiatrists. Many sought to extend Freudian thought to a general psychology. By the mid-twentieth century, general psychology had expanded to include Freud, often ambivalently, but at least as a point of view to be reckoned with.

Certainly the greatest impact of Freud on American psychology was to have solidified a new unit of analysis—the individual personality and life history—and with it a new subfield of psychology—the study of personality. By 1925 Watson had a chapter by that title, and MacDougall (1926) called it "character," but these were in response to Freud. James's (1890) chapter on the self and G. Stanley Hall's (1904) study of childhood and adolescence were leading us to such a focus, but Freud made it inevitable. Allport (1937) made the concept of personality respectable within the confines of mainstream psychology.

The importance of the creation of a new unit of analysis in a science can easily be underemphasized. It changes the map of the science in general. Before we could think of "personality" as a unit of analysis, we couldn't quite make things intelligible to ourselves in the way we do today. For example, if I want to understand psychologically why my boss is angry, I might place that datum in the context of what I know about anger in general or cultural rules in general, or I might place this particular reaction in the context of the particular circumstances in which it occurred. The former two are very general, and the latter is very particular.

However, if I can also place the phenomenon in the context of "what he is like," his personality, I can interpret my boss's anger more particularly than merely as an example of anger in general or cultural rules in general, and more generally than as happening just as it concretely happened this time. If I am able to say, "It is like him to be defensive in the face of challenges to his authority," I am making the datum more intelligible through the use of a concept of his particular personality. And that intelligibility is fuller than what I could understand psychologically without a personality theory. Of course, people have said, "That's just like him," for centuries, but personality psychology elevated such a casual statement to a disciplined study. In this sense, American psychology, and modern consciousness, will never be the same as it was before Freud.

We might conclude, and this is not the first time in this volume, by noting a legacy as yet largely unacknowledged in our science. I have in mind here the following lesson. We may still benefit from the perplexity born of our inability either to accept Freud or reject him. From within the narrower definitions of psychology as a purely experimental science, it is easy to discount him, but from the broader perspective of what in general he has taught us about ourselves, it is impossible to do so.

That fact should tell us that what we understand of ourselves is not, and may never be, restricted to experimental fact. It should tell us that there are levels of our self-understanding, and of our understanding of our science, that are prescientific and certainly nonexperimental. That is, of course, the level at which we, like Freud, define and describe the nature of man, of the mind, of the human situation. Every psychology is explicitly or implicitly based on assumptions of this sort and makes claims of this sort. Whether we locate such questions in philosophy or label them metaphysics, these questions are there, inherent in psychology, and must sooner or later be confronted by psychologists as well as by all thoughtful persons.

NOTE ON FREUD AND THIS BOOK

In Freudian terms, the thesis of this book is that psychological theory has a latent content as well as a manifest content. I may want to be a therapist for all sorts of reasons, many of which I do not consciously appreciate. These reasons are therefore a latent content, from my personal history, of my desire to be a therapist. But if there is also cultural consciousness, then like my personal consciousness, it bears a latent content that also comes from its history.

Such history is not to be unpacked in terms of developmental psychology, of course. It is to be seen in the history of the field, and the field's ideas. Like an ego, a discipline's earliest history is at once its most informative and least appreciated. In the case of the discipline of psychology, the latent content of much of, say, twentieth-century psychological theory is the struggle with the concept of mind (and with dualism) that has plagued Western philosophy since the sixteenth century, or before.

In being therapists, or in being experimentalists, psychologists enact, as Freud did, a latent content of the culture; call it the possibility of rationality in the face of irrationality. Freud himself enacted this theme with his patients. But in his published work he revealed a latent content of human beings by rewriting the story of all human desire and morality, of human happiness, and of war. Perhaps therapists and scientists alike also enact a latent content of psychology, which is as it is for the same reason Freud said what he said: that the human mind is central, that it is not the body, and that it is, as much as any other aspect of modernity, sacred.

10

The Psychology of Edward Tolman

THE LIFE OF EDWARD CHASE TOLMAN (1889–1959)

Edward Chase Tolman got his Ph.D. from Harvard in 1915, trained in the Wundt–Titchener tradition, although he had studied for a year in Germany with Kurt Koffka and also acquainted himself with behaviorism by the time he graduated. The structuralism of the Wundt–Titchener tradition counted for less than his exposure to Gestalt in his research career, and he described his reading of Watson as a "tremendous stimulus and relief" (quoted in Schultz, 1975, p. 219).

After 1918, Tolman taught and did research at the University of California at Berkeley, where his career was uninterrupted except for a brief period during World War II and another three-year break from 1950 to 1953. During these latter years, Tolman fought Senator Joseph McCarthy energetically, against the loyalty oath in the state of California. His more scholarly task, as he saw it through most of his career, was to produce data that were behavioristically respectable, and yet data that bear on hypotheses about mental life. In a 1945 article in *Science*, Tolman stated,

Whereas man's successes, persistences, and socially unacceptable divagations [means "wandering from the path"—Tolman loved words like this] . . . are all ultimately shaped and materialized by specific cultures, it is still true that most of the formal underlying laws of intelligence, motivation and instability can still be studied in rats as well as, and more easily than, in men. (Tolman, 1945, p. 166)[1]

Watson's influence is visible in Tolman's methodology (which was finally true for the entire century), but Tolman's research clearly tested behavioral hypotheses derived from mental theories, often of a Gestalt character, and his subjects were usually rats. His is not only one of the most creative research programs on rodents in American psychological literature, it is also one of the most energetic efforts to keep the field of psychology oriented toward mental life, and to avoid limiting it to behavioral habits or biological adaptation.

The Watsonian taboo against taking seriously anything that smacked of consciousness was not merely a celebration of science as we knew it from physics. Nor was it merely an affirmation that "real" reality is physical. For Watson, it meant that psychological reality is bodily and behavioral. Watson's taboo was indifferent (or hostile) to the dualism that shaped Western thinking since the Greeks. It was, however, an explicit and radical way to deal with exactly that dualism. There was a reason Watson exiled the mind from psychology, and it had everything to do with dualism.[2]

It was sometimes the case that telling psychologists that consciousness does not exist, or cannot be studied, or is not important, was like telling an adolescent boy not to think about sex. Certainly there were psychologists who signed on to behaviorism for methodological reasons; psychology's continuing eagerness to be a "science" tended to lead many psychologists to reject any method that was not positivistically sound. However, some of these psychologists, in spite of believing it necessary to obey the methodological rules, found consciousness to be irresistable to study. Tolman was one such psychologist, and he went so far as to say that not even the behavior of a rat can be undersood without understanding something of the rat's mind.

Tolman did not believe, as Watson did, that the method determines the subject matter. For Watson, the mind was not subject to behavioral experimentation and so it was not a part of psychology. Tolman could not refrain from asking whether mentalistic topics could be studied through behavioral experimentation.

Eventually, American psychologists devised ways of studying the very mind that Watson banned with experimental methods Watson did so much to promote. Tolman stood out, even as early as the 1930s and 1940s, stubbornly insisting that exactly such a psychology should exist. More than any psychologist in the second quarter of the century, Tolman struggled to satisfy the seemingly contradictory demands of the behaviorist methodology, on the one hand, and psychology's traditional obligation to study behavior in all its mentalistic complexity, on the other hand. His 1932 book, *Purposive Behavior in Animals and Men*, was singular among behaviorists at the time.

The scientific strategy that enabled Tolman to do psychology as a certifiable behaviorist and still take up such mentalistic and "metaphysical" topics as purposefulness, expectations, and cognitive maps was the strategy of the *hypothetical construct*. The "purposes" of animals, their "expectations," and even "consciousness" itself, was a legitimate scientific concept for Tolman, as long as there was a clear operational definition for it.

Between S and R lay great complexities, Tolman was certain, and to ignore them seemed to ignore what is most interesting about behavior. But in order to talk of these complexities scientifically, the terms themselves had to refer to something externally and experimentally observable.

The most generic term, "consciousness," was defined by Tolman in 1927 as follows: "Whenever an organism at a given moment of stimulation shifts then and there from being ready to respond in some relatively less differentiated way to being ready to respond in some relatively more differentiated way, there is consciousness" (pp. 64–65). That is, organisms "adjust" their behavior, and they do so in relation to environmental contingencies. Consequently, there "must be an internal representation . . . of the probable stimulus results to be expected from the act" (p. 65). Stimuli and responses are visible to the psychologist who studies them, but the central processes that connect them, like those of consciousness, are not.

In order to study behavior, one had to study these central processes from which behavior emerges. In order to study them, in turn, one had to define one's concepts in terms of operations performed and observed in a behavioristic experiment. To define internal processes in terms of external ones is to offer an operational definition. To define external ones in terms of invisible internal ones is so to create a hypothetical construct, a concept naming something not directly observed but observed in terms of its behavioral results. And the behavioral results themselves, of course, had to be unexplainable without such constructs. Tolman believed most behavior was exactly so.

But it is not the use of hypothetical constructs that most distinguished Tolman, for Hull, Guthrie, and even Watson used them as well. Tolman was also distinctive about which hypothetical constructs to use. Straight Pavlovian constructs could not account for the qualitative variation in the behavior of a normal rat as it is observed every day. And the connectionist theories of Thorndike and others failed to account for the fact that animals could learn without making specific motor responses. That is, they learned "maps," "means–ends relationships," and "signs," not just muscle movements. Therefore, the constructs that populate Tolman's work are explicitly mentalistic, not only because psychology's historic role was to study the mind, but, more important, because he believed that the simpler, more mechanical theories simply could not explain the data. Tolman felt this was no less true of the data of animal experiments than it was of the data of one's personal life.

Tolman's career, therefore, is marked by an extraordinary range of inclusiveness, from MacDougall and Gestalt psychology to Freud and clinical psychology, all to be dealt with through behavioral experiments. Tolman's idea of good psychology was the psychology that could include the most data and incorporate the benefits from different points of view, even in their tremendous variety. His posture was, therefore, the diametric opposite of dogmatism; he felt a responsibility to take every serious psychology seriously, no matter how widely it differed from the behaviorist theories. In order to bring this tremendous variety under the controlled observation of behavioristic methodology, Tolman extended the use of hypothetical constructs far beyond what his more conservative behavioristic colleagues could approve.

Because of Tolman's militant open-mindedness, it is not possible to treat his "system" as is possible with other theorists. One must look at Tolman's career chronologically and watch his psychology grow and develop. Of course, this strategy would be the most fair for all the theorists we are considering, but for Tolman it is absolutely necessary. His importance was not only that he had a systematic position that other psychologists had to reckon with, but, more important, he had an attitude about how to do science. That attitude had to be, and has to be, reckoned with as well.

We shall face that task by treating his psychology developmentally. Furthermore, in the course of reading a collection of his articles, such as *Behavior and Psychological Man* (1966), we traverse nearly three decades of the history of American psychology as he saw it, and his place in it, as it was happening.

THE SYSTEM

We shall attempt our description of Tolman's psychology by envisioning a dialectic that more or less constantly went on in his thinking between what we might call psychology and "metapsychology." The psychology deals theoretically with laboratory data; the metapsychology deals with the theory of the theory about the data: a higher level of theory. These two kinds of theorizing constantly influenced one another through Tolman's career, and we can see (Table 10.1) how papers written in 1933 changed some of his views from earlier meta-

Table 10.1
Tolman's Metapsychological Work versus Psychological Work

Metapsychology		Psychology	
1922–1927	**1, 2, 3, 4, 5, 6, 7**	1933	**8, 9**
1935–1938	**10, 11, 14**	1937–1939	**12, 13, 15**
1941–1945	**16, 17, 18**	1948	**19**

Entries (in bold) indicate numbered papers in *Behavior and Psychological Man* (1966) (selected articles from 1922 to 1948).

psychological papers (1922–1927) to later ones (1935–1938), and how papers written in 1935–1938 changed some of his earlier psychological work (1933) to later work (1937–1939), and so on.

Early Papers on Behaviorism

During the 1920s Tolman published papers on such topics as insight (1922b), instinct (1922a), emotions (1923), purpose (1925a), cognition (1925b), ideas (1926), drives, and consciousness (1927). The struggle throughout these early papers was not only to carve out a position with respect to Thorndike, Watson, McDougall, Kuo, Woodworth, and others, all of whom he read carefully and critically. More important, Tolman used these papers metapsychologically. That is, he attempted to clarify and establish the epistemology of behaviorism, to demonstrate that the methodological strictures of behavioristic psychology do not rule out studying the topics that psychology, even in its prebehaviorist days, took to be the subject matter of psychology.

We may, of course, question whether Tolman's use of operationally defined hypothetical constructs was good science, or whether they allow us to get at the crucial subject matter of psychology, the psyche. We may not, however, question the fact that Tolman struggled valiantly with the task of showing us a science of the mind, one that was respectably scientific and yet loyal to the knottiest questions so conveniently banned by Watson.

Tolman's (1926) own description of what he was doing in these papers cannot be represented better than by him:

I, as nought but a scientist, neither can, nor hope, nor, indeed, would want to attempt anything like a fundamental philosophical doctrine. For it is obvious that questions such as that of the final epistemological and metaphysical significance of ideas must be left to thinkers with wider foundations and a wider interest. (p. 48)

And

If we behaviorists can not present good theories, we can at least present as many bad ones as possible in order that by their successive refutation we may be forced finally either into discovering the correct theory, or, if there be none, into abandoning our behavioristic adventure altogether. (Tolman, 1927, p. 63)

Unlike his behavioristic predecessors, Tolman also sought to distinguish behavior from mere muscular movement or locomotion. Such an impulse toward that distinction rests originally, perhaps, on the recognition that an animal moving in a maze is fundamentally different from a twig floating down a stream. The rat is going somewhere; it has a direction, a purpose, a capability of being frustrated and, when frustrated, behaving differently. The twig does not. Behavior, then, is inherently purposive. But regardless of how this distinction originated for Tolman, he was clear, when accused of anthropomorphism, that experimental data not only defined and justified such a notion as purposefulness. The data also demanded it. Behavior, therefore, "irrespective of whatever muscular or glandular activities underlying" it, has a "new and unique set of properties all its own" (Tolman, 1926, p. 49). Put another way, Tolman's concept of behavior makes psychology into a science not reducible to physiology. On the other hand, he said, "We will undoubtedly have to reduce and explain our more immediate categories of goal seeking and object adjustment in terms of physiological categories" (Tolman, 1925a, p. 47). However, he added a decade later, "A psychology cannot be explained by a physiology until one has a psychology to explain" (Tolman, 1936, p. 118).

That is, psychology necessarily describes behavior, and behavior differs from mere movement in nature because it is purposive. Indeed, it is important to realize that the only way to avoid the reduction of psychology to physiology is to see behavior as having an organization and a character of its own. Behavior, like muscle twitches, may be no less lawful, but psychological laws are different laws from those governing floating twigs or muscle contractions.

Finally, we must note the difficulties Tolman encountered in these early papers in his struggle to show us a science of the mind. We may want to understand his struggle in metaphysical terms, like "mind" and "body," for his constructs name mental events, although their operational definitions are behavioral, bodily events. Tolman surely wants to avoid a mind–body dualism or any metaphysics, but it is indeed difficult to do so in any Western psychology, and so we may ask just how Tolman does see the relation between the mental events his constructs name (X) and the bodily events that make the constructs behavioristically respectable (Y). Within a single article (Tolman, 1927), we see that relation between X and Y as Y *is a sign of* X (p. 65), Y *produces* X (p. 66), Y *is* X (p. 66), Y *involves* X (p. 67), and Y *presents* X (p. 67). To find the right operative verb connecting mind to body is a constant problem for Tolman, and no wonder, given the historic puzzlement with the question. One thing we may say for certain is that behavior itself, according to Tolman's unique and important concept of it, is both mental and bodily and allows us to sense a possible breakthrough, if not for metaphysics, at least for psychology. Many of Tolman's contemporaries did not appreciate the importance of this theoretical achievement; nor, for that matter, did many philosophers.

The Gestalt Papers

Moving from what we have called Tolman's metapsychological work to his psychology proper, we must look at his particular hypothetical constructs and see how, in the 1930s, his earlier work pays off for psychology. Tolman wants to say that behavior must be understood in terms of mentation—even for the rat. He invites us to consider the sequence from left to right in Table 10.2.

Each column to the right contextualizes the column to its immediate left. Just as Gestalt psychologists demonstrated that the Gestalt (whole) determines the sensation (part), so does the network of signs, significates, and means–ends relations (larger whole) determine the perceptual Gestalt (part). A rat will not only focus on elements according to the perceptual laws of Gestalt, it will focus on Gestalten according to the means–ends relations in the environment where it is behaving. It therefore has "propositions" about the environment that guide its behavior just as surely as it has Gestalt percepts that guide its sensitivity to environmental sensations.

This move by Tolman not only contextualized perceptual Gestalt phenomena, but it did so in terms of behavior. Not only does behavior

Table 10.2
Units of Analysis by Theoretical School

Brand of Psychology	Author	Unit of Analysis
Sensationism	Titchener	The single sensation, without context
Perceptualism	Koehler et al.	Figure on, within ground, organized and segregated
Propositionalsim	Tolman	Gestalt caught up in yet a larger whole of behavioral means–ends relations

become inherently mental for Tolman, but mentation becomes inherently behavioral. Furthermore, Tolman attempts to develop a language in terms of which to describe the propositions a rat will have. It will have "expectations" of three distinct types: about what can be discriminated perceptually, what can be manipulated behaviorally, and what will happen if it does manipulate such and so.

The first expectations are about environmental "discriminanda," the second about "manipulanda," and the third about "means–ends relations" (Tolman, 1933). Unaesthetic as this language is, Tolman is attempting to develop hypothetical constructs that will enable us to understand behavior by understanding the mentation embedded in it. If a rat cannot tell the difference between two shades of gray, then these are not discriminanda for it, if it cannot manipulate an object, then it is not a manipulandum for it; if its manipulation is unimportant in terms of its results, then there are no mean–ends relations here for it.

However, the rat's world, from the rat's point of view, is populated by discriminanda it will seek, manipulanda it will manipulate, and means–ends relations whose "sign" it understands. These last relations not only guide the rat's behavior, but they condition what manipulanda and discriminanda matter, depending on the rat's purposes. Note also that each of these terms is, at least in theory, operationally definable.

The Metapsychology of the 1930s

Following the philosophers of logical positivism, Tolman further clarifies in the mid-1930s his notion of behaviorism. Most famous is his distinction between "molar" and "molecular" psychologies, the former studying behavior as he understands it and the latter studying the physiological mechanisms underlying it. These terms have come to mean, in American psychology, larger and smaller units of analysis, although Tolman's original meaning intended to differentiate levels of description and explanation as represented by the two sciences.[3]

More intriguing is Tolman's explicit attempt to deal with the dualism inherent in Western thought since Descartes. The traditional distinction that secretly lies beneath our thought distinguishes external events in the real world ("objective") from experiential events in consciousness ("subjective"). Watson (1930) merely bans the latter and therefore leaves himself, as Koehler (1929/1947) pointed out, unable to explain the experiential basis of his own, or any, science. Tolman follows Koehler in pointing out that immediate experience cannot be said to be merely subjective, for it is also objective; it is pointed at the objective world and it is the origin of our concept of the objective world.

Therefore, Tolman (1935) believes that the crucial distinction is not, as Watson and the entire Western tradition would have it, "between physical entities, and mental entities, but between both of these as mere logical constructs, on the one hand, and immediate experience . . . on the other" (p. 97). "Science," of course, deals with logical entities, not with immediate experience, with the abstracted "rules" that govern the order seen in our experience, rules that can be determined only by observing overt behavior, not by introspecting.

We see here not only a reaffirmation of behavioristic epistemology, now refined by the philosophies of Bridgeman, Carnap, Feigl, Russell, and others, but a further development of Tolman's crucial concept of behavior. Behavior is not merely objective; to the behaver it is also obviously subjective. What is crucial, however, is that it shows us, as scientists, an order, the order of mentation not otherwise visible. As rich and interesting, and Tolman never denies "real" (1935, p. 100), as immediate experience is, mental life itself is not directly studiable by science. Its order, however, is what science studies; its rules are discovered by physics and psychology alike, and their formulation is what enables us to find our way about.[4]

Vicarious trial and error, latent learning, cognitive hypotheses by rats—these are some Tolmanian concepts formulated and supported by experimental data accumulated rapidly in the 1930s. In 1938, Tolman's presidential address to the APA comes as close to a systematic statement of his theory as we have since his 1932 book, *Purposive Behavior in Animals and Men*. The sheer number of hypothetical constructs that Tolman feels obliged to include in his psychology has become immense, and his APA address is a tour de force in organizing them, and the data that support them, into a system.

One solution to the increasing problem of organization is his article entitled, "Prediction of Vicarious Trial and Error by Means of the Schematic Sowbug" (Tolman, 1939), which portrays a hypothetical organism, the schematic sowbug, whose innards are made up of graphs depicting the many variables in behavior. In reading this article, you can almost imagine such a machine as this hypothetical character. And then you look at a rat, and you see one, already assembled and running, just as the schematic description promised! Both this article and the APA address must be read to be appreciated.

The Metapsychology of the War Years

Tolman wrote a book and several articles on war during the early 1940s. This was, no doubt, considered by some to be very strange behavior for an experimental psychologist whose work had been exclusively with rats and whose major concern was to develop the science of psychology. But, indeed, Tolman's major concern, his professional concern, was not really separable from the most pressing questions of human affairs.

In that regard, he wanted not merely to enter the rhetoric of political banter, he wanted also to bring to bear whatever wisdom the science of psychology might have to offer. It never occurred to Tolman that his psychology was separable from humankind's struggles with itself. For him, psychology was an integral part of that struggle. This has not traditionally been, and still is usually not, the case for American psychologists.

In addition, Tolman's thought during this period included two more large chunks of data and theory: psychoanalysis and cultural anthropology. These fields were much too large for most psychologists of the day to assimilate, and indeed too large for Tolman to build into his 1937 "system," and yet they could not be ignored given his uncanny openness to perspectives and data from whatever quarter. So he started over, or at least nearly so, building new theories of how biological drives are converted in human personality into loyalty, neurosis, and war.

This theoretical work (Tolman, 1941) was unrelated to his experimental studies and indeed looks more metapsychological than psychological. It was not, however, unrelated to the reasons behind his experimental work, the purpose of having a psychology at all. Ultimately the task is for human beings to understand themselves. In that underlying region of concern his psychoanalytic and cultural anthropological extrapolations share a common ground with his entire career.

The Psychology of the Late 1940s

Tolman returned after the war, of course, to academic psychology, produced several important summary articles (Tolman, 1945, 1948), and began some new work in social learning and motivation. But he never produced another comprehensive systematic statement as he had in 1932 and 1937.

THE TOLMANIAN LEGACY

Since American psychology eventually caught up with Tolman in its so-called cognitive revolution in the third quarter of the twentieth century, we may say that Tolman's work in the second quarter was decisive. Perhaps it is too much to say that his concept of behavior saved behaviorism from the sterility of Watson's dogmatism, for Tolman did not do it singlehandedly, and it is far from clear that Skinner, for example, whose behaviorism remains untouched by Tolman's work, is sterile. Furthermore, Tolman never occupied a position of cultural or national importance. He was an academic and a scientist, dedicated to psychology, and even most psychologists trained after 1960 have little idea of the quality or quantity of his contribution.

Insofar as Tolman's spirit lives on, we see it not only in the cognitive revolution, but also wherever we see magnanimous openmindedness, undying curiosity, and tremendous energy. These are not, of course, exclusive legacies of Tolman, but to the extent that the discipline has these characteristics, they were developed by concrete psychologists whose dedication set a model for others, and who in turn do so for yet others. Tolman must be counted, perhaps with William James, as one of the heroes of our disciplinary history.

NOTES

1. Unless otherwise noted, page numbers in this chapter refer to the collection of Tolman's papers (1966). Dates refer to the dates of original publication, which are also listed in the bibliography.

2. According to his son, James B. Watson, John Watson shared none of Tolman's philosophical interest or knowledge, but was rather more simply a positivist who was impatient with nonscientific matters (Hannush, 1987). Dualism was, for Watson, a weak and indefensible idea, even if his reason was mixed with a distrust of nonscientific philosophy.

3. The change made by psychologists in the sense of Tolman's terms, "molecular" and "molar," was to change Tolman's intentional meaning from a distinction between levels (physiological versus behavioral) to a mere matter of size (relatively small versus relatively large). We might explain this by the hope psychologists had in the middle decades of the century that psychology and physiology would eventually reduce to a single science. This hope is a denial that psychology is in principle different from sciences like physics, or that behavior is different from a floating twig, or that metaphysical dualism deals with any scientifically real problem. Tolman does not, of course, argue for dualism in a philosophical sense, but his distinction between behavior and physiology is intended to call attention to a difference, to combat the reduction of the behavioral to the physiological, and to combat the reduction of psychology to physics. It also therefore attempts to preserve a psychological level of analysis, which may indeed describe behavior instead of the psyche, but which is not physiology. The language in which we can understand behavior (say, its purpose) simply does not reduce to a physiological language that imitates physics.

4. We see here a way to envision the common scientific ground between psychology and physics that does not reduce the former to the latter. The "rules" of behavior are different from the "rules" of physics: Physical laws deal with things and psychological laws deal with behavior. What is in common is that

they both are abstracted by us as scientists; what is different is (1) the set of data they are abstracted from, and (2) the language in terms of which such rules must be stated. Behavioral data demand hypotheses that are unnecessary about the physical world. And animals may meaningfully and scientifically be said to be pursuing a purpose; a falling body may not. This is as close as Tolman comes to being explicitly a dualist, even though his theory is populated by mental language. He does not move to metaphysics because it is unnecessary in order to write his psychology. All that is necessary is to note scientifically observable difference between floating twigs and purposive behavior. If one wants to do metaphyhsics, one would have to affirm some sort of "reality" to mental (as opposed to physical) life, but that move goes beyond science based on Newtonian physics. The question we might ask, at this point, is whether this "going beyond" really is "beyond"—or is it rather embedded in the data of psychology? Tolman, again quite purposively, does not take the philosophical step. James, we recall, did so.

11

Clark Hull, Carl Rogers, and the 1960s

THE LIFE OF CLARK HULL (1884–1952)

Wolman (1960) says of Hull, "Few psychologists have had such a mastery of mathematics and formal logic as Hull had. Hull applied the language of mathematics to psycholgical theory in a manner used by no other psychologist" (p. 105). Beginning life with poor health and impoverished circumstances, Clark Hull finally received a Ph.D. in mining engineering from the University of Wisconsin at the age of thirty-four. His switch to psychology emerged as an outcome of working with statistical problems in psychological data. He took up a study, *Hypnosis and Suggestibility* (Hull, 1933), as a worthy challenge to his sense that scientific clarification can elucidate intractable problems, and in 1940 turned to learning. In 1943, he produced *Principles of Behavior*, followed nine years later by *A Behavior System* (Hull, 1952).[1]

Hull's psychology, worked out mostly at Yale, was a standard against which to measure research in learning for the middle decades of the twentieth century. He was ingenious at creating hypothetical constructs that could logically and mathematically connect input variables (like motivation, stimulus intensity, and prior training) on the one hand, with output variables (like extinction, memory, and multiple learnings) on the other. His logic was always impeccable, his psychology was always testable, and his influence was inestimable among psychologists dedicated to a behavioristic definition of knowledge and a psychological theory that says that behavior is acquired through learning.

Hull's insistence that anthropomorphic thinking is inherently un-scientific often laid the ground for vivid competition with learning theorists like Tolman, and with certain Gestalt psychologists.[2] His con-cepts included drives (seen as biological needs), reinforcements (seen as drive reductions), generalizations of stimuli, and responses from prior learning, all integrated into complex formulae of various rela-tions among such variables. His insistence on formal theory, with each concept quantitatively defined, yielded more precision than it did ap-plicability to most questions of wide psychological interest, and so his following was strongest among those who felt that criteria of rigor must supercede immediate applicability to practical problems. That group included most academic and experimental psychologists.

Therefore, Hull's emphasis on formal, logically sound theory deal-ing with carefully collected experimental data defined a crucial natural-scientific theme close to the center of American academic psychology at mid-century. Later, we will look at the psychology of Carl Rogers, who understood and respected this tradition, but whose motives and style led him down a very different path. Each saw psychology as a pivotal field, but the pivots on which each turned defined vividly dif-ferent sciences. Rogers, the humanist, could not spend a career on the development of science for science's sake. The betterment of human-kind, and our ability to live full and rich lives, was central to Rogers. Hull certainly understood the seduction of such matters, but for Hull they promised no rewards without a truly scientific psychology, one that would seek and find verification in the laboratory. This was a very different place, in a very different context, than Rogers's face-to-face encounter with counseling clients, whose concrete life crises led Rogers's life course, and his thought, onto very different paths.

Complementing our estimate of what Hull must have thought of Rogers, we may guess that Rogers understood the meaning of a scien-tific laboratory, but he felt no attraction to an experimental focus such as Hull's. Rogers's "laboratory" was the clinic, where he believed he was facing the important problems of clients and was struggling to-ward answers more important than those of Hull's laboratory. This paradigmatic split defined American psychology in the middle de-cades of the twentieth century.

THE LIFE OF CARL ROGERS (1902–1980)

Born on a farm in Elgin, Illinois, the fourth of seven children whose parents were dedicated Calvinists, Carl Rogers was such a good stu-dent in high school that he immediately continued his education at the University of Wisconsin in 1920. He was fortunate enough to visit China, with a religious group, at the age of twenty, an experience likely to jolt anyone out of his or her usual assumptions about human life. After graduation he went to New York, where he attended the Union Theological Seminary from 1924 to 1928, and from there transferred to Columbia where he met Thorndike and began work in one of the very first child guidance clinics. This experience led him to the child study department of the Society for the Prevention of Cruelty to Children, in Rochester, New York. There he produced his first book, *The Clinical Treatment of the Problem Child* (Rogers, 1939).

Clinical psychology was becoming legitimate in spite of hostility from behaviorist psychologists and especially from psychiatrists, so his four years at Ohio State, from 1940 to 1944 were productive, including his *Counseling and Psychotherapy* (Rogers, 1942). In 1956, at the age of fifty-three, he was given one of the first three awards by the American Psychological Association for his contribution to psychological science (the other two went to Kenneth Spence, a close colleague of Hull's, and to Wolfgang Koehler, the Gestalt psychologist). During his career, Rogers was elected president of the American Association of Applied Psychology, and later also to the more inclusive American Psychological Association. He died in 1980.

THE 1960s

Much happened during the 1960s that shaped the face of psychology. Primary among the massive cultural events was the Vietnam War, and accompanying that, the student protests and the counterculture, based in American universities. The cultural competition between Cold War American patriotism and antiwar American humanism has become part of our cultural history. In psychology, a different competition was continuing, between a physicalist and a mentalist approach to psychology.

In terms of historical stereotypes like "hard-nosed" versus "soft-nosed" psychologists, or "humanists" versus "scientists," it is easy to confuse the polarity in psychology with the polarity in politics, especially since university settings all housed both sides of both polarities. If some of the energy of the cultural conflict about the war seemed to appear in the theoretical-psychology conflict, we must be clear that the polarity in psychology between a model based on physical science and a model based on human concern was very different from being for or against the war.

If being mentalistic in psychological vision seemed to some to go along with being antiwar, the connection was and is far from clear. In the case of Carl Rogers, of course, his early experience in China contributed to a vision of the intriguing diversity of humanity, a view somewhat broader and certainly more salient to Rogers than to most

Americans. But the example of Rogers, or that of Hull, whose psychology was very different, must not be generalized to all humanists and all scientists. It is even more irresponsible to associate physicalistic concepts in psychology with war-mongering.

Confusion at this point is, however, quite easy. "Conservative" is a word applicable in various contexts as different as scientific caution and American patriotic pride. Insofar as "conservatism" describes a general character trait, there may be, or may have been, some common dislike or fear of change that characterized both psychological science and the international politics of the Cold War. This rather interesting issue can hardly be made simple. In the 1960s, however, the rush of political events surrounding the war so polarized national consciousness that simplifications were inevitable. The equation, in some popular thought at the time, of traditional interests in science with traditional American patriotism came from a few salient examples whose public visibility easily slipped into stereotypes.

Of course, both "scientific" and "clinical" clusters of psychologists contained many whose attitudes remained unexpressed. But the intensity of feeling about the overriding commitments on both sides of the political controversy made "conservative" and "liberal" or "radical" into badges of honor and damning insults. The clothes one wore, the music one liked, the mind-altering chemicals one consumed (booze versus pot, for example) all became politicized. It was a confusing time, and the confusion easily leads to misunderstanding, even of the history of psychology.

We see here a vivid interaction between psychology and the culture. In terms of views of psychology as held by psychologists, we must recall that the tradition of the separation of facts from values was an important part of establishing psychology as a science. Taken more broadly as a general worldview, those who believed that values are inevitable in psycholgy, or even in all science, may have found American foreign policy to be particularly offensive during the Vietnam War. Military technology is not like other technology. The values it serves are more likely to be controversial. The American government, especially its military sector, was ill equipped to deal with such political issues.

That war was, in fact, initially marketed to the public by the government as a routine anti-Communist necessity, as if, like surgery, the apparent violence is necessary to save the patient. As opposition to the war increased, prowar reactions to antiwar protests seemed to insist that the war was as necessary as removing a malignant tumor, and that the protesters were as malignant as the famous Stalinist atrocities of communism. In contrast, protesters of the war thought the same of advocates. In their less defensive moments, the antiwar protesters made the killing of persons the central issue.

As the war widened, more and more soldiers were needed, the draft was reinstated, resistance to the draft developed, and everyone in the nation found themselves facing a political situation as complex as the knotty problem of the competing values of "the sanctity of human life" and "American patriotism." Families became divided; parents whose discipline of their children had exacerbated rebellion faced not simply rebellious children but throngs of "hippies" and pot smokers who threatened to transform their children into "rebellious infidels." Even parents who were manifestly successful at rearing their children saw these same children turn against them, for reasons they could not understand.

The 1960s were turbulent and exciting, but our retrospective understanding of them should not lead us into stereotypes that falsify the history of psychology. Conservative psychologists were scientific, and humanistic psychologists were radical, but the issues in psychology and the issues of the war should not be confounded. The tendency to divide the world into hard-nosed and soft-nosed, whether one is talking about psychology or politics, must be actively resisted in order not to falsify the picture. The fact is that psychology and politics offered different controversies.

THE SPLIT IN PSYCHOLOGY

It is, however, telling to compare the psychologies of Clark Hull and Carl Rogers, since they come from different traditions in psychology. They do typify a split between mentalistic and physicalistic psychologies that has roots as deep as Wundt versus Brentano and Watson versus McDougall.[3]

I hope to explore the idea that the unspoken and unacknowledged philosophical problem of dualism left over from the previous centuries of modern philosophy has a representation in psychology, the great invention of the twentieth century. For physicalists like Hull and Spence (1956, 1960), the substrate of physical reality is essential to understanding human behavior, and for mentalists, like Freud and Rogers, physical language (of Freud's libidinal energy, for example) was totally metaphorical.[4] The underlying metaphysical difference is obscured almost completely by the very real difference in the psychologies. Freud and Rogers did take human experience as both the data and the end point of their work. Spence and Hull did take the physical realities of movement and other physical behavior as the data and end point of their work.

None of the psychologists was doing metaphysics, but all wrote with metaphysical echoes. Such echoes are rarely clear; we often prefer one approach to another without explicitly articulating reasons why, and we rarely ask whether these preferences can be stated metaphysically. They seem to be implicit beliefs about what makes up the "real reality" of psychological life, which in these cases meant either experiential life or behavioral life.

ATTEMPTS TO BRIDGE THE GAP

Certainly there were attempts to bridge the gap, especially at interdisciplinary centers such as Harvard's Department of Social Relations and Yale's Instititute of Human Relations. At Yale, where Hull taught, his influence was obviously strong. Mowrer's (1940) study of anxiety reduction as a reinforcer, and Neil Miller's (1948) effort to establish fear as an acquireable drive, sought to build a bridge between clinical and experimental psychology by offering animal data and theory analogues from experimental psychology to explain clinical and particularly Freudian (the by-then traditional clinical theory) concerns for the role of anxiety in neurosis. Dollard and Miller (1950) restated their earlier (Miller and Dollard, 1941) efforts in these terms as well.[5]

Whiting and Child (1953), from cultural anthropology (and also at Yale's Institute of Human Relations), also tried to explain Freudian concepts in cross-cultural work in terms of behavioral psychology. Hilgard's (1987) comment about these efforts was, "While there was much interest in these writings, the impression was very strong among psychologists that the basic insights had come from psychoanalysis, and the translations provided chiefly some quantitative evidence without greatly advancing knowledge of personality dynamics" (p. 371). Hilgard's report seems to echo the sentiments of clinicians, not all of whom were Freudians; it seems not to express views of psychologists of learning, who often found Freud obscure. It is also important that the psychologists of learning, by the years of World War II, had established sufficient continuity of research and theoretical coherence—a tradition, in a word—that they paid less attention to other specialized bodies of clinical data, anthropological data, or sociological data.

Beyond that, it is noteworthy that interdisciplinary efforts like those at Yale and Harvard, and also those in the Social Psychology Program at the University of Michigan, lasted only a couple of decades. The exception is the Society for the Psychological Study of Social Issues (SPSSI), begun at the University of Michigan by Theodore Newcomb in 1939. Newcomb clearly wanted the rapidly developing psychology to be put into the service of social problems. That interdisciplinary effort does not ask its participants to be interdisciplinary in their research or to abandon their disciplinary tradition. SPSSI has become populated mostly by psychologists, but members of all disciplines can share commitments to study and action on social issues without compromising their identities in one discipline or another. It remains an active and lively organization.

Within psychology, however, the split between experimentalists and clinicians seems to have settled into a mutual indifference, often without the intellectual excitement of interdiscipinary efforts and rarely creating hostilities among psychologists sometimes typical in other disciplines.

And yet psychologists may have deeper conflicts than those in other disciplines insofar as mind and body are a metaphysical latent content of the split between clinicians and experimentalists. Mind and body (1) name unspoken differences in what is taken as the basic reality of the field, (2) dictate the locus of research, (3) define the procedures for getting data, and (4) determine the company psychologists keep. Scientists and clinicians are sometimes the same people, but it is commonplace that the two groups differ on all these dimensions.

CLARK HULL: EXPERIMENTAL SCIENTIST

In the case of Hull, who is a good representative of mid-century behavioristic experimentalism, we see quite vividly his determinism and his sense that mechanics supplies the model for psychology. A very early (1926) comment in his personal journal states the decades-long theme: "It has struck me many times of late that the human organism is one of the most extraordinary machines—and yet a machine. And it has struck me more than once that so far as the thinking process goes, a machine could be built which would do everything that the body does, except growth" (Amsel and Rashotte, 1984, p. 3). At a later time, Hull mused,

In fact the whole thing could probably be reduced to a mathematical formula and it is not inconceivable that an automaton might be constructed on the analogy of the nervous system which could learn and through experience acquire a considerable degree of intelligence by first coming into contact with an environment. (p. 3)

Two features of these private thoughts of Hull are significant. First, his prediction of a thinking machine has been fully realized, although modern computers do nothing without a human to tell them what to do. (This bespeaks a telling limit to Hull's analogy, although hardly a contradiction to it.) Second, he never doubted then, nor would he doubt now, that this result verifies that it is the body (as opposed to something else, like the mind) that does the thinking.

Indeed, Hull's twenty-one years of research effort and writing re-volved around an elaborate formula, revised in hundreds of detailed ways on the basis of experimental research, that would predict learn-ing in an experiment in some probabilistic way, given specific indices of stimulus properties, conditions of presentation, prior learning, ac-quired or innate inhibitions along with motivational variables, and so on.[6] Hull never believed he had covered all the relevant variables, but he believed that such a formula could be specified by laboratory data and was applicable to all species, including human beings. And he believed that was true because behavior, as a natural phenomenon, was no less a part of nature, and of nature's mechanics, than what is studied in physics or chemistry.

CARL ROGERS: HUMANISTIC THERAPIST

Hull's supreme dedication to a science of behavior was matched at mid-century by Rogers's central dedication to therapy. Like Hull's *Principles of Behavior* (1943) was followed by his more mature *A Behavior System* (1952), we have a similar early statement from Rogers, *Counseling and Psychotherapy* (1942) followed by the more mature *Client-Centered Therapy* (1951). Hull died in 1952, while Rogers remained active for a quarter-century more (recall that Hull got his Ph.D. in psy-chology when he was thirty-four—in mining engineering). And yet these four books offer the historian an astonishing parallel in the two very different psychologies at the middle of the twentieth century.

Unlike Hull's 1952 book, Rogers's 1951 book begins with no postu-lates or logical outlines. In fact, Rogers goes to an opposite extreme:

I would willingly throw away all the words of this manuscript if I could, some-how, *point* to the experience which is therapy. It is a process, a thing-in-itself, an experience, a relationship, a dynamic. It is not what this book says about it, any more than a flower is the botanist's description of it or the poet's ecstacy over it. (p. ix)

We can see here already a beginning of the 1960s, a contempt for the "already staggering pile of words about words," not to mention "that final degradation of becoming classroom knowledge" (p. ix).

However, the book (Rogers, 1951) does, finally and ironically, con-clude with exactly nineteen propositions (explained in about forty pages), half of which propositions speak of "the organism," the other half about "the individual." Science, as a record of knowledge about very concrete experiences but stated in very abstract ways, appears as fully in Rogers's psychology as it does in Hull's—without, of course, the controlled collection of experimental data. We see in Rogers, but not in Hull, anticipations of later developments in psychology, such as the existential and phenomenological celebrations that nonetheless, at some point, take on the sober seriousness of science.

Another striking similarity between Hull and Rogers is the peculiar mix of specificity and generality in each of them. Hull's attention to experimental detail and to the systematic verification at each level of generality did not, curiously, envision greatly different principles of learning across species. Of course, there are differences in the neuro-logical equipment of various species, and thus many findings may accordingly be more or less species specific. But the theory of learn-ing—postulates, corollaries, and theorems—becomes differentiated by species only in detail. Hull wrote at a level more general than his data.

Rogers similarly invents a therapeutic strategy that is generally ap-plicable across all diagnostic categories, from paranoid schizophrenia to simple phobia. What all human beings have in common is more important to Rogers than those divisions we make between diagnosed diseases, when it comes to doing therapy. This is similar to the view of Hull that what all organisms have in common is more important than what differentiates species, when it comes to the science of learning. Thus, Rogers also wrote at a level more general than the standard clini-cal data of the day, which was quite diagnosis bound.

Rogers attends to the particular person in front of him, but he wrote about everyone, just as Hull attended to the particular species, but spoke about all learned behavior. In both cases it is the general ap-proach, their particular psychology's general theoretical content, that makes the theory count at the specific level. For Hull, learning must be motivated in order to be reinforced, and "tension reduction" ap-plies for all. For Rogers, the "problem" reveals itself as not simply imposed by others, but also is accepted as "something wrong with me." The content of one person's experienced problem clearly is uniquely tied to the particulars of his or her life, but like for Hull, the generality is crucial. To believe that there is something wrong with oneself is to experience harsh self-judgment when there are among all human beings always other ways to construe one's experience.

CONCLUSION

The experimental–clinical split within psychology at mid-century goes much further than these two theorists. Indeed they are not the most extreme forms. Both Hull and Rogers were also conscious of the personal role each played within the larger context of American psy-chology. Each of them also understood something of what the other kind of psychology was up to, and harbored respect for the other as a part of psychology. Neither of them paid much attention to what the difference between them meant, nor to the historical importance of this difference. Neither would necessarily agree with the interpretation of this book that a seventeenth-century Cartesian (or fourth-century Platonic) problem informs our intellectual efforts centuries later.

Psychology was not, for either of them, a strange embodiment of something mental, like a philosophical problem or a human mystery. Nor did psychology seem to either of them to manifest a gross incongruity within human knowing, which metaphysical dualism represents in philosophical terms. Rather, each seems merely to have been fascinated by different problems. They both were satisfied to follow through on only one of the two points of the traditional intellectual anchor that keeps humanity in place amidst the sea of time.

NOTES

1. It is easy to see Hull as merely a behaviorist who liked logic. In fact, his psychology—fairly unappealing in contemporary eyes—had an enormously interesting larger strategy. Ammons (1962) notes, after a careful study of Hull's notebooks, that "In 1930, Hull's Idea Books refer to the great philosophers— Hume, Locke, Kant, Hobbes—who had attempted to construct a theory of knowledge, thought, and reason on the basis of conscious experience but who, in Hull's eyes, had failed" (p. 812). Ammons goes on to explain Hull's plan: "He planned to attack the same problem using the opposite strategy. He wrote, "I shall invert the whole historical system. I shall start with action—habit— and proceed to deduce all the rest, including conscious experience, from action, i. e., habit" (p. 812). It is perhaps for this kind of ambition that, in terms of influence and importance, Hull is ranked sixth after only Freud, James, Wundt, Watson, and Pavlov (see also Amsel and Rashotte, 1984, p. 506).

2. In a letter to Spence (Ansel and Rashotte, 1984), Hull recalls a conversation with the Gestalt psychologist, Kurt Koffka, in which he agreed with Koffka's condemnation of Watson, but regretted not that Koffka disagreed with Watson but rather that Watson "had not made out as clear a case for behaviorism as the facts warranted" (p. 21).

3. McDougall came to Harvard in 1920, saw himself as a successor to William James, and explicitly rejected the mechanistic and atomistic ("mosaic") psychology of Ward and others, replacing it with a psychology of purpose, which he called "hormic" (derived from the Greek word for "impulse"). His most popular book, *An Introduction to Social Psychology* (McDougall, 1908) outlined a number of "instincts," which he understood as experiences of impulses, which contrasted vividly with the more positivistic psychology of Watson, who eschewed all such formulations. Hilgard (1987) notes, "The differences between McDougall and Watson . . . represented a deep cleavage within psychology in the early 20th Century on several issues, such as the roles of heredity and environment, blind mechanism versus purposive striving, and the relative emphasis to be placed on objective behavior and subjective experience. . . . There was once a famous debate [Watson and McDougall,

1929] between them on these issues" (pp. 326–327). Thus, we see that a Hull–Rogers contrast bears similarities to earlier versions, such as Watson–McDougall. Insofar as McDougall is to Watson what Rogers was to Hull, we might see these are similar. We should note, however, that both Watson and McDougall encompassed both sides of dualism somewhat more than either Hull or Rogers. This fact suggests both the increasing effect of the dualistic split in psychology and an increasing unconsciousness of the historical and philosophical origins of the split itself.

4. Hull did not think Freud was wrong; indeed, in one of his memoranda to his sudents, Hull notes, "It is greatly to be regretted that no sympathetic student of Freud with a taste for systematization has yet exhibited the structure of his theory in formal detail" (Amsel and Rashotte, 1984, p. 17). It is possible that Freud's penchant for bodily metaphors, like instinct, inspired this thought. Or perhaps it may have reflected Hull's interest in logic, and thus possibly even a desire to stay in touch with mental life, to bridge the gap.

5. Dollard and Miller's *Personality and Psychotherapy* (1950) was dedicated "to Freud and Pavlov and their students," as if to state the hope that psychoanalysis and behaviorism, in the persons of "their students" would celebrate a common task, if not find a common ground.

6. To call Hull's theory a "formula" is to misname Hull's efforts, although Hull himself would not have minded the name. It is misnamed because the formula consisted of no less than seventeen postulates with fifteen corollaries for the general theory, and then dozens of theorems for each of the ten kinds or aspects of learning, each dealing with multiple cases. Thus, the postulates are the most general, specific cases the least, while correlaries and theorems lie between very general postualtes and very specific cases (of which there are hundreds, each reflecting an experiment or series of experiments). Hull would not have minded the name "formula" for his theory, for even though it was complex, that was its essence in Hull's mind.

12

The Psychology of Donald O. Hebb

THE LIFE OF DONALD O. HEBB (1904–1985)

Hebb was born in Nova Scotia, received his AB in 1925 at Dalhousie, and wrote his master's thesis in bed while suffering from a tubercular hip in the early 1930s. In 1934 he went to Yale, where he studied with Yerkes, then later with Lashley at Chicago, and at age thirty got his first Ph.D. in physiological psychology, then another one from Harvard in 1936. Hilgard (1987) tells us of Hebb's description of his second dissertation, which Hebb states, "proved what is false: that perception does not require experience" (p. 437). Reexamination of his data later corrected that error.

In 1937 Hebb became a fellow at the Neurological Institute in Montreal, working with Wilder Penfield; from there he moved to Queens University in Ontario and stayed from 1939 to 1942. Between 1942 and 1947 he accepted a position with Lashley at the Yerkes Laboratories of Primate Biology in Florida, where his experience doing brain surgery was less important than his discovery that chimpanzees display vivid panic at the sight of a stuffed chimp head without a body. Hilgard (1987) notes, "Because this reaction was found to increase with age, Hebb postulated that such a display of emotion resulted from learning, as a conflict in which the unexpected perceptual object interrupted the phase sequences appropriate to the normally acquired perception" (p. 438).

Integrating physiology and psychology, Hebb led us to understand that more brain activity and tissue are necessary to acquire information than to retain it. Hence, brain tissue loss in adulthood does not necessarily result in mental losses, certainly not like those of childhood. But it was the research of Lorente de No, a Spanish physiologist, whose concept of reverberating circuits in the brain led to Hebb's theory of the "cell assembly." Hebb returned to McGill as chair of psychology in 1947, and eventually became chancellor. His seminal volume, *Organization of Behavior* (Hebb, 1949), was turned down repeatedly for publication before it was finally accepted in a clinical psychology series, thanks to the intervention of Frank Beach. Hebb later became president of the American Psychological Association and a member of the U.S. National Academy of Science and the Royal Society of London.

A major thesis of this book is that every psychologist since James has had to deal with the question of the relation between the psyche, however defined or described, on the one hand, and the brain, on the other. Through the decades of the twentieth century, this issue was usually dealt with by defining a relationship between the disciplines of psychology and neurology or physiology. Such a recourse is exactly not dealing with the issue. It is burying one's head in the sand of disciplinary independence. And it escapes asking the hardest questions.

Hebb stands out as asking, not avoiding, the hardest questions, defining the relationship between psychology and physiology most vividly and clearly. His 1949 book, *Organization of Behavior*, not only articulated the often implicit position of many psychologists, but also persuaded others that the psyche, in the final analysis, simply is the brain, the psyche's functions are brain functions, and its limits and potentials are the limits and potentials of the human brain. This position was envisioned by Hebb to be opposed to the "weak-kneed discouragement of the vitalist" or the "animist." "There is no separate soul or life-force to stick a finger into the brain now and then and make the neural cells do what they would not otherwise" (p. xiii). But this rejected "mystic" view is only one, and a more cultural than scientific opponent that Hebb sees. Another opponent exists within science itself, "the antiphysiological position" of Skinner (1938), whose positivist view rules out all hypotheses concerning events invisible to the observer because they are internal to the organism.

While Hebb regards Skinner's view as logically defensible, he sees it as a premature rejection of an important source of psychological understanding, and, in fact, he argues that psychology itself assumes some vision of neural events inevitably, and that the "particular formula chosen mainly determines the nature of the psychological theory that results" (Hebb, 1947, p. xvii). Hebb is saying, in effect, the root of our psychological thinking is an (often implicit) theory of brain, and so we really ought, as good scientists, to make that assumption explicit and test it against known neurological facts. *Organization of Be-*

havior proceeds to do precisely that, and to propose as intelligent a neurological theory as possible to guide our thinking in psychology.

The two kinds of brain theories implicit or explicit in American psychology at this time were (1) a connectionist theory, which envisioned sensory cells connected to motor cells after the fashion of a telephone switchboard—"Current forms of the theory tend to be vaguer than formerly, because of effective criticism of the theory in its earlier and simpler forms, but the fundamental idea is still maintained" (Hebb, 1949, p. xvii)—and (2) a field theory, according to which the "sensory control of motor centers depends . . . on the distribution of the sensory excitation and on *ratios* of excitation, not on *locus* or the action of any specific *cells*" (p. xvii).

Hebb's own model combines features of both these theories and therefore suggests new syntheses on the psychological level between such divergent views as Hull versus Gestalt or Guthrie versus Tolman. It takes seriously the psychological (i.e., behavioral) data of Gestalt and Tolman, necessitating a concept of a central process named "set" or "expectation," in spite of the fact that such concepts violate connectionist theory.

On the other hand, Hebb's (1949) model remains "a form of connectionism, one of the switchboard variety, though it does not deal in direct connections between afferent and efferent pathways" (p. xix). The model states, "Any frequently repeated, particular stimulation will lead to the slow development of a 'cell-assembly,' a diffuse structure comprising cells in the cortex and diencephalon (and also, perhaps, in the basal ganglia of the cerebrum), capable of acting briefly as a closed system" (p. xix). Hebb continues this line of thought as follows: "A series of such events constitutes a 'phase sequence'—the thought process. Each assembly action may be aroused by a preceding assembly, by a sensory event, or—normally—by both. The central facilitation from one of these activities on the next is the prototype of 'attention'" (p. xix). Finally, Hebb concludes, "The theory proposes that in this central facilitation, and its varied relationship to sensory processes, lies the answer to an issue that is made inescapable by Humphrey's (1940) penetrating review of the problem of the direction of thought" (p. xix).

Therefore, we have from Hebb a theory that can make such notions as attention, expectation, and thought intelligible, for Hebb believes that such ideas in fact become really intelligible only when they are accounted for neurologically. Without such an accounting, these concepts run the risk of sounding like, or actually indulging in, prescientific mysticism, anthropomorphism, and animism. And according to Hebb's philosophy of science, these nonneurological understandings are fundamentally unintelligible. The only intelligibility, for Hebb (1949), comes from "reducing the vagaries of human thought to a mechanical process of cause and effect" (p. xi).

It is also clear that Hebb is continuing the trend toward a centralist psychology, a psychology that says that events central to the organism are crucial for events observable on the periphery. Like Hull and Tolman, he uses hypothetical constructs to describe these central events. And like them both, the particular constructs he uses, the language in terms of which he describes central processes, define an implied essence of the organism. However, unlike Hull's hypotheticodeductive constructs, or Tolman's mentalistic ones, Hebb's language is neurological. The nervous system thus appears as the essence of the organism.

Furthermore, the mechanistic and materialistic flavors of these concepts are hardly alien to American psychology. Hebb was probably correct that theorists' implicit model of the brain defined their psychology. Tolman stands out, perhaps, as an exception, and one can surely point to others, but the metaphysical materialism implied in Hebb's psychology remained forceful even in the closing decades of the twentieth century for American psychology.

Hebb (1949) believed that his theory not only offered psychology "a new base of operations" (p. 3), but synthesized the attempt of a number of psychologists to account for central processes with various hypothetical constructs, and gave them a scientific rationale. Embedded in this belief is Hebb's assumption that "one cannot logically be a determinist in physics and chemistry and biology, and a mystic in psychology" (p. xiii). Any nonmaterialistic or nondeterministic view is thus "mystic."

Hebb's neurological translation of the problem was seen by him as the only way out of the dilemma psychologists of the 1940s found themselves in. Specifically, "attention" and other centralist concepts necessarily implied animism, some nonmaterial agency, and thus mysticism and an antiscientific view. To resolve this dilemma, psychologists needed to shore up a materialistic explanation, especially after it became clear that to deny such concepts as attention was to deny obvious data. Hebb's formulation seemed, therefore, to account for the data and to preserve the traditional assumptions of science, its materialism and determinism. His definition of intelligibility therefore demanded an explanation in exactly these terms.

Hebb's theoretical constructions were impossible before the invention of electroencephalography (EEGs), which, importantly, indicated brain activity even in the absence of external stimulation. Brain cells are firing as long as one is alive; they do part of the time respond to stimuli, but the perpetual activity of the living brain suggests an entirely different organization from mere "connections."

Hebb's writing shows us a general scientific crisis and resolution that occurs at the level of the philosophy of science. He also makes clear a similar pattern of crisis and resolution that appears at the level of psychological theory. Connectionist theory is switchboard theory. Connections happen at specific locations, and they owe nothing to a central organizing event such as "a field" (from Gestalt and from the field theory of Kurt Lewin, 1935). These latter theories appealed to theorists like Tolman, or to anyone interested in behavioral purposes or intentions. These latter phenomena would require physiological events more central and widespread than connectionist theory permits. Most important, in moving beyond connectionist theory, we perhaps find the human experience of learning, an experience that not only follows an effort and a hope, but also yields a sense that it is I who has learned. Such experiential data at least make Gestalt and field theory attractive, and they may even be said to seriously challenge materialistic and causal theories more generally.

It is not necessary, however, to make such experiential data decisive, especially if one is dedicated, as Hebb was, to purely physical explanations in science. But Hebb did not settle for leaving such data unexplained. He invented new neural concepts (see "cell assembly" and "phase sequence" later) in order to have it both ways: to maintain a science (in the sense of a physical explanation) and to include the data of intention, expectation, and so on.

By very carefully reconsidering the experimental evidence and precisely what theoretical conclusions are warranted and not warranted from it, Hebb is able to reject the idea (of connectionist theory) that behavior is always the direct result of a stimulus without "autonomous central processes" intervening. At the same time, he can preserve the notion that learning occurs at a specific neural location. Field theorists like Koehler (1929/1947), and equipotentiality theorists like Lashley (1950; see also Lashley, Chow, and Semmes, 1951), insisted that learning changes the brain's field of excitation, rather than makes a specific connection.

Before Hebb, if one rejected the connectionist theory (what Koehler [1929/1947] called "machine theory"), one was simultaneously committing oneself to Gestalt field theory, which denied a specific neural locus to learning, and one was accommodating the intuition, for example, that "I" (a single mental reality) have learned. Conversely, before Hebb, the notion of a specific neural locus of connection also committed one to connectionist theory without any autonomous central processes, and no neural correlate to the famous "I" of our experience.

But the intuited "I" was not the only problem for connectionist theory. Connectionist theory may explain the stability of learning, but not generalization of that learning, or transposition.[1] Field theory explained generalization, transposition, and other Gestalt phenomena, but not the stability of learning. Hebb's theory explains both, and the three chapters in *Organization of Behavior* (Hebb, 1949) that sort through the evidence and theory are models of scientific writing, making distinctions necessitated by the data, even though they were never made before, and abolishing distinctions traditionally made but not necessitated by the data.

For example, Gestalt psychologists can demonstrate that primitive sensory unities, such as a white circle in a black field, occur as organized sensory events independent of learning. Other perceptual organization, however, is clearly learned, such as in learning to look at histological slides, or is clearly not determined by sensory factors alone, such as seeing the place in a homogeneous lawn where one intends to put a garden. Both of these are "nonsensory figures"; that is, figures that are not merely sensory but are learned and affected by the past, or are imagined and affected by a central process. Even more complex is the "identity" of what we see in perception, which is more like meaning, the associative network in which it is embedded. But, of course, even more than nonsensory figures, identity in perception is learned.

The point here is that only after making such distinctions can one examine the data and decide whether perceptual organization is inherent, as Gestalt psychologists claimed, or at least implied. Some of it is (primitive unities) and some of it is not (nonsensory figures and identity). Also, posing the issue this way allows Hebb to bring in the little-known data of perceptual learning in congenitally blind persons after vision is restored (Senden, 1932), data that were not generally known because their importance was not apparent before Hebb's formulation of the problem.

We see, therefore, in Hebb's psychology, concurrent and congruent movement at several levels. First, at the level of experimental data, Hebb scrutinizes well-known data with a dispassionate eye and introduces little known data, sifting and sorting so we can see just what we do and do not know for sure. But second, these siftings and sortings are guided by theoretical questions at the level of Gestalt versus connectionist theory. At this level these theories are changed by the data in such a way that previously irreconcilable theoretical differences reveal themselves as quite consistent with one another, if one makes the right theoretical distinctions.

Third, these theoretical controversies have implications at a deeper level of theory, such as associationism and empiricism versus configurationism and nativism, where the "nature of the mind" itself, all learned or having inherent properties of its own, Locke versus Kant, is at stake. And fourth, at the most general philosophical level of the theory of the real, metaphysics, Hebb is able to shore up the materialist–determinist view against the threat of nonmaterialist and nondeterminist views, the threat constituted by data indicating central events formerly attributed to the soul, by postulating a determinist–materialist central process: cell assemblies and phase sequences in the brain.

Hebb may not be equally sophisticated at each of these levels, but he certainly is aware of them and of the importance of his writing for each of them. His philosophical, or metaphysical, arguments are of course the weakest, but he clearly shares the popular view that these questions ought to be answered by science itself, which operates at a more specific level. His greatest relevance, however, is for general psychology, and the balance of *Organization of Behavior* (Hebb, 1949) traces out some of the implications of his theory of the brain for various fields in psychology. We shall treat his "system" first by describing the brain theory, and then move to describing some of these implications.

THE SYSTEM

How can we envision the functioning of the brain in order to account for "(1) perceptual generalization, (2) the permanence of learning, and (3) attention, determining tendency, or the like" (Hebb, 1949, p. 60)? If the essential pattern of brain action in learning is like the reflex arc, then a single sensory neuron becomes associated with a single motor neuron by some physical growth or chemical change. Were the brain like that, data of perceptual generalization and attention could not be explained. However, the data of the permanence of learning necessitates some structural change in the brain. The cell assembly is that structural unit that changes or develops, but it is not a one-cell-to-one-cell connection. Hebb's own diagram (Figure 12.1) schematizes how a cell assembly works (this diagram might represent the neurological correlate of seeing a circle, for example).

Hebb (1949) admits, of course, that this schematic picture must be an oversimplification, and that it is, as neurology, entirely speculative. But it is a neurological speculation that is consistent with the evidence of psychology, and has specific implications for psychology. These ideas would mean "(1) That there is a prolonged period of integration of the individual perception, apart from associating the perception with anything else; (2) that an association between two perceptions is likely to be possible only after each one has been independently organized, or integrated" (p. 77). These two are followed by "(3) that, even between two integrated perceptions, there may be a considerable variation in the ease with which associations can occur" (p. 77). Hebb's line of thought concludes, "Finally, (4) the apparent necessity of supposing that there would be a 'growth,' or fraction-

Figure 12.1
Cell Assembly Diagram

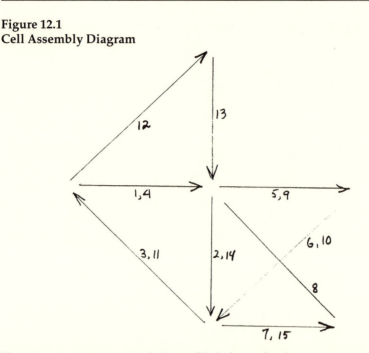

Note: Arrows represent a simple "assembly" of neural pathways or open multiple chains firing according to the number on each (the pathway "1, 4" fires first and fourth, and so on), illustrating the possibility of an "alternating" reverberation that would not extinguish as readily as that in a simple closed circuit. From D. O. Hebb, *Organization of Behavior: A Neuropsychological Theory* (New York: Wiley, 1949), p. 73.

ation and recruitment, in the cell assembly underlying perception means that there might be significant differences in the properties of perception at different stages of integration" (p. 77). These are provocative hypotheses indeed for a theory of perception.

What about motor involvement in perceptual learning? Just because the connectionists are wrong to say that motor firing is the only thing that is learned, that does not mean motor cells are not a part of learning—even of perceptual learning. Indeed, Hebb feels that the "integration" of perception, say, of a triangle, follows complexities of the cell assembly and that some of the firings of the cell assembly may be motoric, especially when one is learning to see complex forms and engages in eye movements. Furthermore, suppose a cell assembly is activated in perceiving a single circle "a" and "a" exists in a larger pattern that includes a triangle, such as in Figure 12.2.

The larger integration of the triangular shape occurs only after learning. Hebb further argues that the actual perception of a triangle "t" occurs within a sequence of fixations to create a cell assembly. Thus,

Figure 12.2
Parts and a Whole

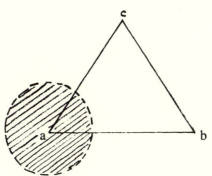

Source: Adapted from D. O. Hebb, *Organization of Behavior: A Neuropsychological Theory* (New York: Wiley, 1949), p. 85.

there is a sequence of fixations, each involving at least one cell assembly. In looking at a triangle, a sequence such as a-b-a-c-b-t-a-t-b-c-t tends to continue, at least until "t" itself becomes thoroughly integrated. This sequence serves to show that "t" emerges only amidst the integrating of separate cell assemblies, and that the whole is, according to Hebb, a matter of association after all. This sequence would also, however, include the motoric elements (not listed in our sequence a-b-a-c), say, eye movements, that become integrated into larger units of cell assemblies.

This larger integrated unit is called a "phase sequence" and is Hebb's (1949) neurological basis not only of superordinate perceptions, but of all complex central activity including thought in human beings: "Within the limits imposed by the needs of exposition, a conceptual system has been elaborated which relates the individual nerve cell to psychological phenomena. A bridge has been thrown across the great gap between the details of neurophysiology and the molar conceptions of psychology" (p. 101). Of course, this program has perils and promise: "The bridge is definitely shaky in the middle, but it is well buttressed at each end; and we have a psychological bridgehead which can be widened and which already includes some strategic points. In other words, the schema has some theoretical value already" (p. 101).

Specifically, Hebb (1949) notes the following advantage: "It shows, more or less explicitly, how it is possible: (1) to conceive of a conjoined action of the primitive figure-ground mechanism, eye movement, and learning (specifically defined synaptic changes), in the development of simple perceptions" (p. 101). But beyond this advantage, there are more.

It also serves "(2) to provide for an action of set, attention, or expectation also defined physiologically, in the perceptual process; [and] (3) to provide at the same time for *Gestalt* completion; similarity; generalization; and abstraction . . . closely related to association itself" (p. 101).

What, then, can Hebb say about learning? Hebb (1949) carefully reviews the data about learning curves (continuous learning) and sudden, insightful (discontinuous) learning and states some facts: "(1) more complex relationships can be learned by higher species at maturity; (2) simple relationships are learned about as promptly by lower as by higher species; (3) the first learning is *slower* in higher than lower species" (p. 116).

How can these facts be explained? Hebb (1949) points out that higher species have a high A–S ratio (amount of association cortex to sensory cortex), and therefore higher species have more ability to handle the potential complexity of phase sequences): "The learning ability of higher species at maturity is not merely the capacity for a greater number of associations or for associations that involve finer sensory discriminations. The behavior also shows a less direct control by the stimulus of the moment, from the immediate environment" (p. 126). Furthermore, Hebb continues, "In larger association areas, the central phase sequence can be more complex: it must still be organized and ultimately controlled by the relatively smaller sensory projection areas, but the phase sequence can escape the direct control more frequently and for longer periods" (p. 126). Finally, the conclusion follows: "The possession of large association areas is an explanation both of the astonishing inefficiency of man's first learning, as far as immediate results are concerned, and his equally astonishing efficiency at maturity" (p. 126).

What about attitudes? Interests? Intentions? These central functions last longer than the attention produced by a phase sequence but are less stable than actual learned habits. They are sequences of phase sequences, reverberating according to a pattern, but not so thoroughly integrated as to be absolutely stable.

What about consciousness itself? It is "to be identified theoretically with a certain degree of complexity of phase sequence in which both central and sensory facilitations merge" (Hebb, 1949, p. 145). Emotional disturbances are incompatible phase sequences resulting from a lack of fit between a centrally induced one (expectation) and a sensorily induced one (perception). Motor equivalence (imagining an action, for example), so important to Tolman and Lashley, is the result of a central phase sequence (purpose) being associated congruently with a sensory one (obeying the particular sensory cues of the movement). Insight is very rapid learning but not different in principle from any other learning, since all learning is both centrally and sensorily determined. It differs from usual motor learning only in its reliance on more complexity of central processing, which is possible in higher organisms with higher A–S ratios. Here as everywhere, Hebb (1949) follows through on his notion of what makes behavior finally intelligible: "Insight . . . has on occasion been defined as a sudden change in behavior, or as a conscious experience that one may have in solving a problem. Neither definition gets at the real meaning, which is that of a causal factor in behavior" (pp. 162–163). That is, the terms "insight," "attitude," "expectation," "emotion," and so on are not intelligible unless they are translated into the language of causality: "Ultimately, our aim must be to find out how the same fundamental neural principles determine all behavior" (p. 166). "Our" in that sentence does not refer to Hebb and his coworkers. It refers to psychology. Hebb is redefining psychology.

Radical as such a redefinition seems to be, Hebb is surprisingly adroit at showing the plausibility and fruitfulness of his task. Excitability, monotony, fatigue, inhibition, drunkenness, sexuality, hunger, pain, pleasure, neurosis, psychosis, and intelligence—only a partial list—are brought under Hebb's explanatory power with his brain model. Hebb's book must be seen as a genuine scientific tour de force.

THE HEBBIAN LEGACY

Throughout Hebb's 1949 book appear many interpretations of existing data that have later been born out by subsequent experimentation, say, in state-dependent or species-dependent learning, for example. They are as commonplace now as was the learning curve then. How could Hebb see farther than his contemporaries? His answer would probably be that the reading of the data by previous theoreticians was always from a point of view of one of the competing theories. Therefore, this earlier reading made assumptions not warranted by the data, even though they were apparently verified.

For example, consider the following assumption: If there is an inherent organization of the perception of a figure, then perception in general is not learned. Both Gestaltists and connectionists tended to think this way and to disagree only about whether perception in general is learned or native. Hebb's advantage lay in the conceptual tools he used, a theory in another language, the language of brain physiology, neutral to such controversies and capable of generating questions not at all apparent from the perspective of earlier thinking.

Thus, we must say that Hebb's scientific contribution, at the level of theoretical hypotheses, has been immeasurable. No longer could the old loyalties hold after Hebb's careful treatment, which flourished from its distance and dispassionate scrutiny of the data at hand.

As noted earlier, Hebb also saved psychology from the dilemma of either ignoring the data of central determinants of behavior, or acknowledging them and sacrificing the mechanistic assumptions of natural science, whose theories simply could not handle the data. He did this, of course, by proposing a mechanistic theory of central processes, holding at bay once again the temptation to resort to spiritual, animistic, or mentalistic explanations.

This achievement, however, is also perhaps Hebb's greatest limitation, in the sense that he never questions the metapsychological or metaphysical assumptions of the psychology of the 1940s. Consider the following passage, where we see both Hebb's (1949) penetrating questioning and his categorical limitation of what can count as a scientific answer:

An animal learning to solve a problem [or a human, for that matter] makes some right moves, some wrong. What is it that reinforces the right ones and discourages the wrong? Why are the right ones remembered in later trials, the rest forgotten? This has been a persistently baffling problem; and its solution is essential to a theory of behavior. (p. 173)

After stating this issue, Hebb reflects, "The difficulty may seem trivial; if so, however, the reader may be begging the question by saying to himself, in a common-sense (and animistic) way, that the animal of course can see that one of his movements has had the right effect, others not" (p. 173). Hebb clearly makes serious intellectual demands:

But if the question is asked, What neural processes constitute the "seeing"? the solution is as far off as ever. The simplicity of the question of reinforcement, or selective retention of some responses and not others, is like the simplicity of the fundamental postulates of mathematics that are taking centuries to ravel out. (pp. 173–174)

Psychology must therefore be ambitious: "A simple common-sense answer has no value whatever; the first thing one has to do is to get away from the animism that saturates common sense. Having done that, there remains an uncommonly difficult scientific problem" (p. 174).

Presumably, a solution to the difficult scientific problem along the lines of a mechanical explanation such as Hebb's will be real understanding, whereas to say that the animal sees what he is doing is a false understanding. But what warrant is there for saying that? Hebb's epistemology is standard fare for scientists: If "the animal sees," what is the causal explanation of that?

Science traditionally implies or assumes a metaphysical proposition that reality is essentially materialistic, deterministic, and mechanistic. This worldview is familiar to us since Descartes, or at least since the nineteenth century. But what warrant do we have for it? Other psychologies could be built on alternative metaphysical bases; are they less legitimate or less scientific? Hebb's implicit equation of science with a materialistic metaphysical view reminds us of the dogmatism of Watson, even as Hebb offers us a loyalty to data and a theory vastly superior to Watson's psychology.

In closing, it must also be noted that Hebb continues to work on the problem formulated by philosophers as "metaphysical dualism." It is clear he does not think that what we call "brain" and what we call "mind" are really different. Attention is mental. Hebb shows us that a fuller appreciation of the physical activity of the physical brain may offer us at least a physical description, if not an explanation. Hebb thus suggest, instead of dualism, that physical events and mental ones are the same phenomena named at two levels of generality, but they reflect no difference great enough to perpetuate older philosophical speculations called "metaphysics."

Our conclusion must be that Hebb's psychology is brilliant, while grounds for his dismissal of metaphysics are speculative. It still remains, in the twenty-first century, for the future to determine whether such a reduction of dualism is a good idea. Half a century has neither made his speculations irrelevant nor confirmed them.

Finally, the decades of research that have been spurred on by Hebb's 1949 book are voluminous and exciting. The discovery of neurotransmitters in recent decades seems to eclipse Hebb's contributions, but actually these merely elaborate, perhaps specify, if not verify, them. To be sure, in 1949 Hebb postulated synaptic knobs growing, whereas we have learned that changes in chemical organization or sensitivity are the material mechanism of brain activity. But we no longer face the scientific scandal of having no causal, materialistic explanation.

In his discussion of waking and sleeping, Hebb seems to suggest that there must be something like a reticular activating system (RAS) that wakes us up. In fact, that term does not appear, but the concept almost does. The excitement surrounding RAS research was merely a continuation of the excitement surrounding neuropsychology in general, for which Hebb's theory was decisive. Sensory deprivation, and the attending research, are also Hebbian outgrowths.

Before Hebb, the role of the brain in behavior, since James recognized it, was appreciated in the spirit of "It must be important." This long-standing intuition was given real specificity and intelligibility by Hebb. We must count him as one of the giants of American psychology in the middle of the twentieth century.

NOTE

1. Transposition is a phenomenon in learning in which one learns to discriminate (perhaps to choose from an array) the larger, darker, or otherwise comparatively distinct stimulus from an array of stimuli. This differs from ordinary learning in that the learned stimulus in not a specific pattern on the retina, but a comparative judgment among the avialable stimuli, thus "transposing" the S–R connection from the stimulus situation that was learned to an analogous but different one.

13

The Cognitive Developmentalism
of Jean Piaget

THE LIFE OF JEAN PIAGET (1896–1980)

Piaget was a remarkably precocious child. His first publication, on mollusks, appeared in a natural history journal when he was ten years old. That same topic earned him a Ph.D. at age twenty-two. He branched out to more sentient species early, but only as a compromise between biology and philosophy. Working in Bleuler's clinic (Bleuler was the most famous psychiatrist in Switzerland), his turn to psychology is characterized by Hilgard (1987) as follows: "Bleuler's lectures on autism warned Piaget not to spend too much time in speculating on his philosophical system lest he fall victim to that form of psychopathology [i.e., autism]" (p. 567). At that time he also was impressed by both Jung and Freud.

At the age of twenty-five he became the director of studies of the Institute J. J. Rousseau in Geneva, Switzerland. His first five books on childhood were based on observations from 1921 to 1925, before he was thirty years old. Between 1924 and 1933, English versions of his work led to lively interest in America. But it was only much later that Piaget formulated the now famous intricate cognitive development involved in the young child, such as the idea that children must acquire the notion that objects are independent of our experience of them. In 1950 a new surge of interest in his work followed an American edition of his *The Psychology of Intelligence* (1950). During his final thirty years, Piaget's reputation in America soared and has continued to do so since his death in 1980.

Piaget, like Freud, made his entry into American psychology from Europe. Like Freud, his work covers nearly half a century and underwent many changes, continually growing and maturing, expanding and consolidating, and again like Freud, Piaget's influence in this country has been subject to the relatively accidental facts of translation. His early books of the 1920s were translated immediately and known to psychologists, but virtually nothing was translated for the twelve years of European preoccupation with Nazism. By 1950 Piaget's books began to appear again in English, and the ensuing quarter-century saw translations appear at a rate even faster than the phenomenal rate at which they were originally written. Piaget is, therefore, both cause and effect of the so-called cognitive revolution that has inspired American psychology since mid-century. American psychologists were not ready for Piaget until the 1950s, and once ready, they parlayed Piaget's work into their own gigantic research output and into a fundamental rejuvenation of child psychology.

Coming from a European context, Piaget's questions and answers were not designed to address the dilemmas of American psychology. Americans thus had to work through, and out of, certain homegrown, historically determined perplexities—for example, the confusion obviously created by the Titchener–Watson sequence—before they could take up a question like the development of the mind. We have seen how Gestalt, Tolman, Hebb, and others all furthered our escape from the birth traumas of American psychology and made it possible to again take up the science of the mind.

Since 1955 Piaget led the International Center for Genetic Epistemology. The title of this research center is important: Piaget always addressed his work to logicians and philosophers as much as to psychologists, and he took a stand in contemporary philosophy that was neither naturalism–positivism nor existential phenomenology, but bears resemblance to both. He called it "structuralism" and saw himself as championing that view along with Levi-Strauss (1963), the cultural anthropologist, and de Saussure (1959), the linguist.

Generally, his studies of epistemology are genetic, which means developmental—showing that knowing develops. To discover just how knowing develops is, for Piaget, a question for science, not philosophy. In that sense he is a naturalist. That he studies knowing, however, gives him common ground with phenomenologists. However, Piaget takes the trouble to argue against the French phenomenologists, Jean-Paul Sartre and Maurice Merleau-Ponty. His main point in that argument is not that they are theoretically wrong; Piaget rather objects to phenomenologists' polarizing themselves from natural science. Speaking as a natural scientist, Piaget says he is not as "dehumanizing" as Sartre says science is.

Indeed, we can see Piaget (1970) resist the typical reductionism, where psychology is explained by biology and biology is explained by physics. Instead, he argues,

The sciences form a cycle rather than a linear series, [and] such a descent from biology to physics would only be preparation for a subsequent return to mathematics, which in the end would bring us back to—well, what exactly? Let us say, to man himself, so as not to force the option between the human organism and the human mind. (p. 138)

But this French intellectual context is totally alien to Americans, for whom psychology is independent of philosophy. In contrast, Piaget thinks he is addressing philosophical questions scientifically. For example, he states that his "most central concern has always been to determine the [relative importance of] the contributions of the person's activities and the limiting aspects of the object in the process of acquiring knowledge" (quoted in Flavell, 1963, p. vii). Thus, Piaget does not believe that stressing the "activities of the subject," even in the scientist, is in the least antiscientific, although Watson, Hull, and numerous other American psychologists would find it rather irrelevant to psychology. There remains, therefore, a tension between Piaget's own sense of doing psychology and that of his more positivistic counterparts in this country.

Even his supporters and advocates in this country do not focus on the philosophical ramifications of Piaget's theory of an active subject. Piaget is understood in the American context as taking the middle road between considering mental development the result of biological maturation and learning based on experience with the environment. This middle road, which tries to construct in theory a picture of the interaction between heredity and environment, addresses the problem of nature versus nurture as American psychologists have asked it. His position was not immediately understood by Americans who tended to think, following Watson, that environmentalism equals science while mental reality equals superstition. But Piaget helped Americans get over that. "Thinking" is now common scientific subject matter in American psychology, as is even the "activities of the subject."

These theoretical advances, heartily boosted by Piaget as well as by more native trends in American psychology such as the "new look" perception (Bruner, Goodnow, and Austin, 1956; Bruner and Klein, 1960), were matched by methodological innovations. Piaget's early work used what he called a "clinical method," followed by experimental work later. Piaget said in 1962, "It is important to understand clearly that in order to explore intellectual development in its creative spontaneity, without distorting it by *a priori* assumptions drawn from our experience with adult thought, it has been necessary to proceed in two phases" (quoted in Flavel, 1963, p. ix). Piaget specifies these phases as "first, to unearth what is original and easily overlooked in the child's successive stages of evolution, and to do this with methods, including verbal ones, which are as free and flexible as possible; then, in a second phase, varied controls and more refined analyses become feasible" (p. ix).

This strategy not only legitimates less rigidly controlled investigative work in order to see what there is to measure later. It also then demands a variety of experimental designs sensitive to the processes initially observed. Testing Piagetian hypotheses in a laboratory requires imaginative experiments, and American Piagetians have responded creatively. The overall effect has been to make psychological methods in this country both more flexible and imaginative than they were before Piaget entered American psychology in the 1950s.

Both the clinical method and the experimental one bear a brief examination. Here is an example of Piaget at work in 1929: Metr (age 5 years, 9 months): Where does the dream come from?—I think you sleep so well that you dreamt—Does it come from us or from outside?—From outside.—What do we dream with?—I don't know.—With the hands? With nothing?—Yes, with nothing" (quoted in Flavell, 1963, p. 25). This interview continues as follows:

—When you are in bed and you dream, where is the dream?—In my bed, under the blanket. I don' t really know. If it was in my stomach (!) the bones would be in the way and I shouldn't see it.

—Is the dream there when you sleep.

—Yes, it is in the bed beside me. (p. 25)

Flavell described the later, experimental phase as "set up to demonstrate [Piaget's theory] rather than to 'test' it in any rigorously predictive sense" (p. 37), but this has become less true as Americans have cast their Piagetian research into purer experimental tests of particular hypotheses.

THE SYSTEM

Key terms in Piaget's system are "structure" and that network of ideas, called "schemata," that humans use in interacting with the environment. The earliest schemata are sensorimotor, such as the repetitive tendency to grasp graspable (and some ungraspable) things. Later, as a child approaches the grade school years, schemata appear that are symbolic and languaged, and in adolescence we see some that are extremely abstract. At any given age the schemata are ordered, in equilibrium, and this order is the cognitive structure with which the individual deals with the environment. The child's overt dealing expresses his or her cognitive structure and his or her cognitions control his or her overt action. Behavior and cognition interpenetrate one another in Piaget's theory, so that, in fact, cognitive structure is simultaneously behavioral structure, which includes the individual's entire interaction with the world.

Structures (often called cognitive structures) endure; they have more stability than what is accounted for in a vision of behavior as largely stimulus controlled, such as Watson's or Skinner's theory might suggest. We could call structures "intervening variables" after the fashion of Tolman, Hull, and even Hebb, except that Piaget is concerned less with the "horizontal" relations to specific stimuli and responses and concerned more with their "vertical" evolution over developmental time. Piaget's theory is not about how a stimulus leads causally to what James called "considerations" (the mental activity of the upper loop; see Figure 3.1) and how these lead causally to motor responses. Instead, Piaget's theory is about how the mind develops over time.

Accommodation and Assimilation

Throughout developmental time, Piaget envisioned the two processes by which structures grow, his "functional constants," assimilation and accommodation:

Every newly established connection is integrated into an existing schematism. According to this view . . . the subject becomes aware of . . . connections only to the degree that he can *assimilate* them by means of existing structures. In other words . . . the input, the stimulus, is filtered. (Piaget and Inhelder, 1969, p. 5, emphasis added)

This filtering by the mind occurs

through a structure . . . which in turn [is] *modified and enriched* when the subject's behavioral repertoire is *accommodated* to the demands of reality. The filtering or modification of the input is called *assimilation*; the modification of internal schemes to fit reality is called *accomodation*. (pp. 5–6, emphasis added)

What Piaget says here is that we change what we see, in our seeing it, into what we can understand. That changing in our perception is assimilation. Hence, I assimilate my father's smile to his approval. However, what I understand changes if these assimilated perceptions are not quite accurate. I refine my categories; I understand more subtle differences; my categories of perception become more accurate. That changing of my way of assimilating is accommodation.

We can see assimilation and accommodation at work in the earliest months of life, what Piaget calls the sensorimotor period. The sensorimotor period is the first of four great developmental periods before adolescence, covering the first year or two, until symbolic processes usher in the second period. A day or so after birth the infant sucks more efficiently than during the first extrauterine hours. This improvement is a kind of learning to be sure, but what is learned? An action, certainly, but more than an action: a schema. There is no concept of nipple versus rattle, and so both are treated alike, as are thumbs, fingers, pillows, and so on. Everything is assimilated to the schema, "to suck." This behavior is schematic, or cognitive, and the earliest schemata are behavioral. As if he were intentionally correcting Pavlov, Piaget states, "A conditioned reflex is never stabilized by the force of its associations alone, but only by the formation of a scheme of assimilation" (Piaget and Inhelder, 1969, p. 8).

Later, stimulus and response differentiations are not mere regularities in behavior, but they signal an internal process, accommodation. This can safely be inferred by what the infant later shows us he or she knows, through his or her enacting means–ends relations, culminating in "insight" of the variety of Koehler's apes, and so on. The child must "construct" reality by accommodating his or her schemata to it, and Piaget has shown us how to do the painstaking observation to verify just how this happens.

Objects become "conserved" only gradually, as the schemata accommodate to reality. At first the child behaves as if an object that he or she sees put under a cloth and is out of sight and does not exist. He or she does not pursue it when it is covered. Later, the child will do so, but only where he or she saw it disappear and not where it would come out if its invisible trajectory were imagined. Eventually, the object becomes an "object," in our sense, to the child. That is, it exists independent of his or her seeing it, independent of place, generally in and of itself. Piaget calls this conservation.

Space

Practical space is mastered also in the sensorimotor period such that the child can solve certain detour problems through a complex structure, which Piaget calls a "group of displacements" (see Figure 13.1). Piaget and Inhelder (1969) explain:

Psychologically speaking, this group has the following characteristics: (a) A displacement AB and a displacement BC may be coordinated into a single displacement, AC, which is still part of the system. (b) Every displacement AB may be reversed to BA, whence the behavior pattern of "return" to the point of departure. (p. 16)

Figure 13.1
Practice Space

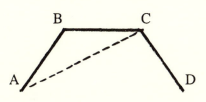

Possibilities in space for the sensorimotor child continue: "(c) The combining of the displacement AB with its reverse BA gives the null displacement AA. (d) The displacements are associative; that is, in the series ABCD, AB + BD = AC + CD" (pp. 16–17).

We have quoted this description of what an eighteen-month-old can do (as can chimpanzees but not hens, notes Piaget) to demonstrate how Piaget understands behavioral abilities in terms of their formal properties, properties that must be understood by a child. These formal properties are the rudiments of logic, later appearing in the verbal and purely mental, as well as motoric, spheres.

The sequence of development of this understanding of formal properties is always the same, whether a sensorimotor child is learning practical space, a concrete operations child is learning dimes and nickels, or an adolescent child is learning algebra. Further, the content of the formal properties of the system are always the same; the system is that known to adults as logic or group theory. All cognitive development is, for Piaget, successive approximations of logic.

Emotion and Cognition

Affective development shows parallels to cognitive development. The focusing of affect into "object relations" parallels the achievement of object conservation. Similarly, a child realizes that rules apply equally to children and adults, and that rules can be established by anyone, even children. This parallels the reversibility of symbolic systems.

Piaget's analogy between cognitive and affective spheres might be seen as his assimilation of observations of emotional life to his cognitive theory, in which case we might expect a later accommodation, in which different patterns will be seen in looking at emotion. Or we might, with Piaget himself, say that emotions follow the same patterns, for they are a part of the larger equipment of organism–environment relations. This latter sphere is what Piaget's work is really about.

At the same time, we must appreciate that the relation between emotion and cognition is not very clear in Piaget's thought. Sometimes emotion is seen as a parallel development; other times it stands to cognition as energy stands to structure. However this is stated, human behavior and organism–environment relations emerge as cognitive— affective–behavioral—all at once. Cognition permeates all human behavior that is of interest to most psychologists, but Piaget is also aware that affectivity similarly permeates behavior:

As we have seen repeatedly, affectivity constitutes the energetics of behavior patterns whose cognitive aspect refers to the structures alone. There is no behavior pattern, however intellectual, which does not involve affective factors as motives; but, reciprocally, there can be no affective states without the intervention of perceptions or comprehensions. (Piaget and Inhelder, 1969, p. 158)

These latter factors then are said to "constitute their cognitive structure. Behavior is therefore of a piece, even if the structures do not explain its energetics and if, vice versa, its energetics do not account for its structures. The two aspects, affective and cognitive, are at the same time inseparable and irreducible" (p. 158).

Is logic the pattern of organism–environment relations as a whole, or does it just capture their structure, with energetics (emotion) as something else? Is Piaget assimilating emotions to cognition when he should accommodate to the special patterns of emotional development? If emotion in Piaget's theory is assimilated to cognition, then we would say that, for Piaget, the essence of human being is logic.

Piaget, in fact, does not go this far. There is no question here whether cognition per se is as he says it is. While it may be conceivable to reduce life itself to the formal terms of his cognitive theory, Piaget never does this explicitly.

However, just as Hebb's terms are inevitably bodily, and thus metaphysical, so are Piaget's mental, and thus metaphysical. We can see that the choice between Hebb and Piaget is not merely an incidental choice of language. Psychologists must chose a language, must make a choice between competing views of the essence of human nature: material causality or logic. Neither Hebb nor Piaget speaks of himself as having only a part of the story, for if either or both were to admit that partiality, they would remain unable to formulate a theory of the whole.

The mental sphere described as logic cannot account for the whole, and the causality of matter cannot account for the whole. It is either both or neither. Dualism has survived to haunt psychology, in spite of psychology's efforts to escape philosophy and simply do science.

Periods of Development

This very general, metapsychological problem should not blind us to the contributions of the rest of Piaget's system. The problems he does not solve do not destroy the value of the problems he does solve, they merely render his solutions tentative, as all science is. The map he draws of cognitive development from birth to adolescence makes a formerly diffuse and vaguely understood territory into familiar ground.

The first period, the sensorimotor period, occupies the child's first two years. In the second, the preoperational period, still before the first grade, cognition is symbolic but not yet logical. The third period, during the early grade school years, sees the appearance of the more logical structures of concrete operations. Finally, only at around puberty do we see the formal operations of abstract logic.

The second period, the preoperational period (say, ages two to five), shows us a marked improvement over the sensorimotor period, and Piaget shows us with painstaking detail how the preschool child's use of language and other representational devices (such as symbolic play) yields a cognitive mastery of the environment far beyond the most intelligent of apes. That mastery is not yet logic in the adult sense, but the complexity of means–ends relations that are daily fare for the four-year-old shows representational intelligence made possible only by the systematic guidance of thought, in turn made possible by the rudiments of logic.

The third period, that of concrete operations (roughly the grade school years), moves the child from symbolic play to organized games. The child's understanding of rules permits him or her to govern his or her behavior beyond the limits of the preoperational child. But at the same time, the child also manifests what Piaget terms "moral realism," a sense of rules as absolute, and a lack of a sense of them as game-specific agreements created by persons. Correspondingly, the child's style of dealing with authority is one of "obedience," an asymmetrical social relationship eventually replaced by a sense of "justice" in adolescence. Later, we shall see that this adolescent sequence, from obedience to justice, is formally identical to the reversibilities of a logical group. According to Piaget, that is far from a coincidence.

Returning to concrete operations (recall that this period corresponds roughly to the grade school years), the most renowned experiments documenting the growth of logical structures through this period involve conservation. For example, is there the same amount of resulting clay when a ball is made into a pancake or a sausage? If the child thinks there is, he has conserved volume.

We once asked children from five to twelve what happens after lumps of sugar are dissolved in a glass of water. For children up to about seven, the dissolved sugar disappears and its taste vanishes like a mere odor; for children seven to eight its substance is retained without either its weight or its volume. (Piaget and Inhelder, 1969, p. 112)

Of course, the developmental process continues:

> After nine or ten, conservation of weight is present, and after eleven or twelve, there is also conservation of volume (recognizable in the fact that the level of water, which is slightly raised when the sugar is added, does not return to its initial level after the sugar is dissolved). (p. 112)

These experiments indicate that the child becomes, over time, less deceived by appearance and more attuned to reality by way of complex cognitive structures. It is an extension of "recentering," making something originally marginal into a center. Recentering can be first noted in the conservation of the object in the first year of life. The object comes to have a reality of its own, instead of being sometimes seen as an extension of oneself. In this third period (grade school years), experiments can reveal exactly when a child understands that matter takes up space. The independent existence of matter in this way extends recentering begun before the grade school years.

Formal operations, seen in the fourth period, after age twelve, are the conclusion of logical development, manifesting the complete set of properties attending logical groups. Logic is available for use by the child on objects not physically present, on propositions he or she does not believe, and on totally abstract symbols, as in algebra. The refinements of logical operations can be mapped in their development by careful experimentation and observation.

This sequence of the four great periods, and of the stages within each, is both a matter of biological maturation and at the same time dependent on experience. It is neither exclusively. Deprived of experiences, the maturational schedule cannot click off. Deprived of maturational time, no amount of learning can reliably speed up the developmental process. In no case is there a reversal in order such that some formal operation appears before its earlier concrete counterpart. And within each stage there is congruence in form among the various regions of the child's functioning: intellectual, social, moral, behavioral, and so on.

THE PIAGETIAN LEGACY

That Piaget spearheaded a renewed interest in child psychology cannot be doubted. But it was not merely making popular again an older field of study. Piaget fundamentally reoriented child psychology in two ways. First, Piaget's work is about cognition, intelligence. This contrasts with the emotional emphasis of psychoanalytic work, whose relatively sparse cognitive hypotheses remain difficult to verify, and it also contrasts with the motor–physical development so carefully codified by Gesell (1934).

We know, of course, that Piaget's focus on cognition spilled over into a "cognitive revolution" in psychology generally, and one of the reasons for this was that Piaget managed to avoid the "pure mentation" emphasis of, say, Titchener, by understanding cognition and action as integral parts of one another. Piaget continues and elaborates James's correction of Titchener.

We are as far from the ethereal "soul" in Piaget's theory as we are in Watson's, for cognition is neither studied nor conceived as separate from the larger network of organism–environment relations. As a genetic epistemologist, Piaget sees epistemology itself as the study of a part of the larger process of biological adaptation, that part wherein behavior becomes intelligent, more than mechanical, more than simply "caused," and in humans intricately logical. If Watson limited organism–environment relations to behavior, Piaget insists that this behavior is qualitatively different in humans, and behavior itself does more than merely adapt to the environment. Behavior plays an integral role in the development of intelligence itself, which in turn reenters the behavioral scene in that vastly superior way humans have of shaping the environment.

Second, Piaget reoriented child psychology by making it developmental psychology. G. Stanley Hall (1904) was a "child psychologist," as opposed to Piaget's "genetic" (meaning developmental) approach. The difference is that Hall studied children and childhood but he did not chart a path of development so clearly. Studying children may have been thought to bear on adulthood, but its primary emphasis did not focus on the orderly sequence of events in the transiton from childhood to adulthood.

In contrast, Piaget's view was that "the child is of considerable interest in himself, but our interest in psychological investigations of the child is increased when we realize that the child explains the man" (Inhelder and Piaget, 1969, p. ix). Therefore, "genetic [developmental] psychology becomes an essential tool of explicative analysis to solve the problems of general psychology" (p. ix). This way of thinking about studying children is essentially the same as Freud's, as Piaget notes. That which puzzles us in adulthood is clarified by looking at it genetically, in terms of its development. Of course, that which puzzled Freud was symptoms, irrationality, and maladaption, while that which fascinated Piaget was intelligence, rationality, and successful adaptation.

This comparison with Freud also allows us to see something of what Piaget considers essential to human nature: his guiding metaphysical assumption about the nature of man. Human nature is marked off from that of subhumans by virtue of the kinds of mental operations the organism actually performs in adapting to the environment. The logic of formal operations is the signal property of human adaptation. Emotions are, from this point of view, less central. The "man" that

Piaget wants to explain is the logical man (in contrast to Freud's neurotic man).

Piaget knows that "man" is also emotional, but the latter is understood as a version of, or complement to (depending on which passage you read), cognition; this ordering of essence is approximately reversed in Freud. Put another way, if Freud blended the nineteenth-century faculties of emotion, cognition, and conation by showing how the latter two are permeated by emotion (around the theme of instinctual desires), Piaget blended the traditional faculties by showing how affects and actions play into the cognitive feats of adapting to the environment.

Of course, a metaphysical issue remains. What is the center, the essence, of human being? This question has important practical implications. How are we to understand, say, the hatreds of war? Through Piaget's eyes, these hatreds are a particular kind of cognition, say, egocentrism manifested in the sphere of morals such that "we" are "good" and "they" are "evil." Through Freud's eyes, these hatreds are projections, displacements, and reaction formations of biological instincts. What indeed is the essence of hatred? Which language enables us to understand it in such a way that we can do something sensible about it?

At the psychological level, Piaget's psychology, like Hebb's, is brilliant, and the two do not particularly contradict one another. A phase sequence is the neurological counterpart to a schema; a schema is the psychological counterpart to a phase sequence. But at a metapsychological level, what is essential to human being differs as brain differs from knowing, and at the metaphysical level, the ultimate reality or base of intelligibility differs as matter differs from logic.

At all these levels, "mind" as a reified entity has disappeared. But the incommensurability of logical patterns with causal patterns betrays that dualism has not ceased to plague psychology. Logic and causality each explain observable sequences. But the two are as different as mind and body. And both are crucial for psychology, but in different ways. Dualism lives.

As with Hebb, Freud, Watson, James, and others, some of the issues raised by Piaget's psychology are resolvable by existing psychological methods, while others seem to escape the net of experimental science because they appear at the more basic metapsychological or metaphysical level. Piaget's impact, of course, goes beyond the experimental level to more basic theoretical issues. But he also inaugurated an explosion of experimental research that, as it accumulates, justifies rethinking at the metapsychological and metaphysical levels as well.

Looking ahead in the historical story, we see that Piaget's work inspired much excitement in the United States, excitement that eventually became what is known as the "cognitive revolution." There is a way that these developments both do and do not deal with the dualistic heritage in Western thought that has been visible in our account.

In our continuing struggle to not be dualistic, psychology has, in its cognitive revolution, retained its methodological insistence, especially in experimental work, that an objective (bodily, verbal, or behavioral) variable be investigated, but such work nevertheless targets mental life once again, as a separable part of human life.

G. Stanley Hall (1904) made the body a center in order to marginalize the mind, or at least to undermine the separation of body and mind. The same langauge is used to analyze both. It was not an explicit parallelism (which would be metaphysics), but Hall recognized various sites at which human being can be investigated. Were the same theories to apply to both, dualism would indeed be a relic of the past, but of course we still have no neurological description of logic, nor do we clearly see a consequence for neurological causal phenomena coming from human logic.

Cognitive psychologists make mental life a center, but not to overcome dualism by marginalizing the body and not to undermine the separation by hoping for a single (perhaps functional) language to bind body and mind together. In fact, they accentuate the separation. They know that brain events could (theoretically) be their focus, but they ignore brain events, and bodily events are reduced to verbal reports, which are (metaphysically) more mental than they are physical. And yet they are necessary for measurement of dependent cognitive variables.

Again, cognitive psychology isolates the mind, but not in the spirit of a metaphysical separation; only in a recognition of various sites that can be investigated. This isolation was provoked, of course, by the neglect of mental life in behaviorism, just as behaviorism isolated the body in protest to the neglect of the body in psychologies like those of Wundt and Titchener. In both cases, the isolation of the body in behaviorism and the isolation of the mind in cognitive psychology were attempts to give the neglected half of the dualism its due.

But in both cases, that isolation inevitably had the effect of perpetuating the separation of body and mind, of further elaborating a language of each that is independent of the language of the other, making the possiblity of a unification increasingly complex and perhaps less likely. Thus is psychology's struggle with dualism a continuing, if not perpetual, phenomenon. If it is perpetual (and perhaps it need not be so), it would suggest that the difference between body and mind is very deep indeed, deeper perhaps than our languaged sciences can overcome.

Such an outcome—continued isolation of these two fields from one another—would continue an unexamined, de facto dualism in psychology. It would not constitute an explicit argument for metaphysical dualism unless one wants to look at the deeper level of analysis, metaphysics, which psychologists are not likely to do. This continued isolation will, however, mean that psychology, the scientific discipline, and metaphysics, the philosophical discipline, are unlikely to ever inform one another very clearly.

14

The Psychology of B. F. Skinner

THE LIFE OF B. F. SKINNER (1904–1990)

B. F. Skinner occupied and revolutionized American behaviorism, building on Watson, Thorndike, and others by bringing an entirely new approach, much more in the spirit of philosophical positivism, to the study of "organisms." Skinner selected that term because he saw his science as very generally relevant to the biological kingdom, and beyond Skinner's pioneering research on pigeons, many applications in prisons, mental hospitals, and schools have become useful and efficient.

Born in a small railroading town, Susquehanna, Pennsylvania, where his father was an ambitious lawyer in a less than warm marriage, youthful Skinner exploited Boy Scouts, orchestra, and sports with an aim to become a writer. Robert Frost had told him, "You have the touch of art" when he was a passionately dedicated student at Hamilton College. His years in Greenwich Village, among other struggling artists in the midst of Bohemian life, ended at age twenty-four when he simply took up psychology at Harvard, where he became, in the course of over half a century of professional work, not only a leading experimental psychologist but also a more positivistically rigorous redefiner of behaviorism, and much of psychology beyond.

Central to Skinner's vision is the "operant principle," whereby behavior is seen as initiated by the behaving organism, not merely responsive to stimuli from the outside that goad the organism to act. Further, spontaneous behavior is not random but is selected by reinforcement contingencies in the environment, in a manner not entirely different from how species were selected according to Darwin.

Skinner's theory is highly data bound; "reinforcement" is not defined by a hypothetical experience of pleasure in an organism, it is simply whatever increases the probability of a particular response. Skinner leveraged knowledge out of controlled observation of organisms; he made every scientific concept clear, defined from the experimenter's point of view, and thus he purified the positivistic integrity of knowledge.

In his retirement, Skinner wrote a three-volume autobiography that reveals personal complexities of an order never seen in his scientific psychology: *The Shaping of a Behaviorist* (1969), *Particulars of My Life* (1976), and *A Matter of Consequences* (1983). The complexities of the man may or may not be illuminated by his own psychological theory, which through its many developments never relinquished the elegant simplicity of his formulations.

B. F. Skinner is a behaviorist, but he is not an S–R psychologist. The distinction is important, for behaviorism has largely become a methodological category, while S–R is a certain theory format. Watson was an S–R psychologist, as was Hull and most of the time Tolman, but in some aspects of their theories the nonbehaviorists Freud, James, and Piaget made use of the S–R format for organizing their theories. One does not have to be methodological behaviorist to be a theoretical S–R psychologist. But even more important is the fact that one does not have to be an S–R psychologist to be a methodological behaviorist. In fact, Skinner can be said to have liberated behaviorism from the S–R format, and it is that achievement that will give Skinner a decisive place in the history of American psychology.

Some of the details of this liberation will be mentioned later, but for now we need to note that Skinner's view of the organism is that it is active, not inert until "stimulated," and further, that the question for psychology is not why the organism is active, for that activity is a biological given. The question is why its activity is as it is; why does it move here instead of there? Do this instead of that? This apparently simple shift of emphasis has profound implications for the science of psychology.

Skinner's behaviorism is clearly a psychology, which is the first and most concrete level of his work The work is also much more, and we must see its context as well. In addition to psychology, Skinner's behaviorism is a metapsychology, a second level of theory that proposes a more general framework within which to understand the questions of psychology. That framework is a creative extension of the Darwinian notion of selection: "For the second time in a little more than a century a theory of *selection by consequence* is threatening a traditional belief in a creative mind" (Skinner, 1972, p. 354). That is, it is the application of no more and no less than the Darwinian notion of selection upon behavior that simultaneously addresses the question of why the organism does this or that (his psychology) and reinterprets the nature of the organism in general (his metapsychology) by reinterpreting once again the old notion of "purpose," offering, as it were, the better behaviorist answer to Tolman.

Before Darwin, it was understood that organisms must have somehow evolved, but inherent in pre-Darwinian notions of evolution was some notion of an invisible guiding hand executing a purpose—an agent, an uncaused cause, a source, or a will—be it God or the organisms themselves who somehow were striving toward the goal of evolutionary advance. Darwin saw selection, a kind of causality not familiar to nineteenth-century push–pull physics, but causality nonetheless, essentially mechanical, without purpose, without an agent. Indeed, most mutations are harmful; selection advances evolution very much by accident. It is orderly and intelligible, but within a causal, not purposive, framework.

The selection of behavior, like the evolution of species, has an apparent "in order to" pattern. Following patterns of survival and evolution, behavior is selected on the basis of consequences. In case after case of apparent purposefulness, Skinner shows this "in order to" to be the effect of environmental contingencies, which are a cause in the evolutionary rather than the mechanical sense. For even human development, Skinner (1974) offers that it merely "remains for us to supplement developmentalism with an analysis of the selective action of the environment. . . . Compared with the experimental analysis of behavior, developmental psychology stands in a position of evolutionary theory before Darwin" (p. 68).

This metapsychological framework, Skinner (1974) thinks, "goes beyond the established facts. I am concerned with interpretation rather than prediction and control" (p. 19). It is, however, an essential part of Skinner's behaviorism, as is yet a third level, the "metaphysical," in that Skinner offers us a view of reality as opposed to illusion. The issue of the mind itself will illustrate this level of Skinner's thought.[1]

"Mind" is seen by Skinner as the middle term in the sequence (1) food deprivation, (2) hunger, and (3) eating behavior. Hunger, a mental event, mediates between physical causes (food deprivation) and physical effects (eating behavior), but in itself "hunger" explains nothing. To explain eating as caused by hunger is to beg the question of what caused the hunger. To say what caused the hunger is to say what caused the eating behavior, and we can now say that one physical event (eating) is a function of another physical event (food deprivation). The mental event, hunger, and all other manifestations of "mind" can obviously be eliminated from the functional equation with no loss of scientific information.

We would call "mind" an unneeded intervening variable, but that term usually refers to something between S and R:

$$S \longrightarrow I \longrightarrow R$$

In Skinner's format, eating (R) is a "function of" (caused by) food deprivation, but food deprivation is not an S; it is a part of environmental contingencies that, temporally, are both before and after the R:

environmental contingencies that deprive an organism of food		the same contingencies that allow eating contingent on some instrumental behavior
	$\longrightarrow R \longrightarrow$	

We see here, again, Skinner's abandonment of the S–R format, and we see how contingencies select instrumental behavior (a kind of causality that is not linear). We simultaneously see the metaphysical statement that mentation plays no independent role in the causal matrix. That is, thinking, in the traditional sense of an activity of the mind, does not matter. Skinner's psychology, metapsychology, and metaphysics are intricately interlocked.

Now it is not entirely true that the events to which we traditionally refer with the term "mentation" do not matter. In fact, for human organisms, they clearly do matter; what is at stake is their nature, whether they are in fact "mental" (as opposed to physical) at all. "What is felt or introspectively observed is not some nonphysical world of consciousness, mind, or mental life but the observer's own body" (Skinner, 1974, p. 17). This physical interpretation of mind states his third, metaphysical level. In this respect, Skinner's notion is reminiscent of Watson, but with a difference. It will be taken up later when we speak of covert behavior. For now it is enough to point out that Skinner's behaviorism reveals itself as a metaphysical as well as a psychological and a metapsychological theory.

A fourth and perhaps most important level of Skinner's behaviorism is his entry into social planning, political policy, and the general ideology of the culture that supports them. In his controversial *Beyond Freedom and Dignity* (1972), Skinner summarizes his recommendations for the "design of culture" first visible in his popular *Walden Two* (1948). Except for this book, Skinner had not "gone public" in the sense that *Beyond Freedom and Dignity* made him the kind of household word that Watson and Freud had been decades earlier. This move to speaking to the general population late in his career was not a mere grab at the fame of TV talk shows, nor was it a senile attempt to remain influential after his professional powers waned (they did not wane). This move continued Skinner's long-standing sense that our culture must adopt a rational, technological attitude in order to survive, and it expressed his (perhaps less long-standing) conviction that cultural change cannot come about without entering popular consciousness in a fairly overt and public way.

His cultural–political recommendations are no less consistent with his psychology than are his metapsychology and metaphysics. In order to get to the thematic center of all these levels of Skinnerian behaviorism, we have to turn to the psychology itself.

THE SYSTEM

In 1932, Skinner published a reinterpretation of the concept of reflex, in which he sought to demonstrate that it was an adequate basic unit for the description of behavior. We know now that Skinner gave the reflex up as a basic unit, but that paper also sorted out our scientific from our unscientific ideas about it. We do know, he argued, that there are observable correlations between stimulus and response. We do not know, on the other hand, that adjectives like "unconscious," "involuntary," and "unlearned" are accurate.

Skinner rightly saw that these latter, negative descriptions came not from scientific research but from a popularly assumed but unacknowledged Cartesian dualism, according to which the organism is divided into two, one part being conscious, voluntary, and capable of learning, and the other part being mechanical. Skinner began to violate this dichotomy in the study of the acquisition, or learning, of reflexive behavior as early as 1932, and he envisioned the complete demise of the Cartesian dichotomy, not by invective and taboo as Watson had done it, but by carefully sorting out what we know from what we unwarrantedly assume.

Nearly twenty years later, Skinner published his important paper, "Are Theories of Learning Necessary" (1950), in which his attack on traditional assumptions and concepts came to include learning itself. Behavior does change, to be sure, and in an orderly relation to its conditions, both contemporary and historical. But the proper scientific statement of these data is that behavior is a function of conditions, not that the organism has learned or is learning. Learning is never observed; it is a hypothetical process assumed to be going on "behind" the observations of performance. The proliferation of hypothetical processes runs the risk of Freudian (or Hullian) fantasy, of course, for theories sometimes trap us into believing our assumptions, no matter how unwarranted.

Skinner believed that the concept of learning in psychology has led to exactly that fate. Neurological, cognitive, field-dynamic, homeo-

static, and other explanations for learning were populating psychological science, and they had as little relation to concrete, observable
data as did their psychodynamic predecessors. Skinner pointed to comparable errors in the history of physics, and he found a vivid contrast
between most of twentieth-century psychology and the positivistic
purity of contemporary physics.

Learning, which is quantity or strength, the degree to which a response is learned, was usually measured by the number of trials to
extinction. Extinction, in turn, is a process opposite to learning. Typically, learning takes place under one set of conditions in which a response is rewarded, while extinction takes place under another set of
conditions in which it is not. Theories of learning and extinction have
avoided mentalistic conceptions of hunger that were thought to mediate between food deprivation and eating behavior, but learning and extinction have the same logical status as the rejected mentalistic conceptions,
according to Skinner. They lead to the same pseudounderstanding that
begs the question parallel to "What causes hunger?" when hunger is
used to explain eating. That parallel question, "What causes learning?" (or extinction), when answered, will give us a functional relationship between conditions and behavior and make the middle term
"learning" (or "extinction") as unnecessary as mentalistic constructs.

As soon as we see that behavior is a function of conditions, and as
soon as those conditions are known, then it becomes a moot point
whether learning requires drive reduction or whether extinction is
some kind of "inhibition" that conflicts with or subtracts from "habit
strength" or "excitatory potential," to use a couple of Hull's constructs.

Perhaps the most central outcome of Skinner's iconoclastic but inci-
sive thinking is his redefinition of reinforcement. Hull had succeeded
in cleansing his language of the mentalistic notions of "satisaction"
and "gratification" through the use of the homeostatic notion of "drive
reduction." A behavior is reinforced when it leads to the reduction of
a drive. Reinforcement was then seen as increasing habit strength, and
the greater the habit strength, the more trials it took to extinguish the
response. The problem becomes, of course, what drives there are, or
more critically, what the drives are. In order to answer this question,
theories turn to biochemistry, neurophysiology, electromagnetic fields,
or even the dynamics of the unconscious mind—virtually anywhere—
and violent ideological arguments ensue, stemming from the various
unscientific loyalties one happens to hold. Skinner argues that the actual scientific work of finding the concrete variables of which behavior is a function gets lost in the shuffle.

Those variables certainly include reinforcement, but is reinforcement
drive reduction? And what are the drives? The question is begged.
Skinner's elegant answer to this whole scientific morass is simply to

define "reinforcement" empirically. Reinforcement is any stimulus that, when applied, increases the probability of the immediately prior response. Food is a reinforcer, but not by virtue of its capability to reduce a hypothetical hunger drive. Food is a reinforcer because (and only if) it works to increase the probability of a response.

This strategy liberates the exploration of functional relationships between behavior and the contingencies in the environment from theoretical loyalties and quarreling. For some organisms, affection or even mere attention is reinforcing, for others the freedom to roam, and so on. Which stimuli are reinforcers for which organisms is an interesting question, and useful to know if one is training organisms, but it is essentially an empirical question whose resulting theoretical debates have delayed the task of doing the empirical work.

Let us look at one more example from Skinner's later work: "Discrimination is a relatively simple case. Suppose we find that the probability of emission of a given response is not significantly affected by changing from one of two stimuli to the other. We then make reinforcement of the response contingent upon the presence of one of them" (Skinner, 1974, p. 92). This procedure yields no surprises: "The well-established result is that the probability of response remains high under this stimulus and at a very low point under the other. We say that the organism now discriminates between the stimuli. But discrimination is not an action, or necessarily even a unique process" (1974, p. 92). The theoretical implications that follow, Skinner notes, are that:

Problems in the field of discrimination may be stated in other terms. How much induction obtains between stimuli of different magnitudes or classes? What are the smallest differences in stimuli which yield a difference in control? And so on. Questions of this sort do not presuppose theoretical activities in some other dimensional system. (1974, p. 92)

Discrimination, extinction, reinforcement, and even learning itself get redefined under the guidance of Skinner's key question: Of what variables is behavior a function? Developmental processes, pathological behavior, verbalization, and political policies all eventually come into the purview of this question. This question is an extension of science, in its purest and most self-critical or at least most parsimonious form, to any sample of behavior. And this, Skinner argues, is psychology, the science of behavior. The psychologist's job is to discover the discriminative stimuli and the reinforcement contingencies of which behavior is a function. Once discovered, behavior will be as predictable and controllable as the actions of antibodies on infections now are.

This psychology does not rule out the phenomena to which mental terms like "thinking" and "imagining" refer. In addition to the extraordinarily rigorous parsimony of Skinner's thought, there is a speculative side of which Skinner is not the least ashamed. "Speculation is necessary, in fact, to devise methods which will bring a subject matter under better control" (Skinner, 1974, p. 19). The difference between his and, say, Tolman's or Piaget's speculation is that his is an extension of known principles into unexplored areas, as opposed to making up new principles that at first describe but later are taken to explain phenomena, such as Piaget's "assimilation" and "accommodation." Of course, "thinking" is a difficult field, and if a behaviorist explanation is not, at this stage, all we should like to have, "it must be remembered that mental or cognitive explanations are not explanations at all" (Skinner, 1974, p. 103).

Mentalism was rebuffed by the methodological behaviorisms of the past, which simply ruled thinking out as a phenomenon to study because it was not objective. Skinner believes this to have been a mistake. While thinking "does not explain overt behavior," it is also true that thinking is "more behavior to be explained" (Skinner, 1974, p. 104). While thinking is most obviously talking to oneself, Skinner does not need to find objective, bodily manifestations of it as Watson did, for he does not try to deny its existence or its importance. What is denied, of course, is our mentalistic conceptions about it, which separates it from the network of contingencies of which reality is made.

For Skinner (1974), "mental" events "have been invented on the analogy of external behavior occurring under external contingencies. Thinking is behaving. The mistake has been in allocating the behavior to the mind" (p. 104). If thinking is behavior, what is thought is what is behaved.[2] What is thought is not concepts, ideas, schemata; what is thought is the behavior in interaction with a contingency-laden world. Thinking behavior omits overt muscular responses, but undergoes them covertly. And there is no reason to suppose that covert behavior somehow follows different laws than those well established for overt behavior. In fact, "Covert behavior is almost always acquired in overt form, and no one has ever shown that the covert form achieves anything which is out of reach of the overt" (p. 103).

Skinner's behaviorism is different, then, from mentalism, and from traditional methodological behaviorism. He terms it "radical behaviorism," indicating that the roots of everything organisms do is fundamentally grounded in behavior: "Our knowledge is action, or at least rules for action" (Skinner, 1974, p. 139), and of course the "knowing" of rules is "quite different from the knowledge identified with the behavior shaped by the contingencies" (p. 139). That is, it is different topologically. The principles according to which it operates are not different: "Thinking has the dimensions of behavior, not of a fancier inner process which finds expression in behavior" (pp. 117–118).

This position of radical behaviorism is relatively new in the history of behaviorist thought. We can see its difference from Watson, who would consider thinking only as subvocal speech, which he then tried awkwardly to discover in minute movements of the larynx, so thorough was his conviction that bodily responses exhausted human functioning. It differs from Tolman's operational definition of thinking in terms of VTEs (vicarious trial and error), which made the concept of thinking behavioristically respectable but led to no extended systematic exploration, and certainly from Tolman's sign–gestalt theory, which "gets at" thinking but is not a behavioristically respectable concept because it adopts the internal point of view of the organism. Skinner's formulation differs from Hull's in the same way that the concept of behavior itself, as operant and emitted rather than as respondent and elicited, differs from Hull's concept. It differs from Hebb's physiological theory in obvious ways, and so on.

I believe we can see Skinner's radical behaviorism as a logical extension of his 1932 article in which the separation between mental and behavioral was seen as Cartesian dualism. Watson resolved the dualism by banishment, Tolman by operational definition, Hull by ignoring it, Piaget by cognizing behavior even as cognition was enbehaviored. Through it all, the tension remains, most vivid in James perhaps, whose psychology was too sensitive to both the subtleties of mind and the palpability of body to settle for any of these solutions, including Skinner's treatment, which does away with the tension by grounding intelligibility in causality and science.

Skinner's radical behaviorism is yet another attempt to deal with Descartes. He believes that while his approach is incomplete, what will complete it is more research. The conceptual apparatus does not appear to Skinner to be wanting at all, for causal science is, after all, the unquestioned ground of intelligibility for radical behaviorism.

THE SKINNERIAN LEGACY

As psychology, Skinner's behaviorism liberated itself from the S–R model, reconceived the organism as inherently active, and changed the scientific question from why there is behavior to why particular behaviors are selected by the organism. These Skinnerian influences have opened up vast new fields for research, from behavior modification with mental patients and teaching machines in schools to the minute events within the Skinner box itself. Apart from its ambitions as pure science, operant conditioning has been useful both in practical settings and as a tool to solve other problems of experimental design across psychology. This latter import has already exceded the uses of Pavlovian conditioning earlier in the century.

The limits of the *psychology* of Skinner are obvious. One response at a time is investigated, and the only theory to account for the more complex patterns so familiar in everyday life is the rather strained notion of chaining. It is not plausible that my eating response is the final, self-reinforcing anchor in a chain of responses having no more connection than their association via the complex processes of behavior selection. Whether Skinner's attempt to deal with cognition can successfully be integrated into an explanation that will account for the coherence of my behavior remains to be seen.

At the *metapsychological* level, Skinner's new connection between behaviorism and Darwinian evolution constitutes one of the more interesting theoretical innovations in psychology in recent decades. To see behavior selection as analogous to organism or species selection puts psychology into a new relation to biology and, in fact, suggests a new definition of psychology itself. Further, since the principles of selection are essentially the same, one glimpses possibilities for the unification of science not previously visible. In the bargain, natural selection moves even closer to the center of the definition of man. Darwin did not intend natural selection to be the essence of man; Skinner is not the first to extend Darwin's concept to that exalted position.

At the *metaphysical* level, Skinner offers us yet another statement of how physical reality is the *real* reality. Mental events are important enough in Skinner's thought, but they are decidedly not dealt with by Skinner as what Cartesians call "mental." They are behavior, and behavior is movement in physical space and physical time. Physics remains the model science and the definitive framework for reality. This metaphysical theme is so strong in Skinner's behaviorism that it creates a vivid tension with other late trends in American psychology, such as the cognitive revolution.

The cognitive revolution could be taken as a mere interest in cognitive variables in predicting behavior, but I believe the cumulative effect of Gestalt, Tolman, Piaget, and even Hebb is to change the notion of behavior itself, from mere movement in physical space to cognized movement, movement with a direction, a guidance from within the organism itself. This "recovery from Watson" or "regression to James" is in direct contradiction to Skinner's repeated emphasis on the environment for the crucial science of the psychological action. That difference is, at base, metaphysical. Is there mind? Or is it a mere figment of human imagination, or of human behavior?

At the social, political, and cultural levels, Skinner entered the fray with as much drama as Watson or Freud before him. Skinner has never been well understood in this arena, although it is probably the case that he has influenced the concrete shape of psychological institutions, such as mental hospitals, schools, and military installations, more than any single person in this century. His line of thought appeals to the cost-accounting concerns of public institutions more than to the general population.

We need to recognize that *Beyond Freedom and Dignity* (Skinner, 1972) was written for some reasons and not for others. Skinner did not write it in a quest for footlights or the glories of a cultural hero or gadfly. Nor is it the ramblings of a scholar whose clout with his colleagues is past. The relation of psychology in particular, but also of science in general, to historical concerns about twentieth-century crises had been important to Skinner for a long time. *Walden Two* was written in 1948.

The essential theme lying behind all Skinner's forays into the culture at large is that science is a better way to do things than tradition, in itself not a shocking idea, nor one that would be expected to generate the depth of reaction that has befallen Skinner. What makes Skinner unique among those who say that science should replace other sources of policy is that he showed us what other such advocates did not; namely, how we can actually do it concretely.

When the concrete implications of this very general thesis are spelled out, something Skinner was never afraid to do, outrageous things seem to happen. His 1945 article on how he and his wife designed a controlled environment for their infant daughter, published in *Ladies Home Journal*, touched off violent feelings of abhorrence. People jumped to the conclusion that he was raising his daughter in a Skinner box, whereas the benefits advertised by Skinner were mostly hygienic and for convenience. Cribs can be improved upon; what's the furor?

During World War II, Skinner and his colleagues developed the idea of a guided missile guided by a pigeon. The complex apparatus worked, given precise training of the pigeon, which Skinner was fully able to supply. The military turned the idea down; it apparently was too unconventional to be taken seriously. Why? Like the temperature-controlled crib and *Walden Two* (1948), the obvious suggestion that science might make things better was rejected outright. And teaching machines never really became educational fare, even though they clearly work for certain kinds of subject matter. From Skinner's point of view, the antiscientific bias in popular thinking must have seemed incredibly strong—and incredibly frustrating.

In *Beyond Freedom and Dignity* (1972), Skinner tried the frontal approach. Popular conceptions sabotaged the rational application of science, and so he attacked popular conceptions directly. His premise seemed to be that people will believe what is reinforcing to believe, and that current traditional notions like freedom and dignity, and the mentalistic theory of human nature that attends them, are reinforcing only in the short run. A rational look at our ability to handle cultural crises—in the environment, in Third World starvation, and in cases of petty dictators—suggests that something more drastic must be done. Skinner hoped that people, through his popular writing, would come to see the long-term contingencies, which favor—and may make necessary—a fundamental cultural change.

Unfortunately, society at large will not be able to follow intellectually much of Skinner's rationale, for we as a culture are dualistic, and thus Skinner's reduction of mind to behavior (mental to physical) will simply not make sense to us. Perhaps Skinner was ahead of his time. Or perhaps dualism is not only ubiquitous, but also necessary.

NOTES

1. I am saying here that Skinner's rejection of metaphysics is a metaphysical position. Such a comment may be disingenuous, for perhaps Skinner should be permitted to disavow metaphysics. However, I do not think so. In fact, I believe it is a level of everyone's cognitive grasp of the world, although its expression in theoretical terms has been most vividly advertised by philosophers. Philosophers may be the most explicit, but philosophy does not own the rock-bottom sense, articulate in theory or not, of reality, a sense that guides our deepest commitments (to reality, for example), and our most profound statements (when we speak of what is really real). Even when we are unaware of our commitment to reality, or make no statements about it, in fact we enact a sense of reality if we act at all, and we speak that sense if we speak at all. To reject metaphysics is to foreshorten human awareness foolishly.

2. We have, at this point, come full circle to William James: "The thoughts are the thinkers" (see Chapter 3). Like Skinner, James invented that formula to avoid reifying an agency like the mind. Unlike Skinner, James did not reject the relevance of metaphysics. He believed, and Skinner did not, that the mental realities of life follow different patterns from the physical realities of life. For James, mental life was never reduced to terms invented to analyze physical behavior. Thoughts are nonmaterial but still real, a position not easy to accommodate without metaphysics.

———————————————————— Part **III**

SPECIALIZATION AND FRAGMENTATION

15

Ideas and Identities in Psychology

This book deals with theory and not with research. This contrasts with other books on the history of psychology, some of which seem to assume that the story of psychology has been substantially determined by the findings of research. While it would be wrong to reject the relevance of research findings in solidifying or establishing one or another of the theories in psychology, I believe the sequence of theoretical ideas makes a better history. Certainly it makes a bettter story.

The motivation that drives an innovation in psychology is very rarely a surprising bit of data.[1] Data count, but they do not speak for themselves. They must always be interpreted by theory, so that theory not only precedes data in telling us what to hypothesize, it also succeeds data in telling us what ideas to cling to and what ones to reject. In this latter role, I think it must be said that psychology, no less than any other science, clings to ideas. Ideas lead to data that are intriguing, and the intrigue of the experimental work of collecting data may sustain ideas beyond their usefulness.

This feature of psychology does not condemn it as unscientific. It is neither unique to psychology nor does it make psychology less of a science. Data continue to prevent psychology from debauching into a matter of religious faith or mere preference, but the accumulation of data does not stand alone. The history of psychology offers us a case study in the compex interaction of ideas, data, and our own intrigue. Does exaggerating the role of data suppose that psychologists, or historians of psychology, ask only data-driven questions? In fact, all scientists, and social scientists especially, follow their curiosity or their hopes, not just a body of facts.

The succession of ideas, from one theory to another, builds on previous ideas, sometimes by reversing them or turning them upside down, sometimes by making only a small change that leads to new research that flourishes in the laboratory. In the latter cases, of course, it never happens that such flourishing simply follows previous data, uninterpreted theoretically.

Brand new theories are, in some measure, related to more than data: the curiosity or hopes of the theorist, perhaps. Even Skinner, whose psychology aims to be totally data bound, did not enter the laboratory without ideas that suggested where to look for better data. Freud had seemingly less laboratory data than anyone, but it would not be wrong to say that his research, that is, the evolution of ways to treat patients, enacted tests of his ideas, basically in the same spirit as Skinner.

What both Skinner and Freud shared, of course, was an intense curiosity, combined with a faith that some things are worth trying, even though (or exactly because) we don't know what will happen. That is, they were both empiricists. They both allowed their ideas to be tested, and, once tested, they sought to formulate them in closer accord with what their respective data told them.

I do not, of course, pretend that Freud and Skinner were alike in the balance of data and ideas in producing their work. But in both, the ideas are the center. Few theorists agonized as much as these two about theory. What does explain behavior? How can we see it with less puzzlement about what it means? Their very different answers came from their very different data, of course, but their very different data, in turn, came from their very different questions. And it is the questions, not the answers found in research, that make the history of psychology such a fascinating story.

What can we finally say about the complex relationship that exists between psychological ideas in America and their cultural context? Generalities are hard to justify, for they will always be too simple. For example, we could cite neither simplicity nor complexity to justify both Freud's and Skinner's enormous popularity in twentieth-century American psychological thought. Skinner was a master at formulating simplicity; Freud was a master at portraying complexity. Something else accounts for the popularity of these two, simultaneously.

Freud can be said to intensify one's preoccupation with oneself, but there is little attraction, for Americans in general, to ideas that simply promote self-examination. Skinner, in contrast, is enormously practical, but practical application is also not a ticket to success that could account for both. In fact, these two well-known and most famous of psychological idea systems appeal to rather different constituencies.

Freud's is, finally, a theory with vivid moral echoes (Rieff, 1959). It recognizes a margin of freedom in a context of coercive forces from biologically based desires on the one hand and from moral standards on the other, a margin of freedom that can grow with insight and can free us of coercions from these two quarters. Skinner's is, finally, a technological theory (Skinner, 1950), whose format is that of a hierarchical situation in which one person controls another's access to rewards and thus can, with Skinner's theory, parlay that power into effective "leadership" or "management" or "manipulation" of the behavior of others. Unlike Freud, Skinner can get immediate practical results.

Freud and others, such as Rogers, spoke to individuals about themselves. Nearly everyone who reads these theories takes them personally, sometimes excusing our shortcomings, sometimes challenging our excuses. Skinner, in contrast, holds rather little gratification in one's self-examination, but appeals to motives that Freud clearly disappoints: the desire to efficiently affect the behavior of others, whether animal or human.

The American population is not a unified factor in our equation. Therefore, these interpretations barely scratch the surface. Unlike Skinner, Freud's and Rogers's psychologies were parlayed into elaborate professional systems of employment roles designed to help people in that quasi-medical way that psychiatrists, who are "doctors," sell their practice as a treatment of diseases, or in that quasi-moral way that "counselors," who are both helpers and moral agents, sell their practice as a way to make life better, one person at a time. The culture that accepted Freud and Rogers, or psychotherapy as a commodity, a treatment, and a profession, is hardly a homogeneous group of people who hold the same cultural values or, even if they do, apply them in the same way or in the same circumstances.

Hardly any Freudian or Rogerian enthusiasts are systematically present in social hierarchies that enable powerful people to control less powerful ones. The therapeutic approach always involves expertise in reflection, not in control. One difference between the Freudian–Rogerian–clinical appeal and the Skinnerian–technological appeal can therefore be stated in terms of behavior and consciousness. Skinner began with behavior and extended his theory to consciousness, but he never promised to control people's thoughts. Freud–Rogers began with consciousness and extended their theory to behavior, but they never promised to change people's behavior.

The polarity between consciousness and behavior, like that between mind and body, continues to exist in our psychology, and the existence of this polarity in popularity betrays the continuation of the unspoken relevance of the mind–body polarity even in identifiable styles or parts of the professional population.

CONSCIOUSNESS

American academic psychology has had a long struggle with consciousness, a struggle that bears some examination. Perhaps a look at Hilgard's (1987) encyclopedic account of American psychology's effort to deal with consciousness will illuminate our understanding. Hilgard reveals how continuingly unsettled, and basically ambivalent, psychology's dealing with consciousness has been. He notes first the important difference between "conscious," the adjective, and "consciousness," the noun. During the early decades of psychology, "Doubts were seldom expressed if one used awareness or consciousness in verbal or adjectival forms; scarcely anyone doubted that we are *aware of* or *conscious of* something, or that we could comfortably speak of conscious experiences" (p. 269). However, as Hilgard continues the thought, "More trouble arose when one referred to *a consciousness*, or the *Unity of consciousness*, and other terms that tended to imply mental substance. It was easier to accept conscious processes than consciousness as an entity" (p. 269).

Hilgard (1987) cites two major scientific facts that helped rid psychology of dualism. First, the theory of the conservation of energy "made it difficult to see how an incorporial mind could add something to the operation of a corporeal entity" (p. 69), and second, Darwin's theory of evolution described how what we call consciousness is a biological, evolutionary product. The metaphysical problem stemming from a dualism that portrays two separate and incompatible realities, tends to dissolve among scientists who study the mind. Scientists can adopt a convenience, like psychophysical parallelism, without making further metaphysical commitments, and this permits the science to procede with a central, but not urgent, unanswered question of what the premise of parallelism means philosophically.

But consciousness presents yet another problem for psychology, even given the more or less intentional neglect of metaphysical presuppositions or implications of psychology. That second problem is epistemological. In Hilgard's (1987) terms, the distinction between a "knower" and a "known," which can be cheerfully acknowledged without metaphysical elaboration, nevertheless leads us always to ask, What belongs to the physical substratum of, say, the brain as an object, and what belongs to the knower as a conscious subject who knows? Even the brain conceived as an object is not comprehensible without a subject who thus objectifies the conscious experiences of scientists who consciously study the brain.

William James did not like intellectual shortcuts, and in his famous "the thoughts are the thinkers" he recognized an inadequate, temporary, and vacuous solution that remained psychology's unpaid debt to convenience. E. B. Holt, a younger colleague of James's at Harvard, among five others, continued the discussion through and after the final years of James's life. Their book, *The New Realism* (Holt et al., 1912), acknowledged the problem and noted that objects appear both in consciousness and in relation to other objects. Those objects of consciousness that have systematic relations to other objects can be called "objective." And we can distinguish them from, say, imagined or hallucinated objects, which we understand as imagined or hallucinated exactly because they do not have such relations.

Thus, there is a scientific definiton of the objective world. When an object is imagined or thought of, we are engaging in responding to that world in perception and memory, and in the case of Washburn's (1916) theory, our response is a motor response, not an entity called "consciousness." Langfeld (1927), also at Harvard, had a theory similar to Holt's, and Kuklick (1977) has called this theory "philosophical behaviorism."

Philosophers did not, to my knowledge, follow this behaviorist lead very far, nor is this line of effort very persuasive. It reorganizes our perceptual experience to account for perceived versus external objects, but it does not approach Descartes's notion of the human soul, which knows, sees, decides, and prays. Nor has psychology, the science, troubled itself again with dualism (there are some exceptions; e.g., Keen, 2000a, 2000c). Instead, the attitude prior to this effort has survived to this day: drawing an impermeable line around psychology so as to exclude issues of philosophy.

In one sense, this is simply sensible. Psychology does not claim to answer all the questions in the world. As a science, it knows what science can address and what science, with its objectifying mode of investigaion (further exaggerated by Watson) cannot. It excludes theories of God and other nonempirical realities, morality and values, and other things taken up by other disciplines such as philosophy and sociology.

Science has indeed taken the "psyche" out of psychology, especially the ever-present psyche of the scientist. Psychological science in America did later, as we know, beginning anew with Piaget's developmental studies, find ways to test his hypotheses of mental development. This has initiated a reclaiming of mental life by psychology in the so-called cognitive revolution. If mental life is visible in behavior, and it is, then a science of mental life is possible (Miller, 1962).

An earlier opportunity that occurred with an earlier European scientist of mental life, Freud, preceded the cognitive revolution but did not gain scientific respectability. Freud's theory, rich in hypotheses about mental life, focused on variables too emotionally nuanced, and too diverse, to achieve a "mental revolution" in respectable scientific psychology.

Cognitive psychology, of course, flourishes without solving the mind–body problem. Metaphysics can be ignored without limiting psychology's subject matter to physical behavior. Social psychology following World War II, and the publication of *The Authoritarian Personality* (Adorno, Frenkl-Brunswik, Levinson, and Sanford, 1950), opened out into the rich data of attitudes and values. It too seems to suffer little from the mind–body problem. Behavior simply is mental, unlike sticks floating downstream; it attends to reality and responds purposively; it is infused with mental life, Freudian wishes, Piagetian schemata, American (or anti-American) values, curiosity, morality, and reverence (or antireverence). Psychology, having recovered from Watson, is regaining the stature of its own name.

Just how all this will matter in the history of ideas about mental life, including powerful theories like Cartesian dualism, remains to be seen. Phenomenology (Chapter 16), first as a philosophy and then as a psychology, does what no others have attempted. It has attacked not only the first problem, which is to find a metaphysical position that includes both mental and physical realities, but it has also attacked the second, epistemological problem by extending its reach from the mental life of those studied to the mental life of the scientist himself or herself.

A PSYCHOLOGY OF PSYCHOLOGY

The interaction between science and culture is as complex or perhaps more complex in psychology as that relation for any other science. In the informal research all psychologists do in the simple process of getting to know one another, an unstable consensus emerges in which three kinds of answers emerge from the question, Why are you a psychologist?

First, the most common and certainly the easiest and least controversial answer is curiosity. An indulgence of fascination with the obvious complexities of behavior and consciousness and life in general is nearly every psychologist's first answer. Especially in the context of nature, whose secrets are revealed by science so dramatically, the satisfaction of curiosity must loom large as a reason to be a psychologist. Consequently, it must be in the forefront of a general answer to the question of why psychology has attracted the enormous effort and talent and produced the extensive knowledge that it has. This includes curiosity about oneself, but that is usually only an initial version of what must extend to others, to societies, and to various species if it is to be a durable motive.

Second, many psychologists confess that indulgence of such a curiosity promised a career, an identity that is respected, and rewards of status and prestige, if not fame. This promise, like that of all sciences, if not all careers, has risks. Few, of course, become famous, but many, with perseverance and hard work, can earn the badges of adulthood, such as income, and the badges of success, such as social position. That psychology can also engage one personally, at the level of curiosity, makes it an especially attractive career choice.

Third, nearly all psychologists committed themselves to this profession as a junior partner in a relationship with a teacher, mentor, or trusted friend. Such relationships are, of course, personal, but they are also cultural. One's mentor represents a segment of the culture, not merely a personal friend. Thus, one's personal decision to become a psychologist, often made tentatively and cautiously, nevertheless is rarely pursued alone. Collegiality is important in any profession, of course; in psychology it is usually mentioned as pivotal when psychologists are asked. This is possibly more true in psychology than in, say, law or medicine or business, where the second factor, the identity or social role, is more likely decisive.

What can we say about curiosity, identity, and relationships in the continual creation of succeeding generations of psychologists? Generalizations about such matters are never safe, especially since the identity of a psychologist is so variable, encompassing some whose mission is morally inspired, others whose intellectual life simply led to psychology, and yet others for whom their career choice has been disappointing. Sometimes curiosity wanes, the rewards of respect and status do not materialize, or relationships explode before either satisfaction of curiosity or achievement of a professional identity occurs. And yet one finds oneself at an age where it is too late to start over.

As a cultural establishment, psychology tends to these matters. National conventions, for example, are elaborate occasions for advertising and indulging curiosity, for granting fame and status to colleagues, and for creating new and recharging old relationships. In fact, these are the primary functions of conventions. In this way, psychology flourishes because there is always more curiosity one can indulge, more hope of achievement that can consolidate respect, and more relationships to have that serve curiosity and identity.

But like all professions, there are disappointments. In terms of curiosity, energetic pursuit of any question in psychology always leads one to the limit of one's science. Every question is contextualized by questions taken up by other disciplines. Biology, sociology, and philosophy are inevitably needed to answer a psychological question in any depth. Every aspect of life, of nature in general, is nested in, overlaps with, or is adjacent to knowledge outside of psychology. Furthermore, every answer to psychological questions has consequences beyond psychology. Some psychologists manage the boundaries of their curiosity by ignoring what is beyond psychology, but most do not.

The rewards of status and respect in an identity can be equally problematic. This aspect of being a psychologist, of having this identity, is made riskier because of the American cultural context of capitalism, which pits individuals against one another in such a way that only a few are stunningly successful, most are moderately so, and some simply fail. Failure in psychology is usually more invisible than the casualties of capitalist economic employment that parlays initial disadvantage into failure, or at least disappoints many and rewards relatively few, who then congratulate themselves and feel no obligation to the less fortunate.

THE SPECIAL CASE OF CLINICAL PSYCHOLOGY

A final feature of the psychology of psychology—of being a psychologist—is that scientists generally and psychologists particularly have reflective moments that seem to throw assumptions into question. It is possible, but actually rare, for a psychologist who deals with people, like clinical psychologists do, to imitate the scientific attitude of physics. Medical doctors, especially surgeons, are trained explicitly to depersonalize their patients, to adopt an attitude of scientific detachment, like that of the physicist. Once one does that, the questions are all "out there." The only content "in here" is a practiced discipline and clarity.

Since clinical psychologists get to know personally the sources of their data, since, that is, their subject matter is not a phenomenon in a laboratory but a person, facing me just as I face him or her, and since this differs drastically from physics, it is well to recognize the implication of this difference.

In the long run, it may be possible to say that the secularization that occasioned science's dominance in the Western world, and that considerably lessened the power of ecclesiastical authority, did not eliminate all senses of the sacred. As transcendental sacred objects faded from cultural centrality, sacred commitments to humanity remained. Secularization did not eliminate the evaluative aspect of human experience.

It may also be necessary to see that differences in gender, so often ignored by psychology (or worse, exploited in employment roles, such as those of nurses and doctors) in becoming a social role becomes more than a convenience for organizing families and professions. The differences between genders have been revealed, by feminists who are psychologists (and psychologists who are feminists), to be crucial differences between male and female perspectives. Feminist psychologists (Chapter 17), like all feminists, seek social justice between genders, but perhaps more important for this historical study, we have come to see feminism as revealing realities heretofore invisible to (male) psychologists.

It appears that social roles and accompanying perspectives have always been deeply gendered. Different perspectives supply different angles of vision. Looking at psychology, its questions, answers, pro-

grams, efforts, and the rest, from a feminine angle of vision came vividly into focus in the closing decades of the twentieth century. As an
oversimple but useful statement about the perspectives of men and
women, clinical problems in psychology mean to women that someone is in need of help; the same problems to men have often meant that
a disease process must be combatted. These are two very different attitudes toward clinical psychology. An exaggeration that falsifies the truth
but nevertheless makes the point is that "mastering nature" and "helping persons" are very different thematic centers of psychology, and
they thematize American constructions of gender, as well.

In clinical psychology, even as I see my client as a person, and even
as I am trained to categorize and to analyze, to study and understand
as a scientist does, therapy involves a perception that both makes and
does not make the person perceived into an object. I may empathize and
"feel his pain" (as I cannot do with an object), but my role demands
that I finally see the other without these sentiments in order to make a
"sound clinical judgment." Any time I tell myself to be "objective," I
am telling myself to mute my spontaneous emotional connections, reactions, and feelings in order to offer an unbiased and professional
reaction.

The feminist psychology explored in Chapter 17 has clarified this
problem enormously. Not only have feminists taught us about the male
character of mastering nature, but they have also taught us about the
female character of helping people. Feminists have also taught us that
the personal is political, that our personal relations are gendered, and
that gender is political. This vastly increases the range of psychology's
self-awareness.

Clearly, this is most easy to see in face-to-face clinical work. Such
face-to-face encounters confront the practitioner with tragedy and pain.
These must be appreciated personally, and yet decisions must be made
in terms of impersonal contexts. Feminists show us how it all is political. The outcome in therapy is a change in a life, and I am responsible,
to some inescapable degree, for that outcome in a way no scientist is
responsible for the knowledge he or she acquires.

This feature of clinical work inevitably makes therapy different from
science. It simplifies too much to say that clinical work is feminine
and science is masculine, for many of both genders do both well. But
feminists have made the issue inescapable. Influencing people is a
moral enterprise. Old themes of mastering a disease, like mastering
nature, limit us all to traditionally masculine sensibilities. The goal of
helping is not the same goal as that of mastering nature. Men were
helpful before twentieth-century feminism, but that feminism has revealed how traditional masculinity has limited our vision, and how
feminist thought enables us to recast old questions.

This polarity between helping people and mastering nature is not new. It has been with us forever, and doctors have always had to deal with this contrast in the practice of their trade. This is, perhaps, one of the reasons that psychotherapy and clinical psychology are seen as allied with the practice of medicine. The medical model and diagnosis that follows it in clincial psychology are impersonal. They come not just from the tradition of medical authority in insane asylums. They come also from what is central to science, a dispassionate quest that must be uncommitted to outcome. All that is masculine.

The uncommitted therapist, whose attitude is simply scientific, who is uncommitted to outcomes and holds nothing sacred, is a poor therapist indeed. This is secularization, which eliminates a sense of something sacred, but it is also a masculinization, which foregoes empathy in the quest for mastery. What is most wholesome in the feminist contribution to psychology is that it has affected not just the clinical enterprise but has also profoundly affected scientific research. Questions never asked about women, or gender relations, or the grounds of our thought have come into focus with the contributions of feminism.

This amounts to a less-than-total secularization. It does not preserve theological interests, it simply preserves a sense of commitment by insisting that something is sacred. Every science has a practical aspect where values inevitably come into play, and where the knowledge of expertise includes a mature sense of ethics. But in psychology the applied field is larger, and is more distinct from the traditional body of scientific culture that sought to master nature. Psychotherapy provokes some suspicion among scientists whose commitment to science is as deep as the moral commitment and sense of the sacred in clinicians. Different moral foci are less easy to tolerate interpersonally and organizationally than different intellectual foci.

This clinical–experimental split (helping people–mastering nature) that was vivid at mid-century (see Chapter 11) became less so by virtue of the impact of feminism. Women have probably made science less imperialistic and therapy more compassionate. Beyond that impact, however, there has been an enormous proliferation of applied settings, employment opportunities, and professional specialties and subspecialties in psychology. This development was inevitable in the context of American culture, which becomes more differentiated technologically and professionally every decade. In fact, the proliferation of psychological roles in American society has changed psychology from a bipolar field to a complexly fragmented and heterogeneous one.

The story told in this volume closes with three chapters that succeed the ideas and events of the enormously productive twentieth century. They cannot, of course, predict the future, and so whatever tentativity has accompanied this tale so far must be magnified in reading Part III. However, phenomenological (Chapter 16), feminist (Chapter 17), and postmodern (Chapter 18) themes will be some part of psychology's future. We include them in this history because they are already there in our history, but unlike much else in this history, they promise change, continued growth, and at least a nudge to the trajectory of this history in particular and describable directions.

NOTE

1. This is an uncommon attitude. Most commonly, historians of psychology see the "science" of psychology as the whole of psychology, and sometimes data as the whole of science. This emphasis on data runs the risk of taking ideas for granted. For example, Terman (1916) began the "testing movement" in psychology, which dominated much of eduational psychology for years. This work began with his and Yerkes's pioneering work on Army Alpha and Army Beta (Yerkes, 1921). They had the idea, the theory, that intelligence could be measured. Their scientific work led to Brigham's (1930) distortions of the findings into a kind of racist ideology. Even Yerkes (1921) himself wrote, in a clearly racist view, "It might almost be said that whoever desires high taxes, full almshouses, a constantly increasing number of schools for defectives, or corrective institutions, should by all means work for unrestricted and non-selective immigration" (p. 365). What eventually settled the matter was indeed data, collected more carefully, attending to sampling bias and test bias. The data won out in the controversy within science, and science won out in the controversy in the minds of many policy makers, but the whole matter would have been of little interest were it not for racist theory. Racist theory is incorrect, which we know for sure only because of the data. But it is the theory—ideas, including of course those we easily call "ideological," and in the case of racism, those that are impressively masculinist—that make data matter. Egalitarianism is also a theory, without which the effort to correct Yerkes may never have come about.

16

Phenomenological Psychology

Doing psychology phenomenologically is paying attention to behavior in a certain way. It describes and explains the behavior in terms of the subjective experience of the person behaving. Many pyschologists, especially James but also Tolman, Piaget, and Freud, included subjective experience in their explanatory repertoire; phenomenological psychology takes this interest a step further.

This further step differs from James and Piaget in that these two theorists more or less assumed that psychologists, the observers themselves, enjoyed the special privileges of objectivity that have accompanied the scientific tradition since the Renaissance. Before the twentieth century, all that one needed to do to enjoy that privilege was to imitate the attitudes of scientists, attitudes such as dispensing with one's personal preferences, being systematic in observing, focusing on reality intently and with as few preconceptions as possible, and being willing to disregard whatever reaction one might receive from others for seeing what one sees.

In the twentieth century, however, this earlier notion of objectivity seemed imprecise. Watson's positivism insisted that only behavior is knowable. Positivism was one way of tightening up the loose joints in knowledge getting. Later, Piaget's theories were immediately subjected to behaviorist–positivist verification in the 1950s and 1960s, after his writing became well-known. Freud's theory, too, somewhat less conclusively, was subjected to empirical–experimental testing during this time. Tolman's work was behavioristic from the start, and his attention to conscious experience was immediately translated into intervening variables in experimental work, which notably improved Tolman's predictive power over other behaviorists like Guthrie because of what he could therefore take into account in his predictions. All these methodological routines were a product of Watson's earlier translation of positivism into experimental psychological terms.

An entirely different, nonpositivist revision of epistemology came with phenomenology, begun by the philosopher Husserl (1900/1954) in Germany with the publication of *Logische Untersuchungen*, which he dedicated to Karl Stumpf, a student of Franz Brentano, who also inspired the development of Gestalt psychology (see Koffka, 1935).

This nonpositivist tightening of the notion of knowledge did not further narrow the range of data that may be considered, as positivism did. Rather, it expanded the arena of knowledge getting to include the scientist's consciousness, all of which had to be investigated. Since Husserl was a philosopher, his work was initially seen as philosophy with little relevance to psychology, especially in America. But Gestalt psychologists did not exclude the psychologist's consciousness. Gestalt psychologists not only systematically examined their own consciousness even as they were scientists doing science; they also wrote their psychology from these data. Applied to others, it provided useful hypotheses for understanding others. This focus by Gestaltists called some scientists to doubt that Watson had all the right answers, or even the right questions.

By the 1960s, existential philosophers, Heidegger (1927/1962) and Sartre (1943/1956), were being read by psychologists, and also psychoanalysts like Rollo May (May, 1950, 1967, 1969; May, Angel, and Ellenberger, 1958). Sartre reopened the challenge of human freedom, particularly, but the larger achievement was to reopen the theoretical question of consciousness to American view. Phenomenology thus became in America more than a French (Sartrean) litereature with an accompanying philosophy, and more than a German (Heideggerian) philosophy that claimed to undercut all other philosophy. Phenomenology became an aspect of American psychology.

Phenomenologists see their psychology as a twentieth-century methodological alternative to positivism in psychology. Of course, not all American psychologists were strict positivists; only the research literature adhered rigorously to that concept of objectivity. But it is true of American psychology that methodology looms large in every university's definition of the "psychology major." Phenomenology thus poses an alternative that cuts very deeply into the assumptions of academic psychology in this country.

The work of cognitive psychologists on human language and thought has roots in the nineteenth century, but it was greatly legitimated by the popularity of Piaget's writing. The cognitive revolution reopened the human mind for scientific investigation, but it has had little effect on the concept of scientific knowledge or the methodology that is taught in universities. Most of the literature of cognitive psychology conforms to the epistemology of positivism. The scientist is a detached observer, whose data always are "out there" in the laboratory, rarely "in here" in my own mind.

However, some psychologists in the past addressed consciousness and went beyond the consciousness of others, back into the consciousness of oneself as scientist. From Freud forward, for example, clinical psychologists knew of countertransference, the insertion of the analyst's feelings into his or her interpretation, forcing every psychoanalyst to analyze himself or herself as a regular part of analytic work with patients. In this sense, Freud might be called phenomenological, and others such as Rogers are also unafraid to call themselves phenomenological (Evans, 1975).

Such a characterization usually refers to an investigative focus on the subjective experience of the behaving organism. But when it refers also to an investigative focus on the subjective experience of the observer, then the impact of Husserl is unmistakable and an entirely new epistemological strategy is required. This is the stronger, broader, and more demanding phenomenological heritage from European phenomenologists (Keen, 1975).

Snygg and Combs (1949) anticipated much of this viewpoint in America, and Binswanger's analysis of Ellen West, in May and colleagues (1958), introduced existential phenomenology to clinical psychologists in America. In the same year, theologian Martin Buber republished his famous *I and Thou* (1923/1937), which later also came to be known by psychologists. Eugene Gendlin (1962) was an early American theorist sensitive to both Buber and Binswanger. Sidney Jourard's (1964) work appeared the same year as the translation from the French of Merleau-Ponty's *Primacy of Perception* (1964), a philosophical work.

Bugental (1965) was an early entry in the psychological elaboration of phenomenology, and R. D. Laing's famous *The Politics of Experience* (1967) was a potent stimulus. Giorgi (1970), Keen (1970), and Van den Berg (1973) all helped consolidate this perspective. Looking back we can see that Snygg and Combs (1949) also anticipated in this approach to psychology at mid-century, and fourteen years before, Kurt Lewin's *A Dynamic Theory of Personality* (1935) did so as well.

EXISTENTIAL PHILOSOPHY AS CONTEXT

Husserl (1900/1954) believed that the immediate translation of experience into terms dictated by Cartesian-based theories of perception led to a falsification of knowledge. This was called "psychologism" by Husserl. Most psychology works within a framework of causal science, which it has cheerfully embraced with Watson. When that set of postulates embraces the study of the mind, even the mind of the investigator, then those crucial origins of human experience lead to prior dynamics and structures of human being.

Of course these dynamics and structures are represented in science, but existentialists insist on human freedom, which the scientific framework of cause and effect cannot represent, except as an exception. Human existence is an exception, Sartre would say, and the refusal to center one's life in that exception—to live one's freedom consciously and rigorously every day—is living in bad faith. Much of psychology encourages this bad faith insofar as it leads people to experience their behavior as effects of causes, rather than as freely chosen paths within the realm of human existence.

Embracing a causal definition of that realm, as science necessarily does, leads psychiatry—and much of psychology as well—to recommend psychological therapy conceived, like other medical routines, as causing health instead of illness. The paradigm case of such treatment is psychopharmacology, the treatment of life problems by prescribing medicines that change the chemical causes of human experience in the brain.

Imbibing a chemical that causes me to feel better is a human possibility. But as a human being committing this act, I am giving myself over to the mechanics of brain chemistry. This is, of course, no different from alcohol or other such self-abdications, but unlike them, this one has the legitimacy of all of modern medicine. It represents the most widespread technological application of psychologism to human life yet devised.

Human history is full of such abdications, such as the giving of oneself over to Nazism in the 1930s or to television in the 1980s, but one can criticize these from a standpoint that is comprehensible to any open mind. In the case of psychopharmacology, the price paid for the convenience of the treatment is much higher than resisting Nazism or giving up television. The former may lead to your death and the latter to your boredom, but neither of these fates bypasses your essential humanity. Psychopharmacology does exactly that. There is little or no conceptual place in pharmacological theory or practice for an individual to realize his or her freedom.

Neither surrendering to Nazism or to television addiction pretends to be utterly humane in the way that the practice of medicine has committed itself. Sartre's theory of mind is strenuous, and it portrays our situation as one of severe demands. Were we committed to, or even acquainted with, Sartre's theory of mind, we would have considerable difficulty giving over our lives to a technology that compromises our very capability to experience anguish.

The current psychopharmacological situation engages the personal lives of hundreds of thousands of persons, who are told by all existing authority that their emotions are part of the material world ("You have a chemical imbalance in your brain. We have ways of treating these conditions"). If emotions have to do with decisions, then the complex struggles with human freedom (with which we are all familiar) becomes central. In psychopharmacology, that complexity is reduced to the single decision to "take your medicine."

THE SYSTEM

Phenomenological psychology has never been a system. But it is an obvious step to examine cases of ordinary persons in terms of their conscious experience, and cases of conscious investigators as well. Human experience, from this point of view, thus becomes the single most important starting point, and it is one that has a describable structure with describable events, limitations, and so on. We nearly always find human experience meaningful, and meanings occur within networks of meanings, called "horizons of meaning" by phenomenologists. Phenomenological psychologists may isolate three such large networks of meaning within which an investigator can begin to analyze, describe, and explore the intricacies of human experience itself (Keen, 1975). These horizons can serve as a starting point for appreciating phenomenology.

The first of these horizons is that of organismic functions, most especially one's own organism. One sees with eyes, and by the time we are adults, we have a sense of the limits of the mechanics of vision. In general, the mechanical substrate of perception occurs as physics would have it, determined and limited by physical variables like stimuli, which become neural energy transfers, and so on.

Vision is, however, more complex than the workings of a camera, because human awareness is more complex than any machine. Organismic functioning, even of the visual system, follows many of the laws of matter, but vision enters human consciousness and thus engages all the complexities of the other levels of human experience, which always give to human seeing such contexts as one's personal identity and social meanings.

In general, this organismic level of human meanings includes the leverages of bodily movement, which is understood in a layman's version of what physics describes more accurately. Also, a rush of emotion in one's body is mechanical and usually beyond the control of the experiencing person. Further, the relation between my physical position and my sensory input, or between effort and the fatigue of effort, are part of the organismic horizon.

Biological phenomena of adaptation occur within this network of meanings, so that maps of the environment and qualities of nutritional and other resources are important meanings. Such meanings permeate human experience, mostly as given facts taken for granted, which can with reflection always be questioned or even changed, and which also change spontaneously in the course of life, sometimes surprising us.

The organism–environment field is thus a coherent, structured network of meanings, many of which are simply given in experience, but some of which are manipulated by decisions I make. The "I" who makes such decisions, however, offers a second level of analysis. Unlike the more topographical and mechanical relations of organismic adaptation, for which cause and effect are inevitable descriptors, persons know they are free to make decisions within certain limits imposed by physical causality on the one side and moral constraints on the other.

This experiencing of self-in-world, this second network, a very different horizon of meanings, is added to organismic ones. Of course, all my organismic functions, caused and chosen, must be tended within the context of my self-in-the-world like everything else (the stringing of words together with hyphens, as in "being-in-the-world," indicates that the meanings of my being and of the world are mutually dependent and interconnected). However, when I see that I can decide not to eat when I am hungry, or not to rest when I am tired, I also sense that my limits are much less coercive than nature's calls. This leads me to experience eating and resting as decisions I make.

This experienced freedom also engages means–ends relations of longer duration, all of which add up to practical contexts. I may also violate practicality, too, "at will," but at costs I can anticipate, including what judgments I may make about myself. The second, practical horizon of meanings lies between the organismic and a third, moral–cultural horizon. Desire from the organism—from rage to fatigue—on the one side, and conscience—from morality to personal goals—on the other side, contextualize any decision I personally make at this second level of experience.

The third horizon of meanings is social. It comes not from biological (and physical or natural) variables and their causality, nor from psychological (and personal) contingencies with their practicality, although it overlaps these two. This level consists of patterns of interpersonal obligations and desires within traditional values represented in how others perceive oneself. In addition to simply obeying my organism, I obey, second, the practicality of my desires and choices, and third, I cannot be free of my embeddedness in a cultural context represented by those who will judge me. Sartre's poignant category of "being-for-others"—knowing one is always seen by others, and knowing that one is not really able to sustain indifference about that fact—is the clearest statement of this feature of human consciousness.

These three networks of meanings are "horizons," a phenomenological term that names enduring structural contexts within human experience. There are other, less universal but nearly always relevant specific horizons, such as a relationship with a life partner, an identity as a member of a profession or group, or a cultural or traditional obligation that is central to one's life. A phenomenological analysis of any human behavior, from being a subject in an experimental laboratory to being a patient in psychotherapy, or being a soldier, doctor, student, or thief, would describe the relevant horizons of meaning and how they are lived by the individual himself or herself.

One's self is always partly free, partly constrained by mechanics, and partly obligated by morality. As a free subject, I chose; as a mechanical object, I am determined; as I see others judge me, I—this self that I am—is perceived and judged by myself as I get through a day. These are what it means to be a conscious human being. I am, first, a subject, a mental agent located "in the world" (being-in-the-world); I am, second, a body and a repertoir of behavior, which I judge constantly (being-for-oneself); and I am, third, seen by others who apply their values to judge me (being-for-others).

THE SELF

William James, Sigmund Freud, and Carl Rogers are just three important psychologists who deal with the self. Each in his own way distinguished between a self-experience that experiences itself to be free to determine its own course through the complexities of life, on the one hand, and a self each of us "objectifies," makes into an object of our reflective self-perception. Freud's "ego ideal," James's "self-esteem," and Rogers's "ideal self" are all objectifications, not experiences of agency. These concepts refer to the experiential nexus that extends morality—our sense of good and evil—into a reflective, personal judgment of ourselves.

Since all human behavior is partly oriented to these horizons, it follows that any psychology about humans should engage the actual pushes and pulls, the meanings and challenges of that subjective experience within one's own consciousness. A psychology that ignores these aspects of human existence is doing so because of loyalty to a method that is closed to what these theorists would call "insight" into what makes us who we are.[1] Such insight pays attention to experience as it is experienced by humans. Because James, Freud, and Rogers all explore this territory, they have been called phenomenologists, which refers to their insistence that an inner life must be explored if psychology is to live up to its name.

Phenomenologists are hardly unique, but are perhaps more explicit, in distinguishing between a "subject self" and an "object self." The former is "inner," my conscious activities of making decisions, appreciating bodily impulses, drawing conclusions. The latter is who I "objectively" reckon myself to be, as seen by detaching and observing myself reflectively. Thus, it is quite inevitable that I have two selves, a self-as-object that I can see and a self-as-subject that sees.

It is not clear whether James, Freud, Rogers, and others, and especially phenomenologists, use conscious reflective experience in this methodological way simply out of loyalty to psychological reality, or even because they are trying to be phenomenologists. Instead, mental life is simply like this. Or is this distinction between self-as-subject and self-as-object, which is so ubiquitous and obvious, actually a latter-day version of what, at a deep level of experiential reality, is a continuation of dualism?

This is a profound question. As a subject I am free; I chose this course or that, every day. But I have limits. My freedom is not absolute. There are constraints, moral and aesthetic, but also causal. As an object I am caused. All together, both subjective freedom and objective causality seem to be true of human being. Perhaps such descriptions are loyal to psychological reality, or perhaps psychological reality appears as it does only because Western patterns of language and experience are powerfully dualistic.[2]

We really cannot be surprised that even after the escape from metaphysics and dualism there is a psychological reason to say that my self-as-subject is a mental life, which is a different kind of reality from myself-as-object, which includes my physical existence. Of course, all thought and perception is mental, but self-perception and reflective thought (about my thinking, for example) are actually formatted, in our experience, by objectifying ourselves, making myself into an object, not in the sense of a thing, but in the sense of that toward which I direct my attention (as opposed to the subject who is paying and directing attention).

This objectifying of the self is inevitable in personal self-experience and in psychology. Western thought simply is not coherent outside a subject–object format. Any self-objectifying experience marginalizes the self-as-subject, and any intense desire focused on an object in the world makes possible a vivid sense of self-as-subject, often marginalizing the self-as-object (i.e., the lack of reflection in the hungry animal or smitten lover).

Everyday experience of life does include both, more or less all the time, making the task of phenomenological analysis of experience necessarily complex, layered, and multimeaninged. It is rare indeed that a single meaning clothes a human experience. Never far from even a simple focus, such as looking at something in the world, for example, lies a marginal (phenomenologists would say "horizonal") sense of who I am.

This is the consciousness that phenomenological psychology describes. It is not quite like any other psychology, and yet it covers much of the same ground, but always in contexts that themselves come not from scientific traditions or former research, but from the phenomenological investigation of human being itself, mostly visible in existential and phenomenological philosopers like Sartre (1943/1956) and Heidegger (1927/1962). In the history of psychology, phenomenology is unique.

THE WORLD

Of all concepts in phenomenological psychology, the concept of the world is probably the most basic and most characteristic of both this psychology and of the philosophy from which it came. Of course, the world contextualizes our action; our action wouldn't be what it is without the world. Of course, the world's many meanings are much more assumed and reside more at the margin of our awareness than the specific meanings of objects. If we think that behavior is affected by what any given stimulus or situation "means" to the individual, then variations in the context of "world" are clearly decisive.

For example, the world of medieval Christianity was very different from our secular world, from which God has (been) withdrawn to the heavens—if God is thought to exist at all. We moderns may find aspects of the world indifferent to us, but some of these same aspects, in a world structured by a medieval sensibility, would be quite sacred. Trees, or other people, or the church, are parts of God's plan; they have an origin in a mystery greater than any person can understand. In this medieval perspective, the world is holy in ways that I myself can merely aspire to, for I am depraved but nevertheless beloved by a God who hopes I can be good.

In these short descriptive sentences about the medieval world we see how a self-understanding and a world-understanding are part of one another. If modern humans believe that how they construe themselves is unrelated to how they construe the world, they are merely illinformed, insufficiently reflective, and, as such, wrong. "World" to the modern eye is in fact a vastly different set of meanings than it was a few centuries ago. Society, too, our group, clearly mediates these meanings of the world, and even primitive peoples knew this. More provincial groups, the Yoruba, for example, never doubted that the superiority of their worldview came from their favored relation to the-istic powers (cf. Prince, 1964/1996).

To demonstrate the point that "world" as we know it is presup-posed, imagine, for example, that you get lost in a city and go about finding yourself, only to

discover that no matter from which side you view [certain] buildings, they are always blue, red, and silver, from left to right. . . . [Your own] circling in space is no longer having its usual effect upon your visual experience. Sup-pose that the faster you run toward the policeman, the farther away he be-comes, even though he is standing still. (Keen, 1998, p. 104)

To continue this phenomenological line of questioning, "Suppose that it is growing earlier rather than later, that it is in fact a different day, snowing whereas it had been summer before. Suppose that the people, instead of going places in a familiar way, are all looking at you, whisper-ing to one another, occasionally sharing suppressed laughter" (p. 104).

These unsettling experiences are of a very different world design from our own; few of us have had such experiences, although some nightmares or psychotic experiences are like this. What is most im-portant here, however, is how the meanings of each person or thing perceived depend vitally on the world design that contextualizes it. In this example, the world design is sufficiently surprising to us that nothing makes sense.

Thus, we see, when we look at different cultures, vastly different world designs within which everything means what it does according to its world context. Even within our own culture there is tremendous variation in the safety or structure of the world. If I grow up in a fam-ily in which love is taken for granted, I will understand the meaning of other people—their behavior, their authority, their obligations—according to a format different from that acquired from a family where everyone was in competition with everyone else that was split into factious camps, or the like.

Where in psychology can the powerful effect of such implicit mean-ings as world, or of self-in-the-world, be articulated as mattering? There is no doubt that such meanings matter to persons; to explore persons' behavior, we must explore their experience. In understanding behav-ior, it is the experience of the world that counts, of course. Once we have understood the role of the experienced world in human life, we can see that science itself also creates a world with a certain causal structure characteristic of physical things. Insofar as we are interested only in physics, this world need not mean anything that physics does not describe. But, of course, in psychology we know that human expe-rience is much richer in human meaning than physics can offer us; the world's meanings in our experience far outstrip what a science based on physics can deal with.

Phenomenological psychology intentionally separates itself from natural science insofar as it not only examines something different (subjective experience), but also finds much that is different from science (human and emotionally charged meanings). These meanings become comprehensible in, and in fact should be comprehended by, psychology.

THE PHENOMENOLOGICAL LEGACY

Psychology in its natural scientific mode examines its subject matter within a framework of natural relations: of causality, of adaptation to conditions, of acquisition of behavior. All of these psychological topics become, in traditional psychology, scientific objects. Even experiences become scientific objects, such as we see in measuring self-esteem the way one measures an object, or seeking a cause of an attitude the way one seeks the cause of a behavioral habit or a disease, or a performance of remembering as a measurable skill. These objectifications do not err; they do not falsify. But they objectify, and make into objective reality phenomena that must also be understood as subjective.

The legacy of the phenomenological alternative to such scientific work is hardly well-known at the beginning of the millennium. However, it can be said, after saying just this much, that phenomenological psychology is at once inclusive and exclusive. It includes most of what already exists in psychology in terms of large topics or subfields that have become very specialized, usually within a causal model of natural science. Often it excludes that causal model, or it understands the human experience of causality as one horizon of meaning amidst many meanings.

In phenomenology, purely mechanical relations, such as physiological relations, are not investigated as science does, but rather are investigated as they are experienced. Also, my free self, seeking practical paths to obvious goals, is studied, but not as seen by a scientist in a laboratory but as experienced by an active person. Similarly, self-in-relation-to-others, who mediate values and traditions, is also examined as experiences, or as aspects of human experience.

Phenomenology is simply not causal science; its goals and descriptions aim to enrich and make more specific and clear our understanding, rather than to specify prior causes or current correlates as explanations. Thus, phenomenology is not interested in distinguishing, for example, what is learned from what is innate, a distinction that was crucial for many psychologists for much of the twentieth century. This distinction simply does not matter very much unless one is seeking causes. For phenomenology, every individual is unique, but with universal characteristics. This distinction, between general and particular, seems more important to phenomenologists, for whom the distinction between learned meanings, motives, and behavior and those that are innate is of little theoretical consequence. In contrast, what is universal and what is particular to an individual are important empirical questions. The goal is to be descriptive of human being, individually, collectively, and universally. But each of these is a different description.

Similarly, the distinction between the healthy and the pathological is of little theoretical interest. A phenomenological quest for a definition of psychological health is not apparent, although such a definition is obviously crucial to scientific diagnoses of "mental illnesses." Even though phenomenologists could, as natural scientists do, statistically determine what is unusual, frequency does not indicate well or ill health. Like the distinction between learned and innate, the distinction between healthy and pathological depends on frames of reference one may use later, in practical contexts. Such considerations do not enter into the investigative work itself, which aims to create an analysis of the conscious (and self-conscious) being of persons.

Nor is it of interest to phenomenologists to create vivid separations between studies of individual persons and studies of social contexts. These may indeed vary independently, and that is not without scientific interest, but for phenomenologists, one's experiential life is always of and in a social (as well as natural) context. Thus, for phenomenological psychologists the interior content of personality and the exterior content of culture are so mutually dependent that they simply have to be studied together. Experience is, finally, the universal context that lies beneath even the natural sciences, which have carved out their domains according to pioneering leadership and political bargaining. Investigating experience phenomenologically seeks to make clear the data of science and of everyday life in a new and basic way, to undercut distinctions embedded in our traditional disciplinary loyalties, and to get at the structures and dynamics of what is universally shared by all persons.

NOTES

1. The concept of "insight" has two earlier appearances in psychlogy. Freud saw it as self-understanding; Koehler's is the more relevant analogue. Indeed, his description of ape "insight" is a description that says the ape is aware of the world, and of itself in the world (as opposed to moving in space the way a twig floats downstream).

2. To call attention to the subject–object duality that structures (at least Western) human experience is to alert us to inevitable biases embedded in our

linguistic coding of objects. To see an object independently of such biases is to somehow purify the categories of the perceiving subject. Indeed, it is to cease being an everyday subject and to begin being a pure subject, uninformed by the history and language that shape human experience. Husserl's philosophy sought to begin there, to achieve experience free of such influence. His argument describes this work, which is commonly called the "phenomenological reduction."

17

Feminist Psychology

The interaction between psychology and the larger culture that supports it is complex. One feature of the 1960s was an increase in cultural awareness of political issues. Racial and ethnic minorities, and the inequalities in their educational and economic opportunities and privileges, came into focus. What special adaptations do we expect of immigrants whose English is poor (an old issue, see Chapter 8)? How can the benefits of American society be extended to those suffering racial or ethnic discrimination? How are these injustices related to other injustices? How can violence and exploitation be prevented and compensated? In the case of women, of course, rape (including marital rape) is a prime example.

A number of writers who put the tragedies of ethnicity into literary form, a genre extending beyond the 1960s, were women (e.g., Morrison, 1970; Silko, 1977; Erdrich, 1988; Cisneros, 1991; Bambara, 1992). This consciousness of American injustice along ethnic lines went hand in hand with women's growing consciousness of gender injustices, which both preceded and succeeded the 1960s countercultural protests and celebrations of human solidarity.

In the early 1970s the Boston Women's Health Book Collective began putting together a volume of information that would help women supplement the information given to women by physicians. Many doctors were not only male, but fairly traditional, with attitudes indifferent to women's special situations, if not outright condescending. Patients generally did not get the information they wanted and needed from doctors, most of whom were overworked and rushed. Female patients asked more questions, and doctors seemed even less responsive in the face of such curiosity. The rather remarkable volume that emerged from this group was called *Our Bodies, Our Selves*, published in 1975; thousands were distributed noncommercially, and in 1984 there followed *The New Our Bodies, Our Selves*.

In addition to literary and medical treatment of women's issues, psychology became an obvious place to see feminist literature both explaining and responding to such prejudice and violence as had accompanied the traditions of male domination. A sample of this rich literature is Butler (1990) on identity, Nye (1990) on logic, Cornell (1991) on law, Bartky (1990) on sexual oppression, and various connections to what came to be called "postmodernism" (Seidman, 1992; Sawicki, 1991; Nicholson, 1989).[1] In 1996 Teresa Ebert published a strong statement that criticized the tendencies of even feminists by concentrating on personal lives and neglecting historical and economic dimensions of patriarchal domination. Ebert argues that neglecting this larger picture tends to trivialize feminism, which she characterizes and explores in her *Ludic Feminism: Postmodernism, Desire, and Labor in Late Captialism*. This volume reminds us all that the enormity and diversity of patriarchal manifestations is being matched by a continuing variety of analyses, none of which is irrelevant.[2]

WOMEN'S WAYS OF KNOWING

There are many psychologies of gender, as noted in the previous chapter, but one of the more remarkable claims is that women have ways of knowing that are to some degree specifically female (Belenky, Clincher, Goldberger, and Tarule, 1986). Knowing for women differs from knowing for men because girls are not raised as boys are. Of course, both boys and girls suffer from a sense that they don't know what adults know, but boys are shepharded through the gates of adolescence into manhood, then and now a very different goal of development than the motherhood and wifehood culturally envisioned for our daughters. Belenky and colleagues (1986) found that psychological development is greatly affected by this difference. The background fact that motivated this research is that girls and women have more difficulty than boys and men in asserting their authority or considering themselves as authorities (see Clance and Imes, 1978; Cross, 1968; Maccoby and Jacklin, 1974; Holmes and Purdy, 1992; West and Zimmerman, 1983).

Building on the work of Gilligan (1982) and Perry (1970), Belenky and colleagues (1986) interviewed 135 women for two to five hours each, producing over 5,000 pages of text. Naturally, the interviewers expressed interest in the subjects' experiences: their points of view, ways of deciding what is true and false, and so on. Of the 135 people interviewed, 90 were college students from five very different colleges. The rest came from the rolls of agencies designed to help families, both urban and rural. Hence, the sample included mostly students, but also women "stuggling to grow up at the edges of society where families are buffeted by such uncontrollable forces as irregular, stultifying, and demeaning work" (p. 14). Also present to some subjects were chronic violence and addiction to drugs, as well as inadequate and unsupportive institutions of all varieties.

Blind coding of the interviews followed Perry's (1970) scheme of five epistemological categories. Some women were (1) silent, simply voiceless, having no confidence that they know anything; others were (2) confident they could receive knowledge, but not create it; others were (3) confident that the knowledge they had was really theirs, but not confident that it would be shared by others; while yet others were (4) confident that they know in ways that could communicate objective knowledge to others; and, finally, others had (5) a sense that all knowledge, including theirs, is constructed and relative to context, but has truth value, both objectively and subjectively.

These are increasingly sophistocated senses of what it means to "know." The exploration of women's ways of knowing was motivated by an appreciation of the gendered inequalities embedded in obvious social roles (like "housewife"), with particular appreciation that cultural influences during development account for differences in how they know, and further, that these differences also explain why some women know similarly to men, but most do not.

Because of the traditional neglect of obvious gender discriminations, the psychology available for such work was inadequate to such "special problems" as various ways of knowing. Nevertheless, the theory and the practice of psychology offer vivid examples of this and other women's issues to be dealt with. First, a number of theoretical advances can be noted.

Nancy Chodorow (1989) and Judith Herman (1992) stand out as bringing feminist concerns directly into the theoretical and clinical literature. Chodorow's work of the 1970s and 1980s deals with socialization, family structure, American ideology of individualism, psychoanalytic theory, and therapeutic practice. She explores the internal dynamics of marriage, including phenomena of blaming (for example, of men by women for not feeling, and of women by men for not thinking). Freudian theory, so rich and useful in some contexts, may require considerable modification in order to accommodate feminist issues, or for that matter, in order to address human issues concealed by Freud's own cultural assumptions about men and women. Indeed, such "correction" of Freud's theory is elaborate among feminist analysts, and often it is designed to save Freud rather than to destroy him.

Or it is designed, by Chodorow (1989), to reread Freud in order simply to appreciate that his reputation as a sexist bypasses the insights he did have about women. For example, it is common to assume that Freud's interest was internal to the individual. True as this may be, it does not amount to an isolation of "human personality" or the "psychodynamic system" from the human context of other people, in families, with traditions, in historical time, and so on. Chodorow states, "An alternative psychoanalytic view of the individual and the self emerges, not from Freud's structural discussions or from the exhortation that 'where id was, there shall ego be,' but from his essay 'On Narcissism'" (p. 156). Chodorow corrects traditional perceptions that Freud is interested only in internal dynamics; in contrast, she points out that for Freud "relatedness is the sine qua non of mental health" (p. 156). She quotes Freud: "A strong egoism is a protection against falling ill, but in the last resort we must begin to love in order not to fall ill, and we are bound to fall ill if, in consequence of frustration, we are unable to love" (p. 156). This passage, from Freud's 1914 essay on narcissism, is as central to Freud's theory as are his theories about internal psychodynamics.

Beyond this kind of consideration, Chodorow (1989) explores how a theory like that of the Oedipus complex is indeed about social roles when stated in the abstract, but generalities like social roles hardly do justice to what Freud was up to. Human beings are always gendered and always sexual, so generalities can be articulated. But in thinking about individuals (and both Freud and feminists must think about individuals), Freud's message is that every individual is gendered and sexual. Thinking about any individual without giving these features of that life its due is to not take Freud seriously. This is as egregious an error as to fail to think of individuals in their individuality. Feminism, Chodorow then concludes, adds to and enriches psychoanaytic theory; it does not contradict it, nor it is contradicted by it.

In the hands of Judith Herman (1992), psychoanalysis and feminism again complement, rather than contradict, one another. In line with feminist traditions, Herman is very interested in the victimization of women by men, the battery, captivity, terrorism, abandonment, and other abuse of women by men that mars the human landscape. Her book, *Trauma and Recovery* (1992), describes in detail her work with victims of such abuse, focusing both on the internal dynamics of undergoing such traumas and on the route to recovery. Her first sentence reads, "This book owes its existence to the women's liberation movement" (p. ix), so her feminism lies at the very base of her work with female victims of male neglect and aggression. "The day-to-day practice that gave rise to this book began twenty years ago [now nearly thirty years ago] with the formation of the Women's Mental Health Collective in Somerville, Massachusetts" (p. ix).

The conflict between the desire to forget abusive trauma, on the one hand, and to proclaim them aloud, on the other, is called by Herman (1992) the "central dialectic of psychological trauma." Thus, victims vascillate between feeling numb and reliving the event, neither of which are therapeutic. And yet these natural reactions form the basis of therapeutic recovery after severe trauma. They interfere with everything else one wants to do, and therein lies the motivation for therapy, which indulges both getting past and acting upon the traumas of abuse. The stages of recovery that are described in detail are (1) the establishment of a trusting relationship with the therapist, (2) the establishment of a sense of safety, (3) remembrance and mourning, (4) reconnection, and (5) commonality.

In spite of Freud's failure to cite patriarchal traditions as misogynous, Freud again looms large in this therapy. The relationship of trust inevitably involves that mix of transference from someone trusted and someone who exploited and abused that trust. Safety, as an experience, is not easy to accomplish after a life-threatening trauma, and whatever earlier safe haven one had in one's life must be built on in order to construct a future.

Remembrance and mourning, clearly the most strenuous recalling and coping with the trauma itself, must at once acknowledge just what trust was violated and what world was destroyed, and at the same time envision the possibility that such a loss can be overcome by new trusts and new securities. Herman (1992) therefore teaches her clients to fight: Even self-defense training is detailed and serious. The loss cannot be recouped, but its repetition can be prevented; the past cannot be undone, but the future can be carefully shaped by physical as well as psychological confidence.

Reconnection, as a part of the recovery, is a step in elaborating the sense of sameness with others, and it often leads Herman's (1992) patients to be helpful to other victims who are at earlier stages of recovery. Once in a while this step yields recruitment of a former victim as a talented therapist. The commonality so created is feminist solidarity, felt at the end of recovery as fully as the most powerful connection any feminist has ever envisioned. It is not antimale, but it is surely antiviolence and, as militantly as any other occasions for feminist advocacy, it is profemale, especially in settings of male abuse.

We see, of course, that such settings as Herman (1992) creates, intensify the support and healing that feminism was made for. It compensates for the most costly outcome of the centuries-long tradition of male domination. However, we must not fail to appreciate a more profound feminist gain in this psychological work. It affects more people than victims of explicit male violence. More people are involved in the psychological pathologies that come from traditions of male domination and misogyny. And more people, especially women but also men, are helped in the treatment and compensation required by these pathologies. The overall effect of feminism as a cultural force is strengthened by these psychological innovations in both theory and practice.

THE RECOVERED REPRESSED MEMORY DEBATE

There also are ways that feminism approaches features of our personal lives that are threatening to some. Psychology from the beginning threatened to expose self-deceptions, to replace mythology (including religious myths) with scientific truth. Defenders of religion felt understandably threatened by the development of psychology, and some psychologists (perhaps Watson) enjoyed the scientific confrontation of religious beliefs a bit too much. Feminist psychology, however, deals inevitably in the currency of different myths, those of feminine inferiority to masculinity. The entire structure of male privilege depends on the myth that women are not moved by the truth, that they are "emotional" instead of "rational," and so on.

Feminist psychology replies in two ways. First, it disputes some of the prejudice that women are by nature more irrational than men, but second, conscious that rationality is not the only value in life, feminism accepts and even celebrates the human creativity, imaginativeness, emotionality, and flexibility that rationality so often rejects.

All these struggles are cultural, and the "memory debate" of the closing decade of the twentieth century is a part of them, and of feminism's broader participation in cultural changes. This debate is quintessentially psychological; it engages the issue of whether it is possible for a woman to recover, in adulthood, memories that were repressed in childhood. As both a professional psychological issue and a cultural one, it became a test not only of the veracity of women, but of the validity of a psychology that made it plausable that therapy allows memories of childhood abuse to surface that had become unconscious.

On one side, Loftus and Ketcham (1994) say that such events as recovering repressed memories of childhood abuse are unlikely. On the other side, Hovdestad and Kristiansen (1996) say that such events are possible and such memories should be taken seriously. At a level of technical science, there either is or is not (depending on how you read it) evidence that memory is sufficiently multimodal for a particular episode to have happened, to have been forgotten, only to reappear again. At the level of cultural struggles between feminists and the traditional culture of male domination, there either is, or is not, justification for recovered memories to be taken seriously. Taking such memories seriously involves many things, such as confronting one's perpetrator (if he is still alive), perhaps suing him, perhaps explaining to the world the origin of other peculiarities in one's personality, and certainly explaining to oneself the origin of such symptoms as sexual unresponsiveness, overresponsiveness, anxiety, and so on.

Insofar as the science of psychology is concerned, there is no better example of the ambivalent relationship that has always existed between psychology and other aspects of the culture that supports it. In this case, the cultural ambivalence follows two lines of thought: First, the culture approves of a psychology that serves the culture by bringing perpetrators of incest to justice, and second, the culture does not approve of a psychology that encourages women to find excuses for their shortcomings by accusing their fathers of incest.[3]

Both of these can be seen as reasonable aspects of the culture, and so the actual possibility of having a psychology of recovered repressed memories, which can, years after the woman was a child, lead to accusations and even convictions for rape, is greeted by the culture with resounding ambivalence. The simple question of whether a father raped his daughter when she was a child turns out to be an enormously complex one in terms of the culture.

Some of that ambivalence is the culture's ambivalence about feminism; it is impossible to say how much. The second line of thought, which blames psychology for causing such trouble, is ill-conceived. Tensions within families are not created by psychology; incest happens whether there is psychology or not. And it is not psychology that leads people to seek and find excuses for shortcomings. Both incest and rebellion against fathers are motivated by motives independent of psychology. But equally ill-conceived is the notion that psychology can answer scientifically such questions as whether a particular person, or persons in general, can attribute certain aspects of adult personality to childhood trauma, and especially whether a father should be convicted of incest on the basis of memories whose veracity is uncertain.

The problem lies in the quest for a simple answer that applies in general. In some circumstances, psychology can answer questions about why one is as he or she is; in other circumstances, psychology cannot do so. Battles between daughters who accuse their fathers of incest and fathers who accuse their daughters of lying, or between psychologists who encourage daughters to do so and those who discourage it, are cultural battles in which feelings run very high. Stakes balloon into the making or breaking of one's reputation, the destruction or preservation of family solidarity, the conviction of acquittal of an accused rapist—and psychology gets caught up in it inevitably. The claim to be a science echoes very strangely when such a deep cultural struggle looks to science for an adjudication.

In 1998 a symposium of the American Psychological Association entitled "Recovered Memories Controversy: A Study in Social Construction," in which I personally was a panelist, revealed the intensity with which psychologists themselves had gotten caught upon the cultural debate. Indeed, psychology took this debate on as its own; the packed room of psychologists attending the symposium seemed to feel every extreme of emotion one can see in other contexts on this issue. It is a testamony not only to the power of such emotional conflicts within the culture, but also of psychologists willingness to participate, many in the hope of one or the other side winning, fewer in the hope of merely elucidating the depths of human feeling that every culture, including our own, must at once believe in and be critical of.

The discussion was so emotional that our time schedule simply collapsed; I and others on the panel had to abbreviate our remarks drastically. For my part, I entirely jettisoned my paper, and produced instead the following diatribe which I scribbled quickly while watching the symposium consumed by emotion:

What I Have Learned from the "Recovery of Repressed Memory" Debate

1. That what we call truth is rarely final; it is always subject to revision.
2. That rules of evidence are mere conventions, in science, in a court of law, in psychotherapy, and in the press.
3. That ambiguity must be tolerated.
4. That this tolerance is especially important when the lack of certainty can be exploited: e.g., by daughters who are certain their fathers need convicting, and by fathers who are certain their daughters need correcting.
5. That people get hurt by such exploitation.

* * *

6. That authorities, procedures, rule-in and rule-out conventions are designed to establish not absolute but merely a "called truth."
7. That such "called truth" will nonetheless be expoited by both sides.
8. That the entire culture needs to deny what it calls truth is really just "called truth" instead of "true truth."
9. That this amounts to a denial of ambiguity in life.
10. That this denial of ambiguity is at once always pragmatic, personally commital, and inevitable.
11. That conflict among people with different interests is inevitable.

* * *

12. That real truth is an ideal construct like "perfect circle," where perfection is asymptotically approached.

13. That imperfection is thus inevitable.

14. That the issue thus becomes *when* to call ambiguity a non-ambiguous truth.

* * *

15. That the everyday operation of a culture depends on calling an ambiguity a simple truth.

16. That doing so always risks hurting someone's interests.

17. That social dynamics of established power usually determine who is hurt.

18. That a power position in a power structure is never safe from upstarts.

19. That such upstarts' claims for truth are no more certain "perfect circles" than the claims of established power.

20. That mobilizing power always unveils pretense.

21. That unveiling pretense always pretends, denies it pretends, and accuses the other of pretending.

22. That these findings—what I have learned—have always been true.

As much as I am convinced that the debate would not have happened without feminism, I am also convinced it really offers no advance, either for feminism or for the culture. Indeed, the attack on the established prerogatives of both male and patriarchal interests may seem heroic, but I do not believe the debate constituted much progress against them. However, the fact that the argument is inconclusive is perhaps less important than the fact that it took place at all. After all, such things are, in polite society, unspeakable. That unspeakability itself has been broached, and in broaching it, some of the traditional power structure has lost a traditional line of defense.

There have always been incestuous fathers, whose power depends on silence. Even if this attack is on innocent fathers, as it sometimes may be, it is clear that the traditional silence no longer cushions any parent or any male from undeserved privilege. As an exercise, then, in feminist political struggle against the entrenched privileges of males, backed up by codes of silence, this inconclusive outcome may be both necessary because of the absolute position on both sides and, in fact, more than inconclusive. Science did not push back the protections of villany, but feminism did.

This is essentially the same kind of victory (over a conspiracy of silence) that Judith Herman (1992) is seeking when she proposes a new diagnostic category: "complex traumatic stress disorder." There already exists a diagnostic category, "post-traumatic stress disorder" that applies to victims of combat, floods and fires, auto accidents, and other assaults on one's body, mind, or both. What is new is the adjective, "complex," and what is signaled with that addition is what Terr

(1991) distinguishes when she differentiates the effect of a single episode, which she calls, "Type I trauma," from "Type II trauma," which comes from prolongued and/or repeated trauma. Herman (1992) notes, about this diagnosis, "Empirical field trials are underway to determine whether such a syndrome can be diagnosed reliably in chronically traumatized people. The degree of scientific rigor in this process is considerably higher than that which occurred in the pitiable debates of 'masochistic personality disorder'" (p. 120).

We may also observe that feminism's impact on psychology is thus palpable. The earlier category of "masochistic personality disorder" relied on an old concept, masochism, which Freud believed sometimes describes especially, but not exclusively, female personality. In that case, "masochism" was absorbed by the culture from very early usage by Freud, and it was parlayed into attributing blame to the victim of battery, especially of wives by husbands.

In other words, the rigor that decades ago was used in establishing such a personality disorder was visibly compromised by popular prejudices of the worst, misogynous kind: "If she is beaten, she must be masochistic." Diagnoses are never particularly accurate, but the difference noted by Herman (1992) between 1992 and much earlier concepts of masochistic personality disorder is a difference that may be attributed to consciousness raising by feminists about the degree to which sexism had been common sense in modern America.

Similarly, the recovered repressed memory debate is about much more than recovered repressed memories. As a closing note in contemplating the effect of feminism on psychology, I call to attention the fact that Division 35 of the American Psychological Association is the Society for the Psychology of Women, and that at the convention in Washington, DC, in August 2000, one of the four miniconvention programs that took place in the first three days of the meetings was "Women in Science and Technology." The impact of feminism on psychology has not only changed the content of textbooks and produced a substantial amount of theoretical and research literature, but also continues to affect the bureaucratic structures of the APA itself.

NOTES

1. I cannot neglect to note how conservative, antifeminist voices continue in the twenty-first century to loudly proclaim the testosterone-driven character, and thus the inevitability, even the legitimacy, of male domination, even in its archaic forms (see, for example, Sommers, 2000).

2. Many feminist have joined the postmodern critique of discourse, for how we state matters not only shapes them but, more important, shapes how we understand them. Ebert (1996) does not quarrel with this thesis, but she

notes that focus on discourse by feminists obscures the effects of class and material conditions. While it is easy to see this protest within feminism as a detail, in fact it brings to the fore the central question of agency. In Marx, the problem of exploitation targets exploiters; ideology and social relations are caught up in what is fundamentally a material exploitation. The turn toward "discourse" as an analytic focus threatenes to make the means of exploitation into a focus that obscures the ends. Such distractions from the agency of patriarchy, and from the ends of such agency, seem to Ebert (1996) to be beside the most cental point of feminism. And we must say that this thought by Ebert is very much to the point of both feminism and psychology.

3. In fact, feminist psychologists were often accused of implanting such memories. Loftus and Ketchem (1994), for example, state that "repressed memories do not exist until someone goes looking for them" (p. 141).

18

Postmodern Psychology

TWENTIETH-CENTURY PSYCHOLOGY AND DUALISM

We must surely say that twentieth-century psychologists took up questions other scientists avoided. It is also true that the answers psychologists pose do not establish, but they are still shaped by, a dualism formulated as a one-to-one correspondence between mind and brain. This has been called "psycho-physical parallelism," which acknowledges a difference between mind and body and simultaneously pronounces a nondifference between mind and brain, at least as far as individual functioning is concerned.

At the level of ideology, on the other hand, collective thinking is in no one's brain and in everyone's brain. This independence of ideas from neurology is like the independence of any shared behavior from any single individual's body. This explains why there seems to be peace on the dualism front in psychology, a consensus that is rarely questioned.

Problems of location (Where is the mind?) and morality (Do I really decide, or do brain events run my life?) are left unresolved, of course. That may be appropriate at our current level of science; that level may not ever be transcended within science as we know it. Hence, the puzzle of free will and determinism not only offers alternative answers to specific questions, but also distinct formats for making life intelligible. The duality in these answers and formats is our dualism, which will be with us for the indefinite future.

Psychology had, indeed, at least by the end of the twentieth century, given up on such matters. This, of course, conforms to the dominate philosophy of science of the twentieth century, a positivism that seeks not wisdom but technological reliability. And, in fact, we see, even as early as William James, a sense of the limits of science. Those limits did not, however, distinguish as sharply between facts and values as positivism in the twentieth century has led us to do.

Social scientists in the nineteenth century, such as sociologists and economists, also offered both descriptions and recommendations (i.e., both facts and values). However their prepositivist format tended to be more coherent. One's recommendations followed from one's descriptions and depended on them. If one had a description of society as a class struggle provoked by the unequal sharing of industrial profits, and the wealthy consolidated their power to maintain this unequal distribution, that description led to the recommendation that the working class rebel and correct matters by force. Clearly, recommending revolution as Marx did depended on his description; the value statements would make no sense without the factual ones.

However, there is, of course, the remaining question that has no resolution, whether the values drive the facts or the facts drive the values. Maybe Marx's descriptions came from the prior values of revolutionary distaste for class privileges prior to industrialization. Maybe the prior values made the descriptive part of Marx's work what it is, instead of the other way around.

Such a question presents an intellectual challenge that is always appropriate. Does science or common sense hold the truth? Does the causality of the brain's material nature determine one's values, or is there some human freedom that decides value questions, and the brain follows a lead originating elsewhere? In the twentieth century, we saw a (modern) tendency to equate facts, their existence, and their discovery by scientists as purely intellectual matters that are totally divorced from more emotionally felt values. Indeed, the entire edifice of scientific methodology is designed to get at the truth independent of the emotional or evaluative quirks of the seeker; in a word, to purify facts by ridding them of human values.

Twentieth-century science thus split facts from values in a way that cancelled out the urgency of dealing with this question by pretending that facts can be value free and stand on their own. This positivist tenet is dogmatic; it neglects to note that facts never simply are what they are. They always "are" for an observing person who is situated in a world, with a personal and ideological history that makes the facts echo one way or another.

The positivist notion of a pure and simple fact is a myth. It may exist in a way, but as soon as it is acknowledged by a human being, the situation and contingent character of that human being determines the fact's meaning. At the same time, many psychologists, among other scientists, could in the twentieth century avoid deciding what any fact evaluatively meant. The tradition of positivism told us, and we believed it, that our own situated context was "merely subjective" (or "emotional" or "involved"), as opposed to the "real" (or "cognitive" or "detached") business of science, which was value-free knowledge.

Trained to understand science this way, American psychologists elaborated the intellectual posture that makes science totally neutral with respect to the value issues of the day. No one who did psychology quite achieved such objective purity in the twentieth century, but we pretended we did, or worse, we defined our discipline in this way.

Postmodern trends sometimes point out that this is absurd. Any person's attention to a question that precedes the acquisition of a fact or the recognition of a fact is driven by a consciousness that is engaged in the world's struggles as fully as it is engaged in eating food or keeping warm. Science is an extension of these motives, not a free-standing, extrahuman endeavor. And to pretend otherwise is a serious compromise of one's self-conscious recognition of the value-laden character of all that one does.

It is, of course, true that much science is equally available to doctors who would cure disease and dictators who would manipulate populations. But to reduce psychology to such technological status demeans it in the larger picture. Even though psychologists may have believed that science had no moral content—and in traditional terms, it did not—they never doubted that they were benefiting humankind by doing this science, and had they had serious doubts along these lines, they and most scientists would see themselves and their careers differently than they did; for example, as merely "self-serving."

To the extent to which this "self-serving" conclusion became true in late twentieth-century psychology—and it is not all wrong—psychology became something very different from what it was early in the century. It did not occur to psychologists a century ago that they were indulging personal motives. Science was, it seemed, their guiding value. But with the suspicions of postmodern thought, psychologists must consider how their motives have affected their science. If my motives for doing science affect the content of the science, then my motives are embodied in the facts. And pure, value-free science is an ideal, not a reality.

In other words, the scientific enterprise, carried out by human beings, is not as mechanical as the scientific universe is envisioned to be. Entire bodies of knowledge embody ideology. Nazi science did so; modern medicine does so. These are different ideologies, to be sure, but neither science occurs in a political and ideological vacuum, bereft of values and interests. Is the flourishing of American psychopharmacology, financed largely by the pharmaceutical industry, an enterprise unaffected by pharmaceutical interests?

In addition to the mechanical universe envisioned by science, there is the historical, human universe that contains and motivates the science. The root metaphor of science is "causality"; the root metaphor of human behavior is "motive." Bodies are caused; motives are chosen by free-willed minds.

The mind–body question is still alive in psychology, and psychologists now, like psychologists earlier, offer important corrections to Watson's reduction of reality to physical bodies. But as specialized as it became, psychology's connection to the metapsychological issues of facts and values became further obscured.

POSTMODERN STUDY OF PERSONS

Postmodern thought criticizes the ideology that says that knowledge stands alone, independent of human motivation. Further, human beings not only chose their knowledge; they bring nonscientific motivations to its very creation. With postmodern thought, these nonscientific impulses open American psychology to centuries-old sensibilities so often neglected in the modern rush of technological mastery. Romanticism, for example, as we saw it in American letters in the nineteenth century, offered much to psychology in the centuries that follow it (Hartman, 1954, 1964, 1987, 1997; Krystal, 1988; Lane and Schwartz, 1987; Mayer and Gaschke, 1988; Mayer and Stevens, 1994, Sundararajan, 2000a).

More specifically, to say that knowledge is a social construction, to deny that our knowledge is forced on us by the stubborn and intransigent shapes of the real world, is to deny to science its central claim. It is to say that knowledge is shaped not by the objective realities of matter and energy and events but rather by (or at least also by) intersubjective social, historical, and ideological factors that inform human knowing.

The postmodern claim, if it is true at all, is clearly true more for some knowledge than for other knowledge. Studies like those of Thomas Kuhn (1962) and Paul Feyerabend (1975) have suggested to many that even the most robust of physical sciences are not beyond the reach of this claim, at least now and then, under certain conditions, and so on. But the kind of knowledge least able to defend itself against a postmodern critique is knowledge about ourselves, about knowing itself, and especially about our knowing of one another.

To attempt to combat these ideological pushes and pulls, so characteristic of the modern period, we imported the methods of the physical sciences, which in turn led to an entirely modern body of "social science." This establishment has become elaborate—in professions, careers, academic departments, entire colleges, and certainly in compartments of government, business, and the nonprofit or NGO sectors of human effort on one another's behalf. Nowhere do we find an antidote to the postmodern suspicion that our knowing of one another says less than we think about the persons known and more than we think about the knowers themselves, we ourselves, our social–historical projects, our way of locating ourselves in the historical drama of humankind, and our moral judgments.

It is more and more commonly agreed now that even though we can tell the difference between men and women, our concepts of femininity and masculinity are socially constructed. It is only slightly less commonly believed that these socially constructed concepts are then read back into nature as properties of our biological (i.e., "natural" rather than "historical") reality. If we have socially constructed our fundamental concepts of gender, then our trust in both common sense and social science, which assume that our concepts follow nature, must be reassessed. The discovery of this misattribution of the source of our concepts, our very knowledge of ourselves and one another, undermines social science as surely as it does common sense.

Current critiques of social science suggest its descriptions of persons are indebted to the common sense that somehow escapes our scrutiny. We do *not* know when we are correct to attribute our descriptions of persons to their "natural endowment," or to some other inherent property of persons known. Another vivid example of the postmodern critique of psychology comes with uncovering the metonymy (a kind of sleight-of-hand with words) concealing the agentic nature of emotions and feelings. What was nature (physiology, acquired by way of evolution) becomes, in postmodern analysis, history (socially constructed concepts in a rhetorical context). What was seen as the center of emotion, its physiology, becomes not the whole but merely a part, a mechanism or means of expression, of a different center. The new center is human action carried out within a network of rhetorical meanings in an historical context.

Our "knowledge" of emotion has suffered from an understandable but fatal tendency to reify it. Psychologists are bound to ask what emotion is (Candland, 1967). Any answer presumes a frame of reference or model of behavior. The model of human being inherited from Descartes, as a ghost in a machine, leads us to assume that emotion is a physical event in the mechanism of my body, which I, as a ghostly consciousness, can perceive. James (1890) assumed as much in his theory of emotion.

Reification has taken place here in ways that are less obvious than the Titchenerian tendency to identify emotion as a thing. The more subtle reification is that the event has come to be understood as an event happening in the mechanics of the body. Emotion is, in most psychological lexicons, a bodily event. This reification is subtle because it seems so unquestionable. It is as if our only other way to think about emotion is to describe something in the ghostly consciousness that perceives the machine (Sartre, 1957, of course, sees emotion as a choice).

Those of us engaged in clinical psychology have a different but not necessarily better way of conceiving emotion, following a somewhat different metaphor adopted from Freud. Emotion is some kind of energy, flowing through an apparatus that regularly discharges that energy in cathexes and catharses. Another reification has occurred here: Emotion for Freud builds up over time, and thus it moves, in the twinkling of an eye, to energy that accumulates as in a battery, a central concept of nineteenth-century physics. Humors had been such a stuff, a much older format for reification. The mechanical metaphor still underwrites both twentieth-century reifications, even though a stuff that accumulates has quite different properties from events that are sensed in the body.

STRUGGLING WITH THE
REIFICATION OF EMOTION

Emotion may be seen as neither a bodily event nor an accumulating stuff. Instead, emotion can be seen as a quality of human action. It thus acquires an adverbial status, modifying the verbs of our lives, nowhere being a noun (Sarbin, 1964). I quarrel angrily; I love passionately; I confess fearfully. The anger, passion, and fear are not nouns, not things. They are how I do what I do. They are qualities, with intensities, which in turn are accurate expressions of the character and degree of involvement I have in the action at the time.

But if emotion is neither an event nor a stuff, what does one study when one studies emotion? Emotion may be accompanied or even implemented by bodily secretions and exertions, suggesting the relevance of the mechanical body. And it might appear in one situation when it originated in another, suggesting the accumulation of stuff that gets displaced or transferred. But to say we have thus understood the emotion may miss much of what emotion is and how it works in our lives.

Indeed, the role we give emotion in our lives is the role that we allow it by the model of human life that we employ. Thinking in terms of narrative psychology (Sarbin, 1986), emotion becomes a part of historical action rather than a part of mechanical or biologically conceived nature. Emotions are a part of life, and life is paying bills, fixing a flat tire, falling in love, suffering an illness. Life can be seen as mechanically moving through the environment driven by energy or humoral accumulations, and such models make lucid some of those aspects of life formerly not understood. But life is, we should insist, a matter of being a person, with an identity, a past, and a future, and some concern for the moral status of our identity, which we know is being judged by others (Sarbin and Keen, 1997).

Life so described is the stuff of narrative, in brief. The root metaphors of matter and energy adopted from physics, including the machine analogy, falsifies our theories in psychology. The tendency to reify emotion leads us to investigate it without reference to its most important role in life, which is to "modify" (to use the grammatical word) or qualify, intensify, or variously color our actions.

Just as the machine analogy leads us astray from this cardinal point, so also does the biological–evolutionary perspective lead us to interpret emotion in an errant way: as a signal, to oneself or others, with evolutionary significance. That it has significance cannot be doubted, to ourselves and to others toward whom and in the presence of whom we feel emotion. But that meaning has little to do with evolution; it has to do with who we are and what we think, and want others to think, of what we are doing. Its meaning frame, in other words, is the narrative we are and the narrative we are enacting whenever we act.

When we psychologists are not caught up in the modern historical project of transforming moral choices into naturally caused events, meanings that are insurmountable to us assert themselves, and we engage the rhetorical context within which emotions, indeed, all behavior, takes place. Human behavior is rhetorical. It makes a statement in a context of social relationships. It enacts a story, which is offered to others as having a point—at the very least, the point that I exist. I am part of the context of social relationships and their many meanings.

The analysis of such a context is necessary in order to understand behavior. This is true of all human behavior, for all human behavior is social. It addresses a world in a fashion intending to be noticed, and in a world that intends to notice.

The isolated frontiersman may seem, for example, to address only the natural elements in order to hew wood for heat and catch game for food. But why does he do so? The commonsense notion of survival tells us why, in a biological framework. But why does he want to survive? As an effect of an evolutionary cause, we have an explanation. But post–twentieth-century psychology must see more. Even frontiersmen mean various things in surviving. Some want to provide for a family, others want to please God, and yet others want to rebel against the politics of village life.

Most of us would find mere survival to be an impoverished explanation for why we do what we do. Indeed, mere survival is also a narrative plot, without which the physical fact of survival is meaningless. Hence, the narrative becomes the center. To assume that nature with its mechanical or organic order makes life meaningful ignores what must be emplotted in order for human meaning to exist. Mere survival without such meaning yields little of interest to survivors themselves. In real life, we conceive of ourselves in a context of human relationships, institutions, and historical actions by others that address us and to whom we respond when we act. If life is like that, so also should be our theory.

NARRATIVE PSYCHOLOGY

As clinicians we have heard, from patient after patient, stories— *their* stories. The stories were not always clear, and sometimes we had to help to tell them, but invariably people have stories to tell, and those stories are who they are. Narratives have all the structures of human experience: central actors and events, against a setting, with a past that is remembered and a future that is anticipated, in a context of relationships of love and hate and a culture defining good and evil.

It may have been only in the last several centuries that the narratives people live are so singularly personal; that is, centered around the person of oneself, with the time span bounded by birth and death, the characters limited to self and auxiliaries, and the space one's residences and haunts. Certainly, before the sixteenth century, the story lived by most people in the West was the story told in sacred texts, and it was about the people themselves as only minor actors in a drama of God in the cosmos, interacting with mankind but not primarily about themselves as individuals. The time boundaries and the space markers—indeed, the world design—was different.

As we look back at Christian Rome, we see an integration of local and cosmic stories, and the same is true with the ancient Hebrews and Egyptians. The first-century Christians and the fourth-century Athenians are especially interesting to us, for they show us stories in the process of radical and yet lasting change.

"Myself" appears somewhat differently in all these periods, but never so vividly as in modern times. In the eighteenth, nineteenth, and especially twentieth centuries, cosmos is reduced to mere backdrop, and even local units like nations and families eventually give way to my self as the central focus of the narratives we live. I recall a conference on autobiographies, where one of the participants was a publisher, who said that there had been periods in his memory when it seemed everyone had an autobiography to publish. Movie stars and sports figures, cab drivers and prostitutes, old people and the most recent addition, young people. He was especially skeptical of the value of this last group and reported one agent who was trying to sell him the autobiography of an eleven-year-old. He was not reassured by the agent's guarantee that the author had the wisdom of someone twice his age.

Everyone's story is, of course, bound to his or her own perspective. Therapists cannot help but notice, let us say, that an account by a client of a fight between the client and his son tells "only one side of the story." Furthermore, the father is often unaware of the limits of his own perspective, or how his particular slant on things is just that—a particular slant—instead of the objective truth. As we listen to stories, we are sometimes impressed with how one's particular slant on things throws into bold relief whatever would justify the storyteller and would obscure whatever might implicate him or her. Therapists especially notice how a teller's perspective seems to exaggerate his or her own weakness, fault, and culpability. This is also—and we shall return to this point—a kind of justification, a self-explaining if not self-serving kind of perspective.

One's story guides one into the future as well. It ties future options to past determinants by the coherence inherent in narratives themselves. That is, a narrative demands a certain order and interrelatedness of parts in order to be recognized as a story one can follow. These "stays of coherence" are exactly the same things that make one future option appear to be the right one, given who we've been, and other options to be wrong, incoherent, or—according to rules never quite articulable—somehow dissonant.

But the most important feature of much narrative is beyond even these considerations. It is the fact that my narrative makes myself intelligible to my self (and the story of psychology makes being a psychologist intelligible to myself). My story is my intelligibility. Insofar as I am not a nervous stutterer in the babble of life, grating abrasively against my past, my future, and my present situations, it is because I understand who I am, or perhaps I should say I have an understanding of who I am, and that understanding protects me from the chaos and anxiety of being not intelligible, of having no place, no identity, no roles, no functions or ways of mattering in the context of everyday experience. It is practically impossible to imagine my life without my story. Indeed, it could no longer be mine, for my self is that story. There is no me or mine without it.[1]

Returning now to our patients, we all have listened to many stories and we find that they may be characterized from the outside as biased and self-serving, but they have to be characterized from the inside as the framework within which everyday experience becomes intelligible. Patients differ from other people in that they are also telling us about something that is *not* intelligible. There is a catch somewhere, a symptom, a thought, or an emotion that seems to them ego-alien, or a relationship that keeps getting out of control, or a mood they cannot explain, or at the very least a person who tells them that something is drastically wrong even if they themselves do not sense it. Almost always, of course, they do; they sense something is radically out of joint in the narrative they tell, enact, and are.

In one sense, that out-of-joint something is part of, even the center of, the story they have to tell. That which was unintelligible to them becomes intelligible as one of those psychological misfortunes that befall people, as symptoms, by definition unintelligible but, because they fulfill that qualification of symptoms or psychological distur-bances of some kind, become intelligible.

This intelligibility of what was unintelligible is, in our culture, the last defense against meaninglessness. If the plot or events or people are meaningless in their narrative content, that fact at least is mean-ingful in a clinical context—as a disease. That last-ditch, desperate meaning is the by-product of telling one's story to a psychologist. Such an act not only "adopts the patient role," as we say, it also changes the former narrative of someone who didn't have a psychological prob-lem to a new narrative of someone who for a long time did not and then did, or someone who has always had one but only now realized it, and so on.

SELF-REPRESENTATION AND DUPLICITY

Inevitably, presenting one's story to a psychologist (or to a biogra-pher, or a clergyman, or to oneself) involves one in a duplicity. The main character described has motives that are "spelled out" in the telling of the story. Intentions, hopes, plans, and reasons are all elabo-rated. What is not spelled out are the motives, intentions, and reasons for telling the story in just this way. The person created is lucid as to his or her motives. The person creating the story is not. In telling one's story, there are always two stories: that told and that enacted in the teller telling. Mead, James, Freud, and others, recognizing this duplicity, distinguish the "me," the protagonist whose motives are made lucid in the story, from the "I," the storyteller whose impression manage-ment is not spelled out.

"Adopting the patient role" thus is a late edition of what we have all done, at least now and then, in everyday self-conscious reflection. Psychology interacts with the requirements for coherence in a narrative by loosening them, by allowing essentially incoherent and unintelli-gible elements to become parts of the story without damaging the in-telligibility of the story as a whole. Psychology tells our self-consciousness how to make a kind of sense out of what in ourselves is unintelligible. That intelligibility states that the anomaly is a "symptom."

There have always been such loosening influences. Erikson (1958) reports that Luther had no difficulty assuming that unexpected noises or even his own fainting were the work of the devil, the personage of evil and chaos itself. Similarly, some people blame voodoo, Odysseus blamed Poseidon, Orestes claimed Apollo told him to kill his mother, and so on. Psychology today plays the role played by supernatural personages in the past: giving the unintelligible a kind of intelligibility that enables the coherence of one's narrative to stay more or less intact in the face of things about ourselves that don't make any sense, given the narrative we are living.

Psychology does this by enacting a professional role of healer, which casts over the client the reciprocal role of patient, the adoption of which bestows on the patient's "I," the teller of the tale, license to hide his or her motives and to believe that the motives of the "me" in the tale are his or her own. Furthermore, the anomaly fits nicely into the role, and the story appropriate for that role, as something that has befallen one. We return, at this point, to the issue of reification.

Playing the patient role is the most common way to not change. Our psychological theories of emotions as natural events that mechanically click off according to Pavlovian patterns and that we can perhaps extinguish or perhaps will merely have to suffer become a powerful part of the patient role, of the narrative of "me" who now suffers an illness, and "I" take real comfort in the natural pattern that is presented by psychology and that justifies my being who and how I am.

The new chapter in the patient's personal narrative revises the meaning of earlier chapters. Such revisions could be enormously healing, if they forced one to struggle with who one is and was, who one's parents were, what one's motives were, and so on. Rewriting one's narrative, overcoming the falsifications and idealizations, can make intelligible the anomaly one begins with. But the patient role works against this, and our reified theories of emotion work against this as well.

These factors enable the patient to continue the self-deception built into his or her narrative by modifying only as much as allows a mechanical or biological explanation of the out-of-joint feeling, thought, or impulse. They encourage the patient to see himself or herself as the object such theories make of him or her, and insofar as they succeed, insofar as we enact our roles as doctors who operate on the machine, insofar as we persuade the patient to trust us, and to believe the elaborate ideological, bureaucratic, and fiscal realities that support such theories, the person is harmed, not helped with his or her problem.

Indeed, patients who avail themselves of psychology in this sense are maintaining most of their former narratives as an alternative to changing them. The symptom, the anomaly that motivated the visit to the psychologist both protested that story and at the same time supported it. While the patient is listening to the pain, he or she is also indulging a style that is part of the pattern that is the problem. To quiet the pain while continuing that indulgence is to become dependent on psychology, on therapy, perhaps on medication. It thus pays to remain a patient, for one can merely add patienthood to one's identity and one can have it both ways.

Like earlier superstitions, a mechanical psychology can mobilize enormous public support, and the cures of mechanical psychology are effective just as were ritual cures of the past. In both cases the person is made to surrender anything like a radical doubt he or she may have about his or her narrative. "Everything is really all right," we seem to be saying in such a psychology: "You couldn't have understood these technical matters at the time, and now that you do, you can see there is nothing much to be upset about."

How many patients, on the verge of breaking through a past of life-long self-deception, driven to a practitioner by a symptom too painful to ignore, are quieted in this way? We have no data on this question, but we can see that our theories and our routines come perilously close to guaranteeing such failure.

CLINICAL PSYCHOLOGY TODAY

The final irony is that most clinical psychologists I know are really much better than our theories. We confront patients with moral dilemmas and self-deceptions and offer little comfort from the tragic character of human experience apart from our own example of somehow coming up with the requisite staying power. In spite of the shape of our theory, we manage to be therapists, and sometimes to do good work with patients. We often provoke growthful cognizance of the inevitable duplicities of life. In struggling with the ambiguities of who they are and testing narratives for their fit and malability, our patients make changes now, in the present, guided by a self-conscious desire to change, without knowing into whom they should change.

Struggles inevitably engage cultural characters, but these are also stand-ins for changes in who patients have been. For example, if a patient were to discover that he really is worthy of being loved—that his sense that his parents did not love him can be forgiven instead of believed—then he might become a self who finally, in fact, is lovable and loved. Such a movement of growth combines his desire to be loved with a reflective consciousness that he is a self who is loveable, which in turn can guide his behavior so as to be perceived by others in exactly that way. Such a person does not tell others to love him because his parents did not, or because he was caused to feel they did not. He simply becomes loveable.

Why, then, is our theory so bad? Whenever most psychology is relevant to our therapy it leads to bad therapy; when our therapy is good it has nothing to do with most of the major theoretical paradigms in psychology. It is not unreasonable to inquire into this anomaly.

In 1973, Gergen's "Social Psychology as History" pointed to the study of the authoritarian personality in the spirit of understanding what psychological science is up to. His conclusion was that psychology is history, which means, among other things, that it is not nature, not a matter of recording the universal properties of objective reality. This accords with the postmodern spirit with which we began this chapter. Psychologists are in history and of history. We do not operate in a historical or rhetorical vacuum.

The writing of *The Authoritarian Personality* (Adorno, Frenkl-Brunswik, Levinson, and Sanford, 1950) not only addressed and thus became history, it did for us as a civilization something like what therapy does for an individual. It confronted us with a reality, all too familiar to some of us, but understood by none of us because it lacked coherence with major themes of progress and optimism about Western civilization. In so doing, it forced us to reexamine the narrative of our civilization, and thus the metanarrative of each of our lives, and to take account of Fascism in its full and florid reality. At the same time, it made the unintelligible intelligible by offering explanations, in terms of psychology, of what we did not understand.

There had been such voices before. G. Stanley Hall's (1904) early studies of adolescence are only an example of how psychology at the turn of the twentieth century was full of moralisms and commentary about the presence of good and evil in our souls and in society. Like *The Authoritarian Personality* (Adorno et al., 1950), these efforts pretended to be scientific. And in both cases the major detractors of such studies won the rhetorical battle, not by defending a worldview worn ragged by time, but by declaring that such moralisms had no place in science.

It is perhaps possible now, with the coming of postmodern thought, that the cleansing science of values, insisted on by those who see science as beyond the influence of historical rhetoric, can be over. To see the rhetorical nature of psychology is to put psychology into a different historical narrative than the modern one of self-correcting, universal, and objective science. It is time to revise our theory. I wonder if good clinicians have not always known this.

NOTE

1. It is interesting in this regard that psychology, or being a psychologist, no longer is a very specific identity, nor is it a story that I share very vividly with other psychologists. The contrast between 1900 and 2000 is absolutely

telling in this respect. No one since Skinner has tried to define the field all at once, nor is that ever likely to happen again. Let us move from thinking about patients, whose struggles with life are struggles to achieve coherence in a narrative morass that feels overwhelming, to thinking about psychologists. Psychologists may or may not struggle with what it means to be a psychologist, but insofar as one does so we must say that it is at once easier and more problematic after the twentieth century. During the twentieth century, there were identities within psychology: Freudian, Skinnerian, and so on. The sense of onself as a "psychologist" constituted an identity in the early twentieth century. By the end of the century, to acquire a self-definition within the great diversity that psychology had become, the label "psychologist" named too diverse and multifarious a group to mean very much, and so specifying "clinical" or "experimental" was necessary to achieve the specificity required for an identity. As the universe of actual psychologists continues to differentiate and diversify in the twenty-first century, such specifications become less and less recognizable, let alone servicable as an identity. What is an "information processing consultant"? How do you explain to your mother that you are a "gender specialist" or an "organization development professional" or a "cognitive child clinical" expert?

19

Toward Some Conclusions

PSYCHOLOGY AND CULTURE

Psychology in America was never as isolated from its cultural context as scientific histories have portrayed it. To be sure, the greatest and most obvious influence on the thoughts and practices of psychologists have been those of prior psychologists, but there is a larger backdrop to the meaning of every thought of American psycholgists.

Twentieth-century America is a singular phenomenon in world history: Its technological accomplishments translated into consumer goods enjoyed by the population; its prosperity led to the highest standard of living for such a large population in the history of humanity; its political democracy, free-press journalism, and wide reading of newpapers give Americans more information about themselves and the world than has ever happened before.

Historians of psychology have not taken up very fully the question of how the twists and turns of American cultural history have shaped psychology. I have suggested that secularization in the nineteenth century was a key cultural factor at the time psychology was first being invented, and that American skepticism about European entanglements—political and intellectual—was an important impetus in the enthusiastic acceptance, or affirmation of behaviorism in the early decades of the twentieth century. What can we see in American culture that influenced or augmented the rapid developments of multiple theories at mid-century?

Certainly, former trends continued. Secular pluralism and national pride were comfortable, while racial conflict became more focal than class conflict.[1] Individualism, a traditional concept, became for some a right to self-development, which justified the seeking of racial justice even as it fostered for others a blaming of themselves for failure. As gigantic corporations replaced individual free enterprises in mediating commerce and employment, Americans at mid-century enjoyed having defeated Nazi brutality and entered the Cold War with what came to be called the Soviet Bloc.

As these enormous cultural trends became more separate in our conscious thinking from psychological theories and laboratories, their influence became impossible to specify. What we can say for sure is that the proliferation of employment roles, which is to say jobs in psychology, fed back into university curricula. The proliferation of theories refined the differentiation of curricular possibilities, which matched the increasingly diverse range of research questions, theoretical foci, and eventually professional roles for psychologists.

This expansion is reflected vividly in the growth of the American Psychologial Association. In 1948, when the APA and AAAP joined, there were twenty divisions, which by 1960 had become twenty-three. In the 1960s, eight were added. In the 1970s, nine, and in the 1980s, seven more. In the 1990s, four more were added, and beyond them four more await approval. After approval, that will be a total of fifty-five divisions, thirty-five of which came in the last four decades of the twentieth century.

The proliferation of psychological subfields is more related to the proliferation of employment roles for psychologists than it is to, say, the number of theoretical innovations. While measures of the scope of psychological research show vast expansion, with cognition (information processing), school psychology, consumer psychology, and other hot areas leading the way, psychologists practicing some kind of therapy constitute the largest collection of specialities. Of fifty-four divisions of the APA, thirteen (nearly one-quarter) are explicitly centered in the delivery of therapeutic services.[2]

I should add to these data the elaborate and concerted effort by psychologists to participate in psychopharmacological practice. The law currently permits the prescription of pharmacological agents only by those with medical degrees. This includes all doctors and some nurse practitioners, but no psychologists. Elaborate training of psychologists, primarily by the Prescribing Psychologists Register and its adjacent organizations, including twenty hours of training in a miniconvention preceding the APA meetings in Washington, DC, in August 2000, focused on political advocacy and a national strategy for changing the prescription privilege laws.

SOME CLOSING THOUGHTS

It is, of course, impossible to summarize this book. But the narrative was written by one person, suggesting that there was a guiding orientation, a way of seeing things, all along. This orientation has now been extended into an interpretation of American psychology over the dozen or so decades of its existence. I recognize this interpretation as my own, and I have offered it with some themes and not others, selecting according to assumptions I hardly knew I held. When I look at where they have taken me, I recognize myself anew. And for better or for worse, I hope to close in such a way as to claim them more openly, to expose more baldly what can be so easily concealed in the manufacture of a thousand details.

I want first to argue that American psychology is, more than we psychologists know, a vintage product of American culture. Second, the narrative I tell has content; there were decisive turning points and unexpected developments that I hope I have made sense of. Third, American psychology thinks of itself as a science, which is to say, an exploration of a reality that simply is what it is. The science in turn reveals that reality loyally. I want to argue that this creation was much less driven by reality than we pretend and much more driven by a creativity we rarely acknowledge. Science, it seems to me, has helped in some ways, and hindered in others, the expression of that creativity. Finally, as the twentieth century gives way to the early decades of the twenty-first, postmodern and postcolonial thought continue to offer an alternative to science that solves some problems and creates others. I hope it is explored by coming generations of psychologists.

RECALLING THE HISTORY

In this context, the history of psychology is helpful in seeing what psychology contemporaneously is. In the early decades—the late nineteenth century—psychology was founded on the project of bringing to the mind–body problem a more secularized and scientific approach. Considerable optimism and enthusiasm accompanied the idea of resolving a philosophical problem with science. We see dualism here in this joining of a physical method with a mental subject matter.

In America in the second decade, Watson's revolution recentered psychology from a study of the mind scientifically to the study of behavior scientifically, thus driving underground the original vision and substituting a more purely scientific one. This also re-created psychology so that it was no longer about the psyche.

As the century progressed, both Tolman and Gestalt preserved the psyche in psychology, but in fact it remained implicitly there even apart from these efforts to yet again redefine the science. Dualism never again surfaced as a focal problem, but it came to be enacted in using a physicalistic methodology on a mental content. This movement within, say, the academic and scientific communities, represented by the rapid growth of the American Psychological Association, did not include the also rapidly growing proliferation of counseling, child guidance, and psychiatric testing roles, nor the academic interest in Freud's psychoanalysis, organized in the parallel group, the AAAP. The AAAP and the APA joined together in the vastly expanded APA in 1948.

This was an occasion of great hope for unity among all psychologists, which indeed was represented in the curricula of academic psychology departments across the land by mid-century. In Chapter 11 this polarized unity (or unified polarity) is represented in the persons of Clark Hull and Carl Rogers. Hebb's physiological psychology continued to struggle with the problem of how the phenomena of mental life might be accounted for in the functioning of the brain. Piaget's developmental explorations of mental life and Skinner's renewed ingenuity for exploring psychology in physical terms represent the continuing, and perhaps final, explicit statement by psychologists that dualism is a problem still engaging psychology.

PSYCHOLOGY AND POETRY

The intense complexity of psychology is absent in many sciences, present in other (perhaps social) sciences, but vivid and inescapable in psychology. Psychology is much more like poetry than other sciences. In poetry, the consciousness of the poet is decisive, if not exhaustive, of the work. Poems are, of course, usually about something outside the poet, but the poet's consciousness of that something is constitutive of the very poem itself.

Like psychologists, poets work within a traditon, so their personal consciousness is obviously contextualized by that of other poets. And yet without uniqueness, a poem is nothing. This bears a similarity to scientific ideas, including psychological ones. Some scientific literature replicates earlier work, but none of it does only that, and that which is most original is the most valued. In science as in poetry, the cultural context also supplies a "reality," which must at once be obeyed and yet transcended if the work is to matter.

Of all sciences, of course, psychology is the most personal. Part of this fact comes from our subject matter, which I, the psychologist, share with all psychologists in some way. Even if I study psychosis, I presumably share with psychotics a world, a culture, and specific existential possibilities. But beyond that, I share behavior, physiology, and some kind of consciousness—which is at once mine and theirs. In studying theirs, I cannot escape studying whatever is also mine in my perception of their manifestations. As a psychologist, I personally am present as both subject and object in my work.

So it is, of course, with poets. Celebrated in poetry, this connection, this fertile interaction of a perceiving mind and a world to perceive, this intertwining of subject and object is denied in psychology. The goals of science itself motivate such denial, of course, and of all the sciences, such denial in psychology is the most difficult and thus the most strenuously sought. If this denial is there in other sciences, it is most vividly there in social sciences, and of them, psychology seems most desperate to separate subject and object, to call our knowledge "objective" and to rule out, or deny, or punish, the intertwining that is simply inevitable.

The most objective knowledge began as a just-glimpsed reality, whose presence as external is invisible except for my internal meeting with it, my casting around for a meaning, clothing it in language, writing theory in my head even as I try not to impose but simply to receive. What eventuates as an explicit cognition, clear as the light of day, true and clean of subjective entanglements, began as an intuitive mixture from multiple sources. What comes out can be relatively objective, but finally its value is its virtue as the ultimate verbal–mental product—a truth.

While scientific denial of these intuitive dynamics distinguishes science from poetry, the psychologists' denial of this also impoverishes psychologists' consciousness of their own field. The entire history of ideas in psychology manifests vivid testimony to the personal creativity of psychologists, and to the dependence of the science itself on what it ironically denies. Fortunately, scientists are human, and humanity is larger than science.

POSTMODERN AND POSTCOLONIAL POSSIBILITIES

The scientific project, beginning in the late medieval context of the breakdown of institutional religious hegemonies, was an attempt to find truth. This vision assumed that reality is what it is, and nothing more. The scientific vision saw all elaborations on reality, particularly those meanings placed upon it by religion, to be in error, merely human elaborations pasted onto the real reality, which is what it is, independent of such myths, meanings, and elaborations. This vision resolved to return to a reality independent of such fanciful elaborations, to have, in a word, truth about the world: real truth, true truth, objective truth unsullied by subjective distortion.

Modernity, therefore, our "modern" way of understanding our own knowledge, construes science as the royal road to objectivity, the cleansing knowledge of all subjective biases, distortions, hopes, and other fantasies that had distorted knowledge so long. Of course, subjective distortions remain, and many of them are collectively shared. For this reason, a rulebound procedure that eliminates subjective distortion appears to be genuinely useful. Continuing disagreements in the contemporary world signal the fact that science simply has not been used to resolve the conflicts. Modernity is surely incomplete, worldwide, but it has not been just mistaken.

But there are mistakes. The history of psychology certainly testifies to the fact that very different psychologies coexist within a scientific context. Many scientists, many psychologists among them, believe that the diversity among different psychologies is temporary. In time, the data will win out completely over subjective biases; the sciences will be unified within each field and there will even be a unification of the sciences themselves, since they share the same commitment to bias-free, objective knowledge.

Can there be knowledge whose content is purely objective? Whose origin is not somehow rooted in, even indebted to, collective assumptions that are themselves not scientific? The agreement among scientists that science is the criterion of truth is not itself a scientific product; it is rather an assumption shared by certain social groups. The possibility for bias remains, even within science itself. Scientists know of many cases where a shared assumption was exposed by a finding that did not fit the conventional scientific wisdom, but that did prove to be true in the eventual sorting out of further scientific data. Such events suggest that science is, after all, self-correcting. Postmodern thought disputes this.

Postmodern thought is often allied with what is called postcolonial thought, that theory native to, say, Caribbean scholars whose education is as good as any but whose sense of the distortions wrought by colonial domination in centuries past (and present) have less to do with subjectivity and more to do with culture. Colonial thought by Caribbean scholars is important French thought, or American thought, or English thought.

Postcolonial thought, however, is not to colonial thought what objective thought is to subjective thought—a correction of an identifiable source of error in the service of eliminating error and achieving truth. It is a more serious relativism of truth itself. Scientific methods may be able to eliminate subjective distortions of the truth, provided all agree that science supplies a clear look at objective reality, but they cannot eliminate cultural distortions, which have less to do with subjectivity and more to do with history. Knowledge is not only compromised by subjective hopes and beliefs that science can correct. It is compromised by a much more subtle infusion of historical and cultural perspective, for which there are no corrective procedures.

Further, there is no knowledge that is not so infused. Science, it can be argued, especially imposes on knowledge a kind of instrumental agenda built basically into the consciousness of a scientist. Since colonial powers have in recent centuries always been powers that are more scientifically advanced, these powers have failed to see the biases in their science itself or those biases in their native culture itself that make science seem so irrefutable.

NOTES

1. The proliferation of psychologies specific to ethnic groups is very American, and the entire field of social psychology has hardly contained such subfields as black psychology. The emphasis on African Americans among ethnic minorities reflects the fact in the twentieth century that African Americans are America's oldest, most discriminated against, and certainly largest minority group. As a sample of this rich literature, see Fanon (1967), Lerner (1972), Guthrie (1976), and Marable (1995).

2. The thirteen divisions are as follows: Clinical Psychology (#12), Consulting Psychology (#13), School Psychology (#16), Counseling Psychology (#17), Psychopharmacology (#28), Psychotherapy (#29), Psychological Hypnosis (#30), Psychoanalysis (#39), Clinical Neuropsychology (#40), Independent Practice (# 42), Group Psychology and Group Psychotherapy (#49), Clinical Child Psychology (#53), and Pediatric Psychology (#54).

References

Adorno, T. W., Frenkl-Brunswik, E., Levinson, D. J., & Sanford, R. N. (1950). *The authoritarian personality*. New York: Harper.

Allen, G. W. (1967). *William James: A biography*. New York: Viking.

Allport, G. W. (1937). *Personality: A psychological interpretation*. New York: Holt.

Allport, G. W. (1960). Personality: A problem for science or for art? In *Personality and social encounter* (pp. 3–15). Boston: Beacon Press. (Original work published 1938).

Ammons, R. B. (1962). Psychology of the scientist: 2. Clark Hull and his "Idea Books." *Perceptual and Motor Skills, 15*, 800–815.

Amsel, A., & Rashotte, M. E. (Eds.). (1984). *Mechanisms of adaptive behavior: Clark L. Hull's theoretical papers with commentary*. New York: Columbia University Press.

Angell, J. R. (1907). The province of functional psychology. Presidential Address to the American Psychological Association in 1906. *Psychological Review, 14*, 61–91.

Angell, J. R., & Moore, A. W. (1896). Reaction time: A study in reaction time and habit. *Psychological Review, 3*, 245–258.

Bagley, W. C. (1922). Educational determinism: Or democracy and the I. Q. *School and Society, 16*, 372–384.

Baldwin, J. M. (1895). Sensory reaction time. *Psychological Review, 2*, 259–273.

Baldwin, J. M. (1896). Reply to Professor Titchener. *Mind, 5*, 81–89.

Baldwin, J. M. (1913). *The history of psychology* (2 vols.). London: Watts.

Bambara, T. C. (1992). *Gorilla, my love*. New York: Vintage.

Bartky, S. L. (1990). *Femininity and domination: Studies in the phenomenology of oppression*. New York: Routledge.

Beauvoir, Simone de. (1961). *The second sex* (H. M. Parshley, Trans.). New York: Bantam Books.

Beer, T., Bethe, A., & Uxkuell, J. V. (1899). Vorschlaege zu einer objectivierended Nomenklatur in der Physiologie der Nervensystems. *Biologische Zentralblatt, 19,* 517–521.

Belenky, M. F., Clinchy, B. M., Goldberger, N. R., & Tarule, J. M. (1986). *Women's ways of knowing: The development of self, voice, and mind.* New York: Basic Books.

Benjamin, W. (1969). *Illuminations* (H. Zohn, Trans.). New York: Schocken Books.

Binswanger, L. (1958). The case of Ellen West. In R. May, E. Angel, & H. Ellenberger (Eds.), *Existence* (pp. 237–364). New York: Basic Books.

Boring, E. G.(1927). Edward Bradford Titchener. *American Journal of Psychology, 38,* 489–506.

Boring, E. G. (1950). *A history of experimental psychology.* New York: Appleton–Century–Crofts.

Boston Women's Health Book Collective. (1975). *Our bodies, our selves.* Distributed noncommercially.

Boston Women's Health Book Collective. (1984). *The new our bodies, our selves.* New York: Simon and Schuster.

Brentano, F. (1960). The distinction between mental and physical phenomena. In R. M. Chisholm (Ed.), *Realism and the background of phenomenology.* Glencoe, IL: Free Press. (Original work published 1874).

Brigham, C. C. (1923). *A study of American intelligence.* Princeton, NJ: Princeton University Press.

Brigham, C. C. (1930). Intelligence tests of immigrant groups. *Psychological Review, 37,* 158–165.

Bruner, J. S. (1960). *The process of education.* Cambridge: Harvard University Press.

Bruner, J. S. (1986). *Actual minds: Possible worlds.* Cambridge: Harvard University Press.

Bruner, J. S., Goodnow, J. J., & Austin, G. A. (1956). *A study of thinking.* New York: Wiley.

Bruner, J. S., & Klein, G. S. (1960). The functions of perceiving: New look retrospect. In B. Kaplan & S. Wapner (Eds.), *Perspectives in psychological theory* (pp. 121–140). New York: International Universities Press.

Buber, M. (1937). *I and thou* (R. S. Smith, Trans.). Edinburgh: T. & T. Clark. (Original work published 1923).

Bugental, J.F.T. (1965). *The search for authenticity.* New York: Holt, Rinehart, and Winston.

Butler, J. (1990). *Gender trouble: Feminism and the subversion of identity.* New York: Routledge.

Candland, D. K. (Ed.). (1967). *Emotion: Bodily change.* Princeton, NJ: Van Nostrand.

Candland, D. K., Fell, J. P., Keen, E., Leshner, A. I., Plutchik, R., & Tarpy, R. M. (1977). *Emotion.* Monterey, CA: Brooks–Cole.

Carden, M. L. (1976). *The new feminist movement.* New York: Russell Sage Foundation.

Chodorow, N. (1989). *Feminism and psychoanalytic theory.* New Haven: Yale University Press.

Cisneros, S. (1991). *Woman hollering creek.* New York: Vintage.

Clance, P. R., & Imes, S. A. (1978). The imposter phenomenon in high achieving women: Dynamics and therapeutic intervention. *Psychotherapy: Theory, Research, and Practice, 15,* 241–247.

Contratto, S., & Gutfreund, M. J. (Eds.). (1996). *A feminist's guide to the memory debate.* New York: Hawthorn Press.

Cornell, D. (1991). *Beyond accommodation: Ethical feminism, deconstruction, and the law.* New York: Routledge.

Cross, P. (1968). College women: A research description. *Journal of the National Association of Women Deans and Counselors, 32,* 12–21.

de Saussure, F. (1959). *Course in general linguistics* (C. Bally & A. Sechehaye, Eds., Wade Baskin, Trans.). New York: Philosophical Press.

Descartes. R. (1970). *The philosophical works of Descartes* (E. S. Haldone & G.R.T. Ross, Trans.). New York: Cambridge University Press.

Dewey, J. (1896). The reflex arc concept in psychology. *Psychological Review, 3,* 357–370.

Dewey, J. (1922). *Human nature and conflict.* New York: Holt.

Dinnerstein, D. (1976). *The mermaid and the minotaur.* New York: Harper and Row.

Dollard, J. (1937). *Caste and class in a southern town.* New Haven: Institute of Human Relations, Yale University Press.

Dollard, J., and Miller, N. E. (1950). *Personality and psychotherapy: An analysis in terms of learning, thinking, and culture.* New York: McGraw-Hill.

Ebbinghaus, H. (1913). *Memory: A contribution to experimental psychology* (H. A. Ruger, Trans.). New York: Teachers College Press. (Original work published 1885).

Ebert, T. L. (1996). *Ludic feminism: Postmodernism, desire, and labor in late capitalism.* Ann Arbor: University of Michigan Press.

Erdrich, L. M. (1988). *Tracks.* New York: Holt.

Erikson, E. (1950). *Childhood and society.* New York: Norton.

Erikson, E. (1958). *Young man Luther: A study in psychoanalysis and history.* New York: Norton.

Evans, R. (1975). *Carl Rogers.* New York: Dutton.

Fanon, F. (1967). *Black skin white masks: The experiences of a black man in a white world.* New York: Grove Press.

Festinger, L. (1957). *A theory of cognitive dissonance.* Evanston, IL: Row, Peterson.

Feyerabend, P. (1975). *Against method.* London: Verso.

Figes, E. (1970). *Patriarchal attitudes.* New York: Faber and Faber.

Firestone, S. (1972). *The dialectic of sex.* London: Palidin.

Flavell, J. H. (1963). *The developmental psychology of Jean Piaget.* Princeton, NJ: Van Nostrand.

Freud, A. (1937). *The ego and the mechanisms of defense.* New York: International Universities Press.

Freud, S. (1900) The interpretation of dreams. In *Standard edition of the works of Sigmund Freud* (entire vols. 4–5). London: Hogarth Press.

Freud, S. (1961). *Civilization and its discontents* (James Strachey, Trans.). New York: Norton. (Original work published 1930).

Freud, S. (1962). *The collected papers of Sigmund Freud* (James Strachey, Ed.). New York: Basic Books.

Freud, S. (1962). Thoughts for the times of war and death. In James Strachey (Ed.), *The collected papers of Sigmund Freud* (vol. 4; pp. 288–317). New York: Basic Books. (Original work published 1915).

Freud, S. (1962). Why war? In James Strachey (Ed.), *The collected papers of Sigmund Freud* (vol. 5; pp. 273–277). New York: Basic Books. (Original work published 1932).

Frey, M. (1983). *The politics of reality: Essays in feminist theory*. Freedom, CA: Crossings Press.

Friedan, B. (1963). *The feminine mystique*. New York: Penguin.

Gendlin, E. T. (1962). *Experience and the creation of meaning*. New York: Free Press.

Gergen, K. J. (1973). Social psychology as history. *Journal of Psychiatry and Social Psychology, 26*, 309–320.

Gergen, M. M., & Davis, S. N. (1997). *Toward a new psychology of gender: A reader*. New York: Routledge.

Gesell, A. (1934). *An atlas of human behavior: A systematic delineation of the forms and early growth of human behavior patterns: Vol. 1. Normative series; Vol. 2, Naturalistic series*. New Haven: Yale University Press.

Gilligan, C. (1982*). In a different voice: Psychological theory and women's development*. Cambridge: Harvard University Press.

Ginsberg, G. P. (2000). Emotions are narratives. In L. Sundararajan (Ed.), *Emotional life-narratives: The good, the bad, the creative*. Washington D.C.: National Convention of the American Psychological Association, APA Symposium.

Giorgi, A. (1970). *Psychology as a human science: A phenomenology based approach*. New York: Harper and Row.

Gould, S. J. (1981). *The mismeasure of man*. New York: Norton.

Greer, G. (1971). *The female eunuch*. New York: McGraw-Hill.

Group for the Advancement of Psychiatry. (1975). *Pharmacotherapy and psychotherapy: Paradoxes, problems, and progress*. New York: Mental Health Materials Center.

Guthrie, E. R. (1935). *The psychology of learning*. New York: Harper and Row.

Guthrie, R. V. (1976). *Even the rate was white: A historical view of psychology*. New York: Harper and Row.

Haaken, J. (1998). *Pillar of salt: Gender, memory, and the perils of looking back*. New Brunswick, NJ: Rutgers University Press.

Habermas, J. (1968). *Knowledge and human interests* (J. J. Shapiro, Trans.). Boston: Beacon Press.

Hall, C. S., & Lindsay, G. (1957). *Theories of personality*. New York: Wiley.

Hall, G. S. (1904). *Adolescence: Its psychology, and its relations to physiology, anthropology, sociology, sex, crime, religion, and education* (2 vols.). New York: Appleton.

Hall, G. S. (1922). *Senescence*. New York: Appleton.

Hannush, M. J. (1987). John B. Watson remembered: An interview with James B. Watson. *Journal of the History of Behavioral Sciences, 23*, 137–152.

Hartman, G. H. (1954). *The unmediated vision*. New York: Harcourt, Brace and World.

Hartman, G. H. (1964). *Wordsworth's poetry*. New Haven: Yale University Press.

Hartman, G. H. (1987). *The unremarkable Wordsworth*. Minneapolis: University of Minnesota Press.

Hartman, G. W. (1997). *The fateful question of culture*. New York: Columbia University Press.

Hayes, S. C., Hayes, L., Reese, H. W., & Sarbin, T. R. (Eds.). (1993). *Varieties of scientific contextualism*. Reno, NV: Context Press.

Hebb, D. O. (1949). *Organization of behavior: A neuropsychological theory*. New York: Wiley.

Heidbreder, E. (1933). *Seven psychologies*. New York: Century.

Heidegger, M. (1962). *Being and time* (Trans. John Macquarrie & Edward Robinson). New York: Harper and Row. (Original work published 1927).

Herman, J. L. (1992). *Trauma and recovery: The aftermath of violence—From domestic abuse to political terror*. New York: Basic Books.

Hilgard, E. (1987). *Psychology in America: A historical survey*. San Diego: Harcourt Brace Jovanovich.

Hodge, C. (1874). *What is Darwinism?* New York: Putnam.

Holt, E. B., Marvia, W. T., Montague, W. P., Perry, R. B., Pitkin, W. B., & Spalding, E. B. (1912). *The new realism*. New York: Macmillan.

Horkheimer, M. (1972). *Critical theory* (Trans. M. J. O'Connell and others). New York: Seabury Press.

Horney, K. (1937). *The neurotic personality of our time*. New York: Norton.

Horney, K. (1967). *Feminine psychology* (H. Kelman, Ed.). New York: Norton.

Hovdestad, W. E., & Kristiansen, C. M. (1996) Mind meets body: On the nature of recovered memories of trauma. In S. Contratto & M. J. Gutfreund (Eds.), *A feminist clinician's guild to the memory debate* (pp. 31–46). New York: Haworth Press.

Hull, C. L. (1933). *Hypnosis and suggestibility: An experimental approach*. New York: Appleton-Century.

Hull, C. L. (1943). *Principles of behavior*. New York: Appleton-Century.

Hull, C. L. (1952). *A behavior system*. New Haven: Yale University Press.

Humphrey, G. (1940). The problem of the direction of thought. *British Journal of Psychology, 30*, 183–186.

Husserl, E. (1954). Logische Untersuchungen. In *Husserliana: Edmund Husserl: Gesammelte Werke* (vol. 1). The Hague: Martinus Nijhoff. (Original work published 1900).

Inhelder, B., & Piaget, J. (1958). *The growth of logical thinking: From childhood to adolescence* (A. Parsons & S. Milgram, Trans.). New York: Basic Books.

James, W. (1890) *Principles of psychology* (2 vols.). New York: Holt.

James, W. (1892). *Psychology: Briefer course*. New York: Holt.

Janis, I. L. (1982). *Groupthink: Psychological studies of policy decisions and fiascoes*. Boston: Houghton-Mifflin.

Jourard, S. (1964). *The transparent self: Self-disclosure and well-being*. New York: Van Nostrand.

Jung, C. G. (1960–1979). *The collected works of C. G. Jung* (Vols. 1–20, E. Read, M. Fordham, B. Adler, & W. McGuire, Eds.). Princeton, NJ: Princeton University Press.

Keen, E. (1970). *Three faces of being: Toward an existential clinical psychology*. New York: Appleton–Century–Crofts.

Keen, E. (1975). *Primer in phenomenological psychology*. New York: Holt.

Keen, E. (1998). *Drugs, therapy and professional power*. Westport, CT: Praeger.

Keen, E. (2000a). *Chemicals for the mind: Psychopharmacology and human conciousness*. Westport, CT: Praeger.

Keen, E. (2000b). Depression as sadness; Anxiety as fear. In L. Sundararajan, "Symposium: Emotional life narratives: The good, the bad, and the creative." American Association Convention, Washington, D.C., August 7, 2000.

Keen, E. (2000c). *Ultimacy and triviality in psychotherapy*. Westport, CT: Praeger.

Koehler, W. (1925). *The mentality of apes* (E. Winter, Trans.). New York: Harcourt Brace. (Original work published 1917).

Koehler, W. (1947). *Gestalt psychology: An introduction to new concepts in psychology*. New York: Liveright. (Original work published 1929).

Koehler, W. (1959). Gestalt psychology today. *American Psychologist, 14*, 727–734.

Koehler, W., & Wallach, H. (1944). Figural aftereffects: An investigation of visual processes. *Proceedings of the American Philosophical Society, 88*, 269–357.

Koffka, K. (1935). *Principles of Gestalt psychology*. New York: Harcourt Brace.

Krystal, H. (1988). *Integration & self-healing: Affect, trauma, alexithymia*. Hillsdale, NJ: Analytic Press.

Kuhn, T. (1962). *The structure of scientific revolutions*. Chicago: University of Chicago Press.

Kuo, Z. Y. (1924). A psychology without heredity. *Psychological Review, 31*, 427–428.

Ladd, G. T. (1887). *Elements of physiological psychology*. New York: Scribners.

Laing, R. D. (1967). *The politics of experience*. New York: Pantheon.

Landfield, A. (Ed.). (1976). *Nebraska symposium on motivation*. Lincoln: University of Nebraska Press.

Lane, R. D., & Schwartz, G. E. (1987). Levels of emotional awareness: A cognitive-developmental theory and its application to psychopathology. *American Journal of Psychiatry, 144*, 133–143.

Langfeld, H. S. (1927). Consciousness and motor response. *Psychological Review, 34*, 1–9.

Larson, C., & Sullivan, J. (1965). Watson's relation to Titchener. *Journal of the History of the Behavioral Sciences, 1*, 338–354.

Lashley, K. S. (1950). In search of the engram. In *Symposia of the Society for Experimental Biology* (vol. 4, pp. 454–482). New York: Cambridge University Press.

Lashley, K. S., Chow, K. L., & Semmes, J. (1951). An examination of the electrical field theory of cerebral integration. *Psychological Review, 40*, 175–188.

Leeper, R. W. (1948). A motivational theory of emotion to replace "emotion as disorganized response." *Psychological Review, 55*, 5–21.

Lerner, B. (1972). *Therapy in the ghetto: Political impotence and personal disintegration*. Baltimore: Johns Hopkins University Press.

Levi-Strauss, C. (1963). *Structural anthropology*. New York: Basic Books.

Lewin, K. (1935). *A dynamic theory of personality. Selected papers* (D. K. Adams & K. E. Zener, Trans.). New York: McGraw-Hill.

Lewin, K. (1936). *Principles of topological psychology.* (Fritz Heider and Grace Heider, Trans.). New York: McGraw-Hill.

Lewin, K. (1938). *Contributions to psychological theory.* Durham, NC: Duke University Press.

Lewin, K. (1948). *Resolving social conflicts.* New York: Harper and Row.

Loeb, J. (1889). *Der Heliotropismus der Tiere and seine Uebereinstimmung mit dem Heliotropismus der Pfanzen.* Würzburg: Georg Hertz.

Loeb, J. (1918). *Forced movements, tropisms, and animal conduct.* Philadelphia: Lippincott.

Loftus, E. F., & Ketcham, K. (1994). *The myth of repressed memory.* New York: St. Martin's Press.

Lotze, H. (1886). *Outlines of metaphysics* (G. T. Ladd, Trans.). Boston: Ginn. (Original work published 1881).

Maccoby, E., & Jacklin, C. (1974). *The psychology of sex differences.* Stanford, CA: Stanford University Press.

Marable, M. (1995). *Beyond black and white: Transforming African-American politics.* New York: Verso.

Marcuse, H. (1966). *Eros and civilization: A philosophical inquiry into Freud.* Boston: Beacon Press.

May, R., Angel, E., & Ellenberger, H. (1958). *Existence: A new dimension in psychology and psychiatry.* New York: Basic Books.

Mayer, J. D., & Gaschke, Y. N. (1988). The experience and meta-experience of mood. *Journal of Personality and Social Psychology, 55,* 102–111.

Mayer, J. D., & Stevens, A. A. (1994). An emerging understanding of the reflective (meta-) experience of mood. *Journal of Research in Personality, 28,* 351–473.

McDougall, W. (1908). *An introduction to social psychology.* New York: Methuen.

Merleau-Ponty, M. (1964). *The primacy of perception.* Evanston, IL: Northwestern University Press.

Meyer, M. (1911). *The fundamental laws of human behavior.* Boston: Badger.

Meyer, M. (1921). *Psychology of the other one: An introductory textbook of psychology.* Columbia: Missouri Books.

Meyers, F.W.H. (1903). *Human personality and its survival after bodily death* (vols. 1–2). London: Longmans, Green.

Miller, G. A. (1962). *Psychology: The science of mental life.* New York: Harper and Row.

Miller, G. A., Galanter, E., & Pribram, K. H. (1960). *Plans and the structure of behavior.* New York: Holt.

Miller, N. E. (1948). Studies of fear as an acquired drive. 1. Fear as motivation and fear-reduction as reinforcement. *Journal of Experimental Psychology, 38,* 89–101.

Miller, N. E., & Dollard, S. (1941). *Social learning and imitation.* New Haven: Yale University Press.

Millet, K. (1970). *Sexual politics.* New York: Doubleday.

Mitchell, J. (1974). *Psychoanalysis and feminism.* New York: Vintage.

Morrison, T. (1970). *The bluest eye.* New York: Holt.

Mowrer, O. H. (1940). Anxiety-reduction and learning. *Journal of Experimental Psychology, 27,* 497–516.

Nicholson, L. (Ed.). (1989). *Feminism/Postmodernism*. New York: Routledge.

Nye, A. (1990). *Words of power: A feminist reading of the history of logic*. New York: Routledge.

Pavlov, I. (1904). Sur lu secretion psychique desglandes salvaires (phenomenes nerveux complexes dans le travail des glandes salivarires). *Archiv internationale de physiologie, 1*, 119–1135.

Pavlov, I. (1927). *Conditioned reflexes*. (G. V. Anrep, Trans.). London: Oxford University Press.

Perry, W. (1970). *Forms of intellectual and ethical development in the college years*. New York: Holt, Rinehart, and Winston.

Piaget, J. (1950). *The psychology of intelligence*. New York: Harcourt Brace.

Piaget, J. (1970). *Structuralism*. (Chaninah Maschler, Trans.). New York: Basic Books.

Piaget, J., & Inhelder, B. (1969). *The psychology of the child*. New York: Basic Books.

Plutchik, R. (1980). *Emotion: A psycho-evolutionary synthesis*. New York: Harper and Row.

Prince, M. (1906). *The dissociation of personality*. New York: Longmans, Green.

Prince, R. (1996). Indigenous Yoruba psychiatry. In A. Kief (Ed.), *Magic, faith, & healing* (pp. 192–223). Northvale, NJ: Jason Aronson. (Original work published 1964).

Quinn, S. (1987). *A mind of her own: The life of Karen Horney*. New York: Summit Books.

Radnitzky, G. (1970). *Contemporary schools of metascience*. New York: Humanities Press.

Rich, A. (1976). *Of woman born: Motherhood as experience and institution*. New York: Norton.

Rieff, P. (1959). *Freud: The mind of the moralist*. New York: Viking.

Roback, A. A. (1961). *History of psychology and psychiatry*. New York: Collier.

Rogers, C. R. (1939). *The clinical treatment of the problem child*. New York: Houghton-Mifflin.

Rogers, C. R. (1942). *Counseling and psychotherapy*. Boston: Houghton-Mifflin.

Rogers, C. R. (1951). *Client-centered therapy: Its current practice, implications, and theory*. Boston: Houghton-Mifflin.

Ryan, J., & Sackrey, C. (1984). *Strangers in paradise: Academics from the working class*. Boston: South End Press.

Sarbin, T. R. (1964). Anxiety: Reification of a metaphor. *Archives of General Psychiatry, 10*, 630–638.

Sarbin, T. R. (1977). Contextualism: A world view for modern psychology. In A. Landfield (Ed.), *1976 Nebraska symposium on motivation* (pp. 1–41). Lincoln: University of Nebraska Press.

Sarbin, T. R. (1993). The narrative as the root metaphor for contextualism. In S. Hayes (Ed.), *Varieties of Scientific Contextualism*. Reno, NV: Context Press.

Sarbin, T. R. (2000). Narratives of emotional life. In L. Sundararajan, "Emotional Life-Narratives: The good, the bad, the creative." American Association Convention, Washington, D.C., August 7, 2000.

Sarbin, T. R. (Ed.). (1986). *Narrative psychology: The storied nature of human conduct*. New York: Praeger.

Sarbin, T. R., & Keen, E. (1997) Sanity and madness: Conventional and unconventional narratives of emotional life. In W. F. Flack (Ed.), *Emotions in psychopathology: Theory and research* (pp. 130–142). New York: Oxford University Press.

Sartre, J.-P. (1956). *Being and nothingness.* New York: Philosophical Library. (Original work published 1943).

Sartre, J.-P. (1957). *Existentialism and human emotions.* New York: Philosophical Library.

Sawicki, J. (1991). *Disciplining Foucault: Feminism, power, and the body.* New York: Routledge.

Schultz, D. (1975). *A history of modern psychology* (2d ed.). London: Academic Press.

Seidman, S. (1992). *Embattled eros: Sexual politics and ethics in contemporary America.* New York: Routledge.

Senden, M. von. (1932). *Raum und Gestaltaffassung bei operierte Blindgeborenen vor and nach der Operation.* Leipzig: Barth.

Silko, L. M. (1977). *Ceremony.* New York: Viking.

Skinner, B. F. (1932). Drive and reflex strength. *Journal of General Psychology, 6,* 22–37.

Skinner, B. F. (1938). *The behavior of organisms: An experimental analysis.* New York: Appleton-Century.

Skinner, B. F. (1945). Baby in a box. *Ladies Home Journal, 62,* 30–31.

Skinner, B. F. (1948). *Walden two.* New York: Macmillan.

Skinner, B. F. (1950). Are theories of learning necessary? *Psychological Review, 57,* 193–216.

Skinner, B. F. (1957). *Verbal behavior.* New York: Appleton–Century–Crofts.

Skinner, B. F. (1969). *The shaping of a behaviorist.* New York: Knopf.

Skinner, B. F. (1972). *Beyond freedom and dignity.* New York: Knopf.

Skinner, B. F. (1974). *About behaviorism.* New York: Knopf.

Skinner, B. F. (1976). *Particulars of my life.* New York: Knopf.

Skinner, B. F. (1983). *A matter of consequences.* New York: Knopf.

Snyderman, M., & Herrnstein, R. (1983). Intelligence tests and the Immigration Act of 1924. *American Psychologist, 38,* 987–1000.

Snygg, D., & Combs, A. W. (1949). *Individual behavior.* New York: Harper and Row.

Sommers, C. H. (2000). *The war against boys: How misguided feminism is harming our young men.* New York: Simon and Shuster.

Spence, K. W. (1956). *Behavior theory and conditioning.* New Haven: Yale University Press.

Spence, K. W. (1960). *Behavior theory and learning.* Englewood Cliffs, NJ: Prentice Hall.

Sullivan, H. S. (1947). *Conceptions of modern psychiatry.* Washington, DC: William Alison White Institute.

Sundararajan, L. (2000a). Grounding rhetoric in the heart: Wordsworth's challenge to psychology. *The Existential Humanist, 4,* 1–4.

Sundararajan, L. (2000b). The plot thickens—or not: Protonarratives and emotional creativity. In L. Sundararajan, "Emotional Life-Narratives: The good, the bad, the creative." American Association Convention, Washington, D.C., August 7, 2000.

Terman, L. M. (1924). The mental test as a psychological method. *Psychological Review, 31,* 93–117.

Terr, L. C. (1991). Childhoood traumas: An outline and overview. *American Journal of Psychiatry, 148,* 10–20.

Thorndike, E. L. (1903). *Educational psychology.* New York: Teachers College Press.

Thorndike, E. L. (1904*). Introduction to the theory of social and mental measurements.* New York: Science Press.

Titchener, E. B. (1895). Simple reactions. *Mind, 4,* 74–81.

Titchener, E. B. (1895–1896). The type theory of the simple reaction. *Mind, 4,* 506–514.

Titchener, E. B. (1896). *An outline of psychology.* New York: Macmillan.

Titchener, E. B. (1898). *A primer of psychology.* New York: Macmillan.

Titchener, E. B. (1901–1905). *Experimental psychology: A manual of laboratory practice* (2 vols.). New York: Macmillan.

Titchener, E. B. (1910). *A textbook of psychology.* New York: Macmillan.

Titchener, E. B. (1915). *A beginner's psychology.* New York: Macmillan.

Titchener, E. B. (1920). Notes from the psychological laboratory of Cornell University. *American Journal of Psychology, 31,* 212–214.

Titchener, E. B. (1929). *Systematic psychology: A prolegomena* (H. P. Weld, Ed.). New York: Macmillan.

Tolman, E. C. (1922a). Can instincts be given up in psychology? *Journal of Abnormal Psychology, 17,* 139–152.

Tolman, E. C. (1922b). A new formula for behaviorism. *Psychological Review, 29,* 140–145.

Tolman, E. C. (1923). A behavioristic account of the emotions. *Psychological Review, 30,* 327–331.

Tolman, E. C. (1925a). Purpose and cognition: The determiners of animal learning. *Psychological Review, 32,* 287–297.

Tolman, E. C. (1925b). Behaviorism and purpose. *Journal of Philosophy, 22,* 36–41.

Tolman, E. C. (1926). A behavioristic theory of ideas. *Psychological Review, 33,* 352–369.

Tolman, E. C. (1927). A behaviorist's definition of consciousness. *Psychological Review, 34,* 433–439.

Tolman, E. C. (1932). *Purposive behavior in animals and men.* New York: Appleton-Century.

Tolman, E. C. (1933). Sign Gestalt or conditioned reflex? *Psychological Review, 40,* 391–411.

Tolman, E. C. (1935). Psychology vs. immediate experience. *Philosophy of Science, 2,* 356–380.

Tolman, E. C. (1936). Operational behaviorism and current trends in psychology. *Proceedings of the 25th Anniversary of the Inauguration of Graduate Studies* (pp. 89–103). Los Angeles: University of Southern California.

Tolman, E. C. (1938). The determiners of behavior at a choice point. *Psychological Review, 45,* 1–41; APA Presidential Address (1938).

Tolman, E. C. (1939). Prediction of vicarious trial and error by means of a schematic sowbug. *Psychological Review, 46,* 318–336.

Tolman, E. C. (1941). Psychological man. *Journal of Social Psychology, 13*, 205–218.

Tolman, E. C. (1945). A stimulus-expectancy need-cathexis psychology. *Science, 101,* 160–166.

Tolman, E. C. (1948). Cognitive maps in rats and men. *Psychological Review, 55,* 189–208.

Tolman, E. C. (1966). *Behavior and psychological man,* 4th ed. Berkeley and Los Angeles: University of California Press.

Tomkins, S. S. (1962). *Affect, imagery, consciousness.* New York: Springer.

Tomkins, S. S. (1980). Affect as amplification: Some modification in theory. In R. Plutchik & H. Kellerman (Eds.), *Emotion: Theory, research, and experience* (vol. 1). New York: Academic Press.

Van den Berg, J. H. (1973). *A different existence.* Pittsburgh: Duquesne University Press.

Washburn, M. F. (1916). *Movement and mental imagery.* Boston: Houghton-Mifflin.

Watson, J. B. (1913). Psychology as the behaviorist views it. *Psychological Review, 20,* 138–177.

Watson, J. B. (1914). *Behavior: An introduction to comparative psychology.* New York: Holt.

Watson, J. B. (1919). *Psychology from the standpoint of a behaviorist.* Philadelphia: Lippincott.

Watson, J. B. (1930). *Behaviorism* (rev. ed.). New York: Norton.

Weedon, C. (1978). *Feminist practice and post-structural theory.* Oxford: Basil Blackwell.

Wertheimer, M. (1959). *Productive thinking* (enl. ed., Michael Wertheimer, Ed.). New York: Harper. (Original work published 1945).

West, C., & Zimmerman, D. H. (1983). Small insults: A study of interruptions in cross-sex conversations between unacquainted persons. In B. Thorne, C. Kramarae, & N. Henley (Eds.), *Language, gender, and society* (pp. 103–118). Rowley, MA: Newbury House.

Whiting, J.M.W., & Child, I. L. (1953). *Child training and personality.* New Haven: Yale University Press.

Wolff, P. H. (1960). The developmental psychologies of Jean Piaget and psychoanalysis. *Psychological Issues, 2.*

Wolman, B. J. (1960). *Contemporary theories and systems of psychology.* New York: Harper.

Woodworth, R. S. (1918). *Dynamic psychology.* New York: Columbia University Press.

Wundt, W. (1900–1920). *Voelkerspsychologie* (10 vols.). Leipzig: Engelmann.

Wundt, W. (1904). *Principles of physiological psychology* (5th ed., E. B. Titchener, Trans.). New York: MacMillan.

Yerkes, R. M. (1923). Testing and the human mind. *Atlantic Monthly, 121,* 358–370.

Yerkes, R. M. (Ed.). (1921). *Psychological examining in the U.S. Army.* Washington, DC: Memoirs of the National Academy of Sciences no. 15.

Young, P. T. (1943). *Emotion in man and animal.* New York: Wiley.

Young, P. T. (1949). Emotion as disorganized response: A reply to Professor Leeper. *Psychological Review, 56,* 184–191.

Name Index

Adorno, T. W., 108, 194
Agassiz, L., 26
Allport, G. W., 12, 13, 107, 112
Angell, J. R., 69, 75
Austin, G. A., 163

Baldwin, J. M., 64–66, 70, 74
Bambara, T. C., 215
Bartkey, S. L., 216
Beauvoir, S. de, 215
Beecher, H. W., 26
Beer, T., 85
Belenky, M. F., 216
Beneke, F. E., 28
Benjamin, W., 29
Bethe, T., 85
Boring, E. G., 18, 19, 20, 27, 65, 68
Boston Women's Health Book
    Collective, 215
Brentano, F., 25, 90
Bruecke, E., 112
Bruner, J. S., 163
Bugental, J.F.T., 203

Carnegie, A., 27
Cattell, R, 64, 67, 70,
Chodorow, N., 217, 218

Cisneros, S., 215
Clinchy, B. M., 216
Copernicus, 17
Cornell, D., 216

Darwin, C., 65, 70, 74, 76, 112, 114,
    115, 175, 176, 177
De Saussure, F., 162
Descartes, R., 17, 18, 130, 231
Dewey, J., 13, 28, 70, 103, 106
Dollard, J., 107, 145

Ebbinghaus, 59, 103
Ebert, T. L., 216, 224 n.2
Eddy, M. B., 86
Erdrich, L. M., 215
Erikson, E., 120, 236
Evans, R., 203

Fechener, G. T., 19, 93
Festinger, L., 13
Flavell, J. H., 163
Frenkl-Brunswik, E., 108, 171
Freud, A., 120
Freud, S., 13, 63, 87, 106, 108, 111–122,
    145, 162, 171, 172, 190, 191, 207,
    217, 218, 219

Friedan, B., 25
Frost, R. 175

Gendlin, E. T., 203
Gilligan, C., 216
Giorgi, A., 203
Goodnow, J. J., 163
Goldberger, N. R., 216
Guthrie, E., 106, 109

Habermas, J., 28
Hall, C., 112
Hall, G. S., 28, 63, 64, 67–68, 73, 112, 120, 171, 173
Hebb, D. O., 98, 109, 147–160, 165, 172
Heidbreder, E., 58, 96
Heidegger, M., 202, 209
Helmholz, H., 19, 26, 112
Herman, J. L. 217, 218–219, 223–224
Hilgard, E., 12, 13, 128, 109, 110, 147, 161, 192
Hitler, A., 89
Hodge, C., 26
Holt, E. B., 193
Horkheimer, M., 29
Horney, K., 120
Hovdestad, W. D., 220
Hull, C., 108, 125, 135–142, 150, 165
Humphrey, G. 1494
Husserl, E., 203, 204

Inhelder, B., 171

J. J. Rousseau Institute, 161
James, W., 3, 5, 6, 7, 8, 12, 13, 22, 31–48, 49, 50, 59, 63, 64, 70, 74, 83, 98, 103, 172, 192, 193, 207, 231
Jones, E., 63
Jung, C. G., 63, 119, 120

Kant, E., 24, 25, 26, 28, 91, 92
Keen, E., 193, 203, 233
Ketcham, K, 220
Klein, G. S., 163
Koehler, W., 89–98, 103, 112, 130, 137, 212 n.1

Koffka, K., 89, 96, 144
Kristinasen, G. M., 220
Kuo, Z. Y., 83

Ladd, G. T., 68, 74
Laing, R. D., 233
Langfeld, H. S., 192, 193
Lashley, K. S., 147
Leibnitz, G. W., 91, 92
Levinson, D. J., 108
Levi-Strauss, C., 162
Lewin, K., 13, 98, 151, 203, 194
Lindsay, G., 112
Locke, J., 19, 91
Loeb, J., 85, 86
Loftus, E. F., 220
Lotze, H., 28
Luther, M. 236

MacDougall, W., 98, 120, 144–145
Marcuse, H., 28
Marx, K., 7
May, R., 202, 203
Mayer, J. D., 86
Merleau-Ponty, M., 162, 202
Meyer, M., 86
Meyers, F.W.H., 13
Miller, G. A., 193
Miller, N., 107, 113, 145
Morrison, T., 215
Mueller, G. E., 19

Newton, I., 17
No, L. de 148
Nye, A., 216

Pavlov, I., 78, 86, 92, 106
Pearson, K., 63
Pennfield, W. 147
Piaget, J., 68, 109, 161–174, 202
Prince, M., 13

Radnitsky, G., 87
Roback, T. 49
Rockefeller, J. D., 27
Rogers, C., 13, 108, 136–137, 142–146
Russell, B., 112, 114

Sanford, R. N., 108, 194
Sarbin, T., 232
Sartre, J-P., 162, 202, 204
Sawicki, J., 216
Schultz, D., 49, 50, 75, 123
Seidman, S., 216
Senden, M. von, 152
Silko, L. M., 215
Skinner, B. F., 109, 148, 190, 191
Smith, A., 7
Snygg, D. 203
Spence, K. W., 144
Spencer, H., 7, 26
Sullivan, H. S., 120

Tarule, J. M., 216
Thorndike, E., 28, 63, 64, 70, 78, 79, 106, 137, 175

Titchener, E. B., 25, 26, 27, 29, 49–62, 63, 64, 65, 68, 70, 74, 75, 76, 78, 83, 90, 91, 114, 162, 171
Tolman, E. C., 109, 123–134, 149, 165

Van den Berg, J. H., 203
von Uexkuell, J. 85

Wallach, H., 89
Watson, James, 133 n.2
Watson, J. B., 3, 4, 11, 12, 64, 73, 75–87, 103, 112, 114, 120, 125, 130, 133 n.2, 144, 162, 163, 172, 175, 193
Weiss, A., 86
Wertheimer, M., 89, 96
Woodworth, R., 109
Wundt, W., 3, 19, 24–29, 49, 50, 58, 61, 76

Subject Index

Accommodation, 165–166
Action (William James), 41–43
American cultural context, 9, 10, 12, 13, 26–27, 135–146, 245–247
AAAP (American Association of Applied Psychology), 105
APA (American Psychological Association), 9, 50, 105, 244
Assimilation, 165–166
Associationism, 78–79, 152
Atomism, 91
Attention, 150
Attitudes, 108

Behavior as rhetoric, 232–233
Behavior versus mechanical natural event, 128
Behaviorism, 75–85, 102–103, 123–129
Brain, 147–160

Capitalism, 26, 195
Cell assembly, 151f
Christianity, 68, 209
Civil War, 26
Clinical psychology, 136–144, 196, 238–240

Closure, 93
Cognitive development, 168–170
Cognitive psychology, 12, 13, 86, 102–103, 125, 192–194
Concrete operations, 169
Conflict, 116–118
Connectionism, 125, 151
Consciousness, 86, 92, 104, 125, 161–174, 192–194
Consciousness rejected, 75–85, 124
Consciousness studied, 49–61, 124, 161–174, 201–215
Conservatism, 136
Constancy, 92
Contingencies, 175–185
Corporations, 242
Cultural anthropology, 132
Cultural characters, 238
Culture and psychology, 242
Curiosity, 190, 194, 195

Darwinism, 26
Data of Freud, 119
Defense, 117
Developmental stages: Freud, 117–118; Piaget, 168–170
Discrimination, 181

Displacement (Piaget), 167
Dreams, 116
Dualism, 4–6, 19–21, 28, 45, 61, 68,
    85, 97, 100–106, 108, 121–122, 128,
    174, 244
Duplicity, 236–238

Economics, 7
EEG, 150
Ego, 115–116
Elementalism, 25
Emotion, 40–41, 147–153, 167–168,
    181, 231–234
Emotion and cognition, 167
Existentialism, 202
Experiment, 26
Extinction, 181

Facts and values, 50, 227–230
Feminism, 196, 197, 215–225
Field dynamics, 99–104
Field theory, 98
Formal operations 170
Free will, 32–33, 35–37, 45–46, 84
Functionalism, 63, 64, 68–72, 73, 76,
    77, 82; Skinner, 175–185

Genetic epistemology, 161–174
Gestalt, 89, 104, 106, 112, 123, 129
God, 120, 209
Guilt, 118

Healer role, 237
Helping people versus mastering
    nature, 198
History of psychology, 9–10, 19–26
Horizon, 205
Hyponosis, 135
Hypothetical constructs, 125–127

"I" and "me," 237
Id, 115
Identities in psychology, 189
Ideo-motor theory, 41
Individualism, 242
Intelligibility as narrative, 234–236
Intentionality, 25

Insight, 95–96
Internal representation, 125
Interpretive truth, 114
IQ, 14 n.1

Learning, 106–108, 180
Libido, 115
Logic, 135

Machine analogy, 233
Mastering nature, 198
"Me" and "I," 237
Meaning, 205–207
Mechanical psychology, 238
Metaphors in psychology, 35–36, 37
Metaphysics, 17, 19, 28, 37, 82, 125,
    128, 172, 177, 184
Metapsychology, 126, 131, 184
Methodology, 54–58
Mind, 8–9, 33–34, 36–44, 50–52, 106,
    128, 177, 203–204
Molar, 130, 133
Molecular, 130, 133

Narrative, 70–72, 76, 97; in history,
    234–235
National pride, 242
Naturalism, 70–72
Natural law, 104
Nazism, 89, 108, 204, 242
Nervous system, 54
Neurology, 103
Neurosis, 117
1960s, 137

Odeipus complex, 118

Paradigm shift, 77
Parsimony, 182
Patient role, 236–238
Patriotism, 139
Perplexity in confronting Freud, 113
Personal equation, 18
Phase sequence, 147
Phenomenology, 201–211
Philosophy, 5
Politics, 123

Positivism, 8, 9
Postmodern critique of psychology, 230–233
Postmodernism, 230–232
Postmodern possibilities, 245–247
Predictive truth, 114
Preoperational period, 169
Professionalization, 237
Progress, 9
Proliferation of psychology, 242
Propadeutic science, 18
Psychoanalysis, 111–122, 132
Psychology and culture, 12–14, 241
Psychology and physiology, 128
Psychology of psychology, 189–196
Psychopharmacology, 204, 205, 242
Psychophysics, 18, 33
Purpose, 125, 127, 128

Rationalism, 115
Recovered memories controversy, 220
Reductionism, 19, 29, 85, 133–134, 150
Reification, 231, 232, 237f
Reinforcement, 175–186
Renaissance, 17
Repressed memory debate, 220
Rhetoric as behavior (and vice versa), 232–233
Rhetoric in theory, 239

Science, 17, 18, 19, 28, 33, 70–74
Science versus humanism, 114, 135, 140

Scientific pride, 10, 72, 87
Secularization, 12–14, 241
Self, 37–38, 46, 64, 142–146, 207–209
Self-deception, 237
Self-representation, 236
Sensorimotor period, 169
Social Darwinism, 8, 26–27
Sociology, 6, 7
Split in psychology (1960s), 139, 143–144
Stimulus error, 55, 91
Structuralism, 49–61
Structure (Piaget), 164–165
Superego, 116

Taboos, 115
Tabula rasa, 91
Testing 12, 108
Theory 128, 189, 238–239
Therapeutic psychology, 111–122
Titchener-Baldwin controversy, 64–66
Transcendental ego, 38
Transcendentalism, 26
Transposition, 92, 160

Values as neglected by science, 227–230
Vietnam war, 137–149
Vitalism, 19, 97, 175–186

War, 108, 117, 123, 131
Women, 215 F
Worldview, 17–18
World War II, 107–108

ABOUT THE AUTHOR

Ernest Keen is professor emeritus of psychology at Bucknell University. Keen has published widely in the field. Among his earlier books are *Drugs, Therapy, and Professional Power* (1998), *Chemicals for the Mind* (2000), and *Ultimacy and Triviality in Psychotherapy* (2000), all published by Praeger.